The Role
of the State
in Property
Taxation

Books from
The Lincoln Institute of Land Policy

The Lincoln Institute of Land Policy is a school that offers intensive courses of instruction in the field of land economics and property taxation. The Institute provides a stimulating learning environment for students, policymakers, and administrators with challenging opportunities for research and publication. The goal of the Institute is to improve theory and practice in those fundamental areas of land policy that have significant impact on the lives and livelihood of all people.

Constitutions, Taxation, and Land Policy Michael M. Bernard

Constitutions, Taxation, and Land Policy—Volume II
Michael M. Bernard

Federal Tax Aspects of Open-Space Preservation Kingsbury Browne

Taxation of Nonrenewable Resources Albert M. Church

Conflicts over Resource Ownership Albert M. Church

Taxation of Mineral Resources Robert F. Conrad and R. Bryce Hool

World Congress on Land Policy, 1980 Edited by Matthew Cullen and Sharon Woolery

Land Readjustment William A. Doebele

The Rate of Return Edited by Daniel M. Holland

Incentive Zoning Jerold S. Kayden

Building for Women Edited by Suzanne Keller

Urban Land Policy for the 1980s Edited by George Lefcoe

Fiscal Federalism and the Taxation of Natural Resources Edited by Charles E. McLure, Jr., and Peter Mieszkowski

State Land-Use Planning and Regulation Thomas G. Pelham

The Role of the State in Property Taxation Edited by H. Clyde Reeves

Land-Office Business Gary Sands

The Art of Valuation Edited by Arlo Woolery

The Role of the State in Property Taxation

Edited by
H. Clyde Reeves
Lincoln Institute of Land Policy

with the assistance of
Scott Ellsworth

LexingtonBooks
D.C. Heath and Company
Lexington, Massachusetts
Toronto

Library of Congress Cataloging in Publication Data

Main entry under title:
    The Role of the state in property taxation.

    1. Real property tax—Law and legislation—United States—States—
Congresses. 2. Real property tax—Law and legislation—British Columbia—
Congresses. I. Reeves, H. (Herman) Clyde, 1912-   . II. Ellsworth, Scott.
III. Lincoln Institute of Land Policy. IV. Title.
KF6760.A75R64   1983   343.7305'4   82-48536
ISBN 0-669-06292-8   347.30354

Published simultaneously in Canada   *84- 878*

Printed in the United States of America

International Standard Book Number: 0-669-06292-8

Library of Congress Catalog Card Number: 82-48536

Contents

Preface

The Tax Policy Roundtable of the Lincoln Institute of Land Policy held its first meeting in the fall of 1978 and has met semiannually since. At each, save two of its meetings, it received two or more specially prepared papers relating to the property tax. The first eight papers, most of which have been published subsequently by the Lincoln Institute, were calculated to cover roughly the property-tax spectrum—its problems and prospects, incidence, theory and practice, and its variations both among states and internationally.

This approach was taken to give a common orientation to members of the Tax Policy Roundtable. Moreover, among taxes the ad valorem property tax is universal in the United States and has a unique relation to land-use decisions.

During this orientation process we became impressed with several things. Prominent among them were: (1) the property tax, though slightly declining in relative importance, is likely to long continue to be the dominant source of local-government revenue; (2) assessment administration is generally poor; (3) property-tax-relief measures are often ill conceived; and (4) new technologies now make it possible to improve assessments markedly.

Recognizing the legal primacy of the states, we decided, before delving more deeply in the property tax or confronting other land-use and tax-related policy issues, to study the role of the state in property taxation. This book is the result of that exploration.

Initially we commissioned three papers—covering the situations in the states of Kentucky, Maryland, and Washington—to be kind of bellwethers. On the basis of these papers an outline was prepared and eleven other papers were developed in general accommodation to it. These eleven covered Arizona, British Columbia, Florida, Kansas, Maine, Minnesota, New Jersey, New York, Ohio, Texas, and Utah. The eleven papers were reviewed by the Roundtable in one-and-one-half days. In this case the authors did not present their papers. Rather, the principal issues were extracted from the series, and the authors of papers about states deemed to represent the spectrum of each issue were asked to comment. This was followed by general discussion. Roundtable members had previously had an opportunity to read all the papers.

In January 1981, the International Association of Assessing Officers (IAAO) had somewhat similar papers presented on Hawaii and Wisconsin. These papers were made available for review by Roundtable members and are incorporated into this book. We gratefully acknowledge the permission of IAAO and the authors. Subsequently, the Iowa paper was prepared.

The sixteen states (plus one Canadian province) were selected with a view of giving a panoramic and reasonably accurate picture of the fifty— British Columbia was selected because it presents a provocative Canadian approach to a problem identical to ours. The selection process was subjective and sometimes arbitrary. For example, California and Massachusetts were deliberately omitted because we had reviewed Proposition 13 and Proposition 2 1/2 in several other contexts. Other choices had obvious merit, and substitution might have improved the case-study presentation, but we are satisfied that the cases studied gave us an adequate picture and one we hope will be useful to others.

All the papers were then edited and some were rearranged to fit into a format facilitative of state-by-state comparison. The edited versions were submitted to the authors for correction and approval.

Typically, we invite to Roundtable meetings a few knowledgeable guests who participate freely in discussion but are not involved in any decision making. We are grateful for the guest participation of Edward L. Brooks, Florida Department of Revenue; Richard A. Chandler, assessor (Richmond, Virginia), and president of the International Association of Assessing Officers; and John L. Istel, SCM Corporation, New York, and president of the Property Tax Institute at the November 1981 meeting and of Gene L. Burner, Maryland Department of Assessments and Taxation; Professor Lowell Harris, Columbia University; Professor F. Ted Hebert, University of Oklahoma; Douglas R. Holbrook, North Carolina Department of Revenue; and Will Knedlik, Kirkland, Washington, at the April 1982 meeting. Of course, authors of papers were present and participated in discussion when their papers were reviewed.

The dialogue at these two meetings was recorded and the introduction presents a summary thereof. The conclusions and recommendations reflect the consensus of the membership of the Roundtable. No member is bound to any conclusion or recommendation or to its verbiage.

Our membership expresses appreciation to the authors of the case studies for making their study of the states' role in property taxation possible, and the editors are indebted to the authors for their tolerance of the editing process. Arlo Woolery, Charles Cook, and Sharon B. Shea of the Lincoln Institute of Land Policy staff were unfailingly supportive with their attendance and assistance. The Lincoln Institute provided the necessary funding. My moonlighting secretary, Glenda Miller, masterfully deciphered notes and typed and retyped papers. Without her capable help we would never have made it.

Lastly, I should acknowledge with appreciation my great debt to the conference reporter and my editorial colleague, Scott Ellsworth.

Tax Policy Roundtable Members

Roy W. Bahl
Syracuse University
Syracuse, New York

Marion S. Beaumont
California State University
 at Long Beach
Long Beach, California

Kenneth Back
Property Tax Institute
Washington, D.C.

Harvey B. Gantt
Gantt-Haberman Associates
Charlotte, North Carolina

Ralph Gerra
Bethlehem Steel Corporation
Bethlehem, Pennsylvania

William N. Kelly
National Conference of
 State Legislatures
Denver, Colorado

Will S. Myers, Jr.
Advisory Panel on
 Financing Elementary and
 Secondary Education
Washington, D.C.

James Harry Michael, Jr.
U.S. District Judge
Charlottesville, Virginia

H. Clyde Reeves
Chairman, Tax Policy Roundtable
Frankfort, Kentucky

Joel Stern
Chase Financial Policy
New York, New York

Frederick D. Stocker
The Ohio State University
Columbus, Ohio

Deil S. Wright
University of North Carolina
Chapel Hill, North Carolina

Introduction

Scott Ellsworth

On September 13-14, 1981, in Cambridge, Massachusetts, the Tax Policy Roundtable of the Lincoln Institute of Land Policy hosted a conference on the property tax. This gathering drew together over thirty practitioners and scholars. By concentrating their discussion upon twenty major subjects associated with the property tax, the conference participants were able not only to engage in a valuable interchange of information on practices and policy but also to provide a window on the current general status of the property tax.

Seven months later, on April 18 through 20, 1982, at the Quail Roost Conference Center in North Carolina, members of the Tax Policy Roundtable and selected guests met again to discuss the activities at the first conference (and the seventeen chapters contained in this book) and to formulate a series of observations and recommendations regarding the property tax. These findings are also included in this book.

The following is a combined condensation of the primary topics discussed at these two conferences.

Status

Rarely in its history has the property tax in the United States received as much attention as it has in recent years—an era marked by skyrocketing property values, the enactment of Proposition 13 in California and Proposition 2 1/2 in Massachusetts, and renewed debates over property taxation in state legislatures and county courthouses across the land. "The property tax has been a stepchild," stated Douglas Holbrook, director of the Ad Valorum Taxation Division of North Carolina Department of Revenue, "Until the 1960s, it was an extremely low burden and nobody really got miffed about it." Then, reasoned Holbrook, due to the increased utilization of the property tax by the counties and some of the effects of increased spending, the burden climbed higher and higher until the property tax was "brought screaming into a new century."

Conference participants agreed that the renewed concern over the property tax was indeed quite deep and very widespread, but questioned whether the property-tax system has attained a poorer reputation than it deserves. "Someone needs to defend the property tax as a way of raising money," stated one participant, while Roundtable Chairman H. Clyde Reeves asserted that, "The flaws in the property tax are exaggerated."

Reeves then asked: "A fundamental problem is why do we exaggerate the shortcomings of the property tax and mitigate the shortcomings of other taxes?" According to a number of participants, this situation was in part caused by the fact that unlike other forms of taxation, a *third party* establishes an individual's property tax. "One of the things that might cause the property tax to have more serious problems than the income tax or the sales tax," stated Gene Burner of the Maryland Department of Assessment and Taxation, "is that nowhere else does a third party establish the basis of the tax. You, as a taxpayer, certainly establish the basis of the tax with the sales and income tax." Will Knedlik, a former legislator from the state of Washington, on the other hand, asserted that the inability to avoid the property tax might be the source of some of its unpopularity: "There is a gargantuan underground economy, and people are totally opting out of the income system. . . . The property tax is unpopular because you can't avoid it. You can totally avoid the income tax, and you can largely avoid the sales tax, if that's what you are committed to doing." William Kelly, of the National Conference of State Legislatures, speculated that part of the property tax's recent unpopularity might also be due to the fact that people are aware of past abuses with it and may assume that they continue today.

Other participants argued that the primary problems with the property tax have to do more with how it is operating currently rather than with its structure. "The trouble is that the folks who are paying most of the taxes are not getting most of the services," stated one attendant, who argued that in his state, most of the property-tax revenues, which primarily go into the school system, were being paid by older citizens without children in school.

Yet, whatever the causes for its unpopularity, there was a general consensus at the conference that the property tax was indeed under fire. "The tax revolt is very real," one participant said, "People would vote right now to eliminate the property tax in the state, without caring what kind of plan you have to replace it."

The Base

Perhaps the most logical starting point for any comparative discussion of property-tax policy and practice is the tax base itself. How is the property tax base defined in the various states and provinces? What exclusions and total exemptions are granted? How much, if any, have property-tax revenues increased during the recent past? What is the fiscal importance of these revenues in the overall state or provincial budgetary pictures? Not surprisingly, conference participants exhibited a healthy divergence in the answers they provided to these questions.

Exclusions and Total Exemptions

British Columbia, Kansas, and Texas were illustrative of the spectrum in granting exclusions and total exemptions from property taxation. In defining the property tax base, British Columbia employs an extremely wide definition. "Basically speaking," stated J.T. Gwartney, of the British Columbia Assessment Authority, "all property defined as real estate is subject to taxation." Although Gwartney said that there is "a whole raft of exclusions and partial exemptions" in effect in the province, it is notable that the provincial assessment office lists and assesses all property defined as real estate (including churches and schools) as if it were subject to taxation, regardless whether that is indeed the case.

The practices of granting exclusions and total exemptions in Kansas is probably closer to the norm in the United States. According to Lyle W. Clark, an official with the Department of Revenue, "Kansas law requires that all property be listed, real and personal. Some personal property is exempt—again, municipal, state, and federal properties are exempt." Clark stated that while his office is required by state law to maintain a list of all exempt properties, at market value, time considerations make this action extremely difficult to accomplish. "We don't have the time to value those properties that are taxable, much less keep up lists and values of exempt property," he said. Clark informed the conference of some of Kansas's exemptions, including household goods, personal effects, and, most recently, industrial-revenue-bond properties.

Disparities between constitutional requirements and legislative practices have significantly impacted upon the definition of the property tax base in Texas. Kenneth E. Graeber, executive director of the State Property Tax Board, stated that "The state constitution of Texas requires that all property, unless specifically exempted by the constitution, be taxable. That includes real property, personal property, and intangible property." Whereas there have been a considerable number of constitutional amendments granting exclusions and exemptions in Texas, Graeber stated that the state legislature has passed statutes exempting certain property without proper constitutional authority. Moreover, the definition of the tax base has been further clouded in Texas by local assessors who have utilized their own interpretations of the state constitution to exempt certain types of property from ad valorem taxation. Lastly, there exist what Graeber refers to as "unconstitutional statutes," which exempt everything from women's clubs to civic clubs (but which usually get challenged successfully in court). Graeber's enumeration of various properties exempt from ad valorem taxation in Texas included items shared by a number of other states, such as farm machinery, schools, cemeteries, and relligous organizations. He did, however, list one specific exemption of limited currency: "We're probably the only state in the nation that has a statutory exemption for buffalo."

Other participants shared information on various exemptions and total exclusions in their states, from homestead exemptions for disabled veterans in Florida, to exemptions for pollution-control equipment in Minnesota. David Gaskell, executive director of New York's Division of Equalization and Taxation, expressed some concern over the extent of exemptions and total exclusions, giving evidence that during the past six years, nearly 6 percent of the taxable property in that state has been made exempt. "We have this continued movement going on of eroding the tax base and moving the taxable to the exempt, so that now in the cities, 40 percent of the property no longer pays taxes." This commentary, along with that regarding exemption practices in Texas, prompted some speculation on the best manner by which exemptions should be granted. "I believe the real issue here is if you honor only constitutional exemptions, they don't erode on you," asserted Tax Policy Roundtable chairman H. Clyde Reeves. "If the legislature makes statutory amendments, do they always increase?"

Shifts

Perhaps in no other period of our history has the property tax received as much attention as it has during the past half decade—years that have witnessed the so-called taxpayer revolt and the emergence of Proposition 13 and similar legislation with their attendant mentalities in various segments of U.S. society. A key force in the ascendancy of property-tax policy to national concern has been, of course, the mercurial rise in property values and the feeling that, as a result, the tax burden has been shifted unfairly onto the backs of homeowners. While other shifting has occurred—such as corporations shifting these burdens onto labor and consumers; or landlords to tenants—the share that has fallen on the homeowner's shoulders has been paramount. "The real opposition to the property tax," H. Clyde Reeves stated, "is by those who can't shift it—namely the homeowners." Several states and provinces have attempted to grapple with this problem in different ways, as was evidenced by various conference participants.

Ohio's experience in dealing with the tendency for the tax burden to shift to residential property has been extremely complex, and colored both by a uniformity statute and by the state's rather unusual requirement that votes for levy increases must be for only a certain number of dollars. As the situation stands, due to recent legislation and a court decision, the General Assembly will now have the option to increase the rollback for residential property beyond the present level. The degree to which the legislature may increase the rollback is unclear, but nevertheless, conference participant Dr. Frederick D. Stocker, of the Department of Economics at Ohio State University, feels that one major effect may be that the state's uniformity principle ultimately will be abandoned.

The situation in Minnesota has also been rather involved. Lyle Ask, an official with the Minnesota Department of Revenue, informed the conference as to how the state had set a 5-percent limit on annual assessment increases for farms and homesteads, only to soon discover that amount was inadequate in face of 20-percent inflation rates (causing the legislature to raise the limit to 10 percent).

It bears notation that at least one conference participant described homeowners in his state as being "pretty well protected" from shifts. This observation came from Seth Franzman, assessment standards manager for the Arizona Department of Revenue, who described two mechanisms protecting Arizona homeowners: a statutory classification system in which residential property is in one of the lowest classes and, a recent constitutional amendment that provides for a limitation on increases in property taxes on residential property. Arizona's seemingly placid situation stood in sharp contrast to that of neighboring Utah, where Gary C. Cornia of Brigham Young University described the intense political warfare going on between homeowners and the business community over shifts. Although, currently, there appears to have been something of a compromise worked out between various state officials for new property-tax legislation, Cornia feels that this package will indeed be challenged by the state's business community.

Again, in sharp contrast to the highly charged, political atmosphere of Utah's struggles with shifts stands British Columbia's experience. Like most U.S. states, that province underwent significant increases in the market value of its residential property beginning in the 1960s. In 1977, the provincial government developed an extremely flexible classification system—now consisting of eight classes—through which annual assessments are made at market value. What makes the British Columbia system unique, however, is that the assessment authority is a government corporation—and that it is responsible for making a 100-percent valuation. The fraction of the valuation at which the various classes of property are assessed and taxed is not set by the assessment authority but by elected governmental officials. As a result, according to J.T. Gwartney, determining equitable values in British Columbia has been removed from controversy and politics.

Growth in Property-Tax Revenues

During the past two decades, property-tax revenues have grown throughout the United States. Four conference participants—representing British Columbia, Kansas, New York, and New Jersey—were asked to explain the growth in their states/province, and it is interesting to note that their presentations included a wide array of reasons.

Property-tax revenues in British Columbia increased some 8.1 times during the past twenty years, giving it the highest rate of increase of the four subnational governments reviewed. J.T. Gwartney explained this growth as primarily being the result of the dynamic growth of the province, and particularly of property values. Increases in residential property values have been particularly sharp in cities, such as Vancouver, where the market value of the average house rose 65 percent last year (during a twelve-month period). Gwartney also listed the overall effects of inflation as a subsidiary cause of the growth, particularly the inflation of wages.

Kansas's seemingly modest rate of growth (3.1 times) for property-tax revenues contrasts sharply with that of British Columbia. Lyle Clark explained the reasons behind this rate as due to the facts that, basically, the state level for levying taxes has been no higher than 1.8 percent for several decades, and there are limitations placed on how much municipalities annually can increase their budgets. As to why property-tax revenues *did* grow in Kansas, Clark attributed this growth to the increased number of jurisdictions utilizing the ad valorem tax base as a method of financing their budgets and increased spending at the local level—particularly in school budgets.

Raymond L. Halperin, state tax assessor for the Maine Bureau of Taxation, stated that the growth rate of property-tax revenues in Maine (about six times over the past twenty years) is "a direct reflection of inflation, increased spending at the municipal level, and increased school funding." Maine does not have any limitations on the size of a budget a municipality can develop. Interestingly, Halperin pointed out that it is the larger cities in the state—those with professional city managers—that have tended to increase their budgets during the recent past, while smaller towns in the state—such as those governed by town meetings—have been less inclined to do so.

While New York and New Jersey share a common boundary, and fairly similar growth rates in property-tax revenues (4.1 and 4.7 times, respectively, over the past two decades), their representatives at the conference explained their growth rates differently. David Gaskell stated that an important reason for the increase in New York had to do with the facts that his state was not as successful as much of the rest of the nation in capturing federal dollars in the 1970s and that the state was not as anxious to share its funds with local governments—all of which ended in fewer dollars flowing to the local level. "That difference got made up by the property tax," Gaskell stated. J. Henry Ditmars, an official with the New Jersey Division of Taxation, on the other hand, emphasized the slackening of his state's rate of increase in property-tax revenues during the past ten years. He stated that the primary reason for this curtailment of growth was legislation passed by the state in 1977, which limited the increase in the amount of money that municipalities could raise for tax purposes to 5 percent (annually).

Fiscal Importance

Five participants—representing Florida, Kansas, Maine, New York, and Ohio—outlined the relative and actual importance of the property tax in their states' patterns of public finance. While the specifics and causal factors behind each presentation differed, with but few exceptions there appeared to be three common threads that have coursed through their experiences: schools have been the biggest users of property-tax revenues; the property tax has declined in importance (relative to other taxes) within their overall pictures of state and municipal finance; and, actual property-tax revenues have increased during the recent past.

This information engendered another, related discussion on the probable future importance of the property tax. At least two participants took the position that the property tax would either increase in significance in the coming years or at least hold its own. The latter position was adopted by Raymond L. Halperin of Maine, who outlined both how the property tax occupies a central position in school funding in his state and also how the recent fiscal conservatism of the state government should only tend to strengthen that centrality (in Maine, municipalities retain all property-tax revenues they raise). "For a long time to come," he states, " I'm sure the property tax will be fiscally important in Maine."

A more aggressive position on the future importance of the property tax was taken by Gary C. Cornia of Utah. Citing the recent history of the property tax in New York—where property-tax revenues as a share of personal income have risen—Cornia predicted that this situation is likely to be mirrored in other states, particularly due to the reductions in federal funds. As a result, he felt that, overall, the property tax will gain in importance.

Other participants disagreed. Dr. Roy W. Bahl of Syracuse University asserted that the New York experience was unique, due to the overriding importance of local governments in the overall governance of the state. On the overall future of the property tax, Dr. Bahl reiterated the thesis of his monograph, *Property Taxation in the 1980s* (Cambridge, Mass: Lincoln Institute of Land Policy, 1979): while property-tax revenues may increase in the coming decade, the relative importance of the property tax vis-a-vis other forms of taxation will decrease. Lyle W. Clark offered a similar analysis for Kansas.

Two participants also voiced the opinion that the relative importance of the property tax would decline in their home states, although their reasons differed. Taking a historic view dating back to the early twentieth century, Seth Franzman felt that the emphasis in Arizona would be less and less on the property tax, perhaps because of the maturation of the state's economy. Edward Brooks of Florida predicted that other forms of taxation, such as the sales tax, would be relied upon more heavily in his state in the future than the property tax. "At the local level," he said, "if ever there was a message being given to the state level, it concerns property taxes. I think for that reason you are going to see a trend toward some other type of taxation."

At least two participants occupied somewhat of a middle ground in the discussion. Kenneth E. Graeber of Texas stated that for the immediate future, he foresaw a decline in the dependence on ad valorum property taxes in Texas—due in part to the revenues from taxation of the petroleum industry in the state. He added, however, that, "Sooner or later, the well is going to run dry on oil and gas, and then we're going to have a taxing problem in our state." Dr. Frederick Stocker did not necessarily predict a decline in the importance of the property tax in Ohio, but he did assert that there would be a decline in the rate by which property taxes have been cut. This decline would come about, he argued, once people became aware of the symbiotic relation between various forms of taxation: ultimately, the reductions made in one form of taxation will have to be compensated by increases in other forms.

One result of this discussion over the future of the property tax was a feeling among some participants that more attention should be paid to the overall structure of taxation, specifically, what it should look like in an ideal system. Arlo Woolery, executive director of the Lincoln Institute of Land Policy, undoubtedly spoke for most of the participants when he urged the Tax Roundtable to investigate more carefully "the role of balance in the tax structure."

Relief Measures

While the base is the central component of any system of property taxation, unless it is viewed in context it may appear vastly larger than it actually is. Most states and provinces have enacted various forms of *relief measures*—such as classification systems, use-value assessments, or homestead exemptions—which markedly impact upon what are their actual property-tax bases. As was the case in regard to their bases, the various states and the one Canadian province represented at the conference exhibited wide degrees of variance in the numbers, types, and effects of the different relief measures they have adopted.

Classification Systems

Systems of classifying property for taxation purposes are a common form of relief measure utilized by many states. These systems vary greatly, however, in both their make-up and intent, as was well evidenced by the four states' representatives who were chosen as panelists to discuss classification in their home states.

Arizona's classification system—an assessment classification system—is the product of several decades of evolution. Seth Franzman detailed this history, one that has been marked since the 1950s by the interplay of legislative actions, lawsuits by the major railroads in the state, and at least one landmark court decision. Franzman stated that although Arizona currently employs eight different property classifications, with different rates of assessment per class, he feels that there exists a trend toward two general levels of assessment—one for commercial and industrial properties, the other for residential and agricultural properties.

Ohio's system, which dates back to the 1930s, has also been the subject of considerable evolution. While it originally was designed to have assessment ratios for tangible personal property lower than those for real estate, according to Dr. Frederick D. Stocker, this system has reversed itself over the years. "It's a crazy system, in my opinion," he said. Stocker related that the state constitution clearly provides that real estate be taxed uniformly according to value and told how a long line of court decisions upheld this position. In recent years, however, the combination of constitutional amendments on farm use value and the allowance of credits—or *tax-reduction factors*—plus a court ruling that declared a highly controversial statute allowing for an increased rollback on taxes for residential property to be legal, has considerably challenged the uniformity requirement. "What I think we have in Ohio now," Stocker stated, "is a system of classification of real estate with two categories—residential and farm in one and everything else in the other—in which different effective rates are permitted."

The history of Minnesota's classification system, on the other hand, has been marked by an accretion of classes. Established in 1913, it originally contained only four classes. Presently, according to Lyle Ask, there must be close to fifty. Moreover, Ask stated that "they are building classes and credits within a class, so it is kind of difficult to count up all of the classes." As a rule, property is classed according to its use.

Minnesota's system, particularly in regard to the sheer number of classes, was met with some incredulity by other conference participants, some of whom questioned how it could be administered effectively. Roundtable chairman H. Clyde Reeves brought up the related issue as to whether the average taxpayer could understand such a complex classification system, a concern that was echoed by Ohio's Dr. Frederick D. Stocker. According to Charles C. Cook, director of education and research for the Lincoln Institute of Land Policy, Minnesota's public-understanding problem comes in explaining why a property has been placed in a particular class, whereas Ohio's centers around why a property has been assessed and taxed at a particular rate.

Texas has an *equal and uniform* principle in its constitution, and recent movements for establishing a classification system in the state have been halted. According to Kenneth E. Graeber, the opposition of the state's business community, which feels that classification would have a deleterious effect on the state's economic well-being, has been crucial in this regard. "Texas is very unusual in that we have a very dominant business community in our political world," Graeber stated. John L. Istel, tax manager for the SCM Corporation and president of the Property Tax Institute, voiced support for the position taken by the Texas business community, asserting that classification does indeed render harmful effects to the nation's corporations.

A follow-up discussion between Graeber and Istel on whether or not a de facto system of classification has existed in Texas prompted commentary by Seth Franzman of Arizona. "The property tax is but one thread in the fabric of taxation," he said, "and all the threads together that make the fabric are what should be considered." Franzman stated that while he has no trouble with the notion that different segments of the economy should assume different amounts of the overall tax burden, he feels that what determines those loads needs to be explicit. "It is appropriate and necessary," he said, "that the classification system or assessment ratios be out front, so that everyone knows what they are and that they be legitimate and not de facto."

Use Value

Closely related to the topic of classification systems is that of procedures for use-value assessment, particularly of agricultural lands. Here, as throughout the conference, a fairly wide range of practices were revealed by various conference participants.

Arizona has two basic use-value-assessment procedures: one for agricultural land, the other relating to gas- and electric-utility property. The former, which is predicated upon the rental value of agricultural land, received the most attention. It is still, however, in its infancy, as the program was begun only in 1980. According to Seth Franzman, there have been some problems associated with it already due to the fact that the response to filing under the program has been somewhat marginal.

In British Columbia, there are provisions for both farmland being actively farmed and for agricultural land that is capable of being farmed. Owners of land that qualifies under either category receive preferential property-tax treatment. In addition, the province also has use-value-assessment provisions that apply to timberlands (specifically relating to tree farms) and to property upon which there are railway trackage, telegraph lines, and oil and gas transmission pipelines. In the latter case, the provincial assessment authority takes into account any factors that might increase the value of such property—something that has resulted both in relatively high valuations and also in numerous appeals by the corporate owners.

Use-value assessment of Florida's agricultural property, according to Ed Brooks, has caused local assessors in Florida considerable difficulty in interpreting the statutes and defending their interpretations in court. "It is a very difficult job to make the determination as to what is a bona fide, commercial agricultural venture as spelled out in our statutes," Brooks said. "As a result, there are a lot of lawsuits." Although he feels that the provisions have been effective in assisting farmers, Brooks stated that it has been very difficult to prevent developers from taking advantage of them—a problem that has been compounded by questionable court decisions. When asked how orange groves are assessed in the state, Brooks replied that the guidelines, which are based on production, utilize the word *typical*. He stated that there has been a tendency by assessors to assess the land at its highest potential, however, something that has caused citrus lands to be assessed quite high.

Kansas does not have use-value assessment, although a constitutional amendment passed in 1978 apparently opened the door for the state legislature to enact use-value-assessment provisions. So far it has failed to do so, and Lyle W. Clark predicted that there would probably be movement for a new amendment, owing to the questionable constitutionality of the 1978 amendment. "I suspect that we will see some more fighting this year," he said, "but it is very difficut to see what will come of it."

Farm use-value assessment is a topic of no small amount of controversy, as was adequately revealed by the discussion at the conference. Gary Cornia of Utah questioned whether farm use-value-assessment provisions had indeed slowed agricultural-land conversion in the states where they are in effect. J. Henry Ditmars asserted that they had in New Jersey, while David Gaskell stated that they have not been very effective in New York.

There was also some discussion of the effect of such provisions on land use and who, exactly, benefits from such provisions. Richard A. Chandler, assessor of Richmond, Virginia, and president of the International Association of Assessing Officers—who questioned whether use-value-assessment procedures were "just a bonanza for the developers"—asserted that it was the so-called gentleman farmer who was a major beneficiary. While this position was questioned by one participant, it also received some support. Dr. Frederick D. Stocker, author of *Farm-Use Assessment Revisited* (Cambridge, Mass.: Lincoln Institute of Land Policy, 1979), essentially concurred with Chandler's argument. "That's about what I'd expect to happen," Stocker said. "It isn't the dirt farmers, generally speaking, who benefit."

Rate Limitations

The four states chosen to illustrate rate-limitation practices covered a broad spectrum. Maine has no rate limitations, and the state's representative at the conference, Raymond L. Halperin, felt that they were not necessary. Halperin asserted that the property-tax rate in the state was not that burdensome, partly as the result of the rural nature of the state where town governments have done much to hold spending levels in check.

In Minnesota, according to Lyle Ask, one must look at both rate and levy limits together. Ask stated that, generally speaking levy limits are by far the most important, as taxes are levied by dollar and not by rate. It was pointed out, however, that while Minnesota does not employ rate limits for general governmental purposes, there are rate limits for the state's school system.

Ohio, on the other hand, is a "very tough state on property-tax-rate limits," employing a stiff formula that dates back to the 1920s. In fact, the rate limitations are so harsh that, according to Dr. Frederick D. Stocker, the municipalities (and, to some extent, the counties) have virtually given up on the property tax, leaving it to the schools. Stocker pointed out, however, that this situation does not assure the schools, particularly in this inflationary age, of a virtually automatic source of funds. Beyond a certain, very modest, percentage, additional property-tax levies must be voted upon—and sometimes the electorate denies the increases, in some cases threatening the very operation of school systems.

In Texas, the situation regarding rate limits is rather deceiving. "Even though in our state we have statutory rate limitations," Kenneth Graeber stated, "they are not really rate limitations at all." Due to the fact that Texas recently abolished its assessment ratios, and other factors, Graeber stated, their rate limits "are not limits whatsoever." When queried whether local governments in Texas have practiced restraint in the face of this freedom, he replied that, on the whole, they have.

Levy Limitations

A wide spectrum of practices was also revealed in the four states selected for illustration on the topic of levy limitations. Arizona recently enacted legislation that provides for limits on levy increases for cities and towns to 102 percent of the previous year. In Maine, on the other hand, there has been no concerted effort to limit property taxes on a statewide basis—and there thus are no statewide levy limits in Maine. Utah has a number of levy and rate limits, something that has severely impacted upon school funding in the state. Minnesota's system, as was mentioned earlier, is a combination of both rate and levy limits (the latter at 6 percent).

In response to these presentations, David Gaskell of New York questioned why it was those states with lower tax burdens that had these limitations—a seeming reversal of what one might expect normally. His query, in turn, generated an interest in what caused states to adopt limitations—something about which a number of participants voiced ideas. Dr. Roy Bahl, Syracuse University, suggested that the extent to which a state's fiscal system was moving toward the state-government level might create a tendency to limit the property tax and questioned whether the presence of private school systems might also have significant impact. Dr. Deil S. Wright of the University of North Carolina offered a hypothesis in which geography might play an important role. Citizens and public officials in Maine, Wright stated, can readily note how much lighter their tax burden is relative to that in neighboring states—and thus see no great need for placing limitations on themselves. Wright added, however, that he was certain that no one reason can explain the presence or absence of limitations. Lastly, Federal District Judge James Harry Michael, Jr., suggested that there might be a correlation between states with limitations and those that were strongholds of the Populist movement.

Truth in Taxation

Florida's truth-in-taxation law has aroused a great deal of interest in recent years, and at least one of its components—the trim notice—has been adopted outright by another state. This law, designed at least in part to better educate the public in matters of taxation, has led to a whole raft of changes in the functioning of the state's system of taxation, including: changing the name of the tax assessor to *property appraiser*; adoption of the trim notice; and the calling of public hearings on proposed tax increases.

According to the two Florida representatives at the conference, Ed Brooks and Rod Nedeau, the law has been highly successful. They stated that citizens have been attending the public hearings and making their voices heard. Moreover, they claimed that since the law places elected officials much more in the limelight on issues of taxation levels, the stigma of being a tax assessor has been reduced noticeably. "It's working," Brooks said.

Circuit Breakers and Tax Credits

During the past two decades, a number of states have enacted legislation providing for *circuit breakers*—devices that automatically limit the amount of property taxes paid by some citizens, primarily the elderly. Although,

operationally, they vary significantly from state to state, taxpayers covered
by such programs will often pay their property taxes in full and then receive
either a rebate or the ability to make appropriate deductions from their state
income taxes.

While the participants from Kansas and Minnesota testified that their
programs were working quite successfully, others questioned both the value
and effectiveness of circuit breakers. Roy Bahl took such a stance, arguing
that while circuit breakers are often touted as ways to redistribute income,
much better methods are available.

Other participants voiced more specific concerns and criticisms. Gary
Cornia said that a major problem with Utah's recently enacted circuit-
breaker program is that only slightly more than half of the people eligible to
take part in it have thus far done so. As this complaint appears to be
somewhat common, there was some speculation by conference participants
on the reasons behind it. Dr. Marion S. Beaumont, of California State
University at Long Beach, suggested that the complexities of the application
procedure in California probably have a lot to do with the lack of participation in that state's circuit-breaker program. "People find that terrifying,"
Beaumont said. Others felt that a more important reason is the fact that
potential users often equate the programs with a form of welfare and thus
avoid them.

Doug Holbrook of the North Carolina Department of Revenue was
critical of circuit-breaker programs (or any other forms of property-tax
relief) that are tied to a state income-tax system. "All of the people," he
stated, "know the county tax supervisor, the assessor, and they've dealt
with him for years if they've owned property, which is most of them. Now,
if you take the circuit-breaker route, they have to deal with a whole crowd
of folks they don't know, and a whole bunch of forms that they are not
familiar with—because at least part of the people who would qualify here,
many of them have never filed an income-tax form, and the great majority
wouldn't owe any income tax . . . It's not as simple as just saying, 'Take a
credit on your income tax.' It's a whole new initiation. You put them in a
state system that they know nothing about."

Exemptions

Exemptions, particularly partial exemptions and those exemptions that relate
to homesteads, are perhaps the most common form of relief measure. There
is considerable diversity, however, in their operations and eligibility requirements. Florida has a basic $5,000 homestead exemption, which increases
if one is a legal resident of the state for five years. Additionally, the state has
exemptions for the disabled, both veterans and nonveterans. Exemptions for

veterans—including a complete deduction for disabled veterans—are also found in New Jersey, a state that has some rather interesting exemptions, including those for homesteads utilizing solar-energy devices and for residential property in areas with significant air and water pollution. Minnesota, on the other hand, does not have exemptions as such. Rather, non-farm homesteads are assessed and taxed at different percentages based on value.

Texas employs several forms of homestead exemptions, including those for disabled veterans. There is also a local option in the state for exemptions for persons over sixty-five and the disabled, with no upper limit. One unique feature of the Texas law applies to the over sixty-five in regard to school taxes: when a citizen reaches age sixty-five, their school taxes are essentially frozen. According to Kenneth Graeber, this feature has been a political boon to the state's school system, because it has "taken the heat off" of them for increases in taxes from older citizens (who, for the most part, no longer have children in school).

This particular feature of Texas law caused Graeber to inquire whether any of the conference participants had ever been sued in federal court under the equal-protection clause—since, fifteen years from now, there will more than likely be a wide discrepancy in Texas between the school taxes paid by someone aged sixty-five and someone aged eighty. Ed Brooks replied that he had been sued in federal court as an assessor over a considerably different matter, but his response once again engendered discussion of what was one of the conference's major subthemes: the increasing impact of litigation on property-tax policy and practice. One Roundtable member with considerable legal experience stated that he had discovered that the case burden relating to state and local property taxation in the federal courts had risen dramatically during the 1970s. He then offered an explanation for this increase, one that clearly touches upon a major issue confronting property tax-scholars and practitioners in the coming decade: "Plaintiffs have been trying to get away from the widely disparate decisions which they have been getting in state courts."

Assessment Practice

As is the case with virtually any other operation of government, operational and administrative practices impact highly upon the efficacy of any particular grouping of property-tax policies and laws. With the property tax, the major points of focus in this regard have to deal with assessment practices—an area in which there has been considerable change during the past two decades. And while most of the conference participants agreed that assessment practices had improved over the past few years, they also concurred with Marion Beaumont that they need to be made "much more effective." Items of major interest under this heading include the determination of assessment districts and responsibilities; the frequency of assessment; the selection and training of assessors; and the degree to which computerized appraisal systems have been adopted and implemented.

Review

Three participants were selected to discuss assessment-review practices in their home regions. In British Columbia, the twenty-seven regional assessors (who are responsible for the assessment roles) are subject to what J.T. Gwartney referred to as a "tight review system." A central component to this system is the assessment authority's field-audit division, which reviews—including by way of field visits—and reports upon the quality of assessment in each region. Moreover, all of the regional assessors are subject to direct review by their supervisors. One interesting practice in the review process in the province, which was mentioned by Roundtable Chairman H. Clyde Reeves, is that when a particular property is valued higher than comparable properties, the assessment authority tends to upgrade the values of the others, rather than lower the single exception.

Florida utilizes what appears to be a fairly exhaustive review system. Once every two years, in-depth studies are done of the assessment practices in each county. These investigations include computerized study of samples drawn from all strata, plus on-site assessments performed by appraisers. This investigation is followed by a detailed comparative analysis, which also gives the assessor under review ample opportunity to challenge the findings of the appraisers.

Dr. Frederick D. Stocker described Ohio's review system as encompassing an "accessible appeals procedure." He noted, however, that most of the appeals that have been carried forward concern business property, which has caused him to wonder whether residential property owners have received satisfaction at lower levels of review or whether they have in some form been deterred from utilizing the review system altogether. Stocker also provided some evidence on one phenomenon in the review process that is appearing more frequently, both in Ohio and in other states: school districts appealing the assessments of business property. According to Stocker, the reasons for this trend in Ohio have to do with the fact that school districts now view the property tax as an exclusive revenue and, because they are in serious financial difficulty, they have sought to increase these revenues by making certain that business properties have not been undervalued.

Computer-Assisted Mass Appraisal (CAMA)

Computer-assisted mass-appraisal techniques and systems—an area in which the Lincoln Institute of Land Policy has been an educational leader—have received an increasing amount of attention during the past decade. Two participants, from Arizona and British Columbia, briefly reviewed their systems, both of which are undergoing substantial revision. Although it is still not used in all of its counties, Arizona's rather extensive computer-based system has been in use since the early 1970s. Presently, according to Seth Franzman, it is being modified in two major ways: one that concerns the base-home approach; the other that will allow for the establishment of market areas and subareas within counties. British Columbia currently utilizes a batch data-processing system, with minicomputers in the field. In 1982, however, the provincial assessment authority will install an on-line system that should allow for further improvements in their market analyses.

Not all of the news at the conference regarding CAMA systems, however, was encouraging. Gary C. Cornia related how Utah's computer-assisted appraisal system, still very much in its infancy, will most likely cease to exist. Cornia cited the opposition in the state's rural counties, a movement against property assessment, and an ethos that considers such devices as bordering on government intrusion as important reasons. "It's a real retreat," he said. The Utah experience also prompted some participants to question how general public resistance to computer-based appraisal models might be overcome.

Frequency

The multifarious nature of laws and requirements governing the frequency by which property is to be assessed for tax purposes in the United States and Canada was well illustrated by a handful of conference participants. In British Columbia, the assessment authority is required to come up with the market value of all properties each year—but there is not a requirement that actual, on-site assessments be made annually. The degree to which these on-site assessments are made, J.T. Gwartney stated, is primarily a function of planning priorities and staff availability. Recently, the assessment authority finished its first complete reinspection with standardized field cards, a device Gwartney feels will significantly expedite that process in the future.

Ohio's frequency requirements have undergone considerable change during the past decades. According to Frederick D. Stocker, for many years the state required that, for all intents and purposes, all property must be assessed once every three years. In 1972, the General Assembly enacted a provision providing for an annual update, but that provision was repealed some three years later. Currently, the state operates under a sextennial reappraisal system, with an update every three years.

In New York, on the other hand, assessors work under what appear to be considerably less well-defined guidelines. According to David Gaskell, while not explicit, the pertinent statute implicitly requires that assessments be made annually. The result is that some appraisers do indeed make annual reassessments, while some never do. "We have the full range," Gaskell stated.

Standards

Assessment standards as discussed at the conference were also a study in contrasts. There were considerable variations in de jure assessment levels from state to state (ranging from 30 percent to 100 percent), a situation that was mirrored in de facto assessment levels (which ranged from 5 percent up). An interesting sidelight to the relatively brief discussion of standards was the wealth of terms and definitions employed by various states as to what their assessment standards would be measured against. A number of states utilize just, or full, market value. Others, like Ohio, utilize what appear to be somewhat more homegrown concepts—in this case being *taxable value*, which is a fraction of true market value.

Assessors

The front line of any system of property taxation is, of course, composed of its assessors. Evidence was provided by a number of conference participants on the selection and training of assessors in their state—yet another aspect of the property-tax system in the United States and Canada that has experienced considerable activity and evolution in recent decades. One conference participant well summarized the overall thrust of this recent history: "We have come to a time of trying to make assessment a professional, technical job."

Exceptions, needless to say, do exist, and there is considerable diversity in both the selection and training procedures utilized in the various states. Assessors in Florida are elected, and although a certification process and numerous training and education programs are offered, they are not mandatory. A similar dearth of requirements also exists in some assessment districts in Maine, where assessors are appointed. In New York, assessors are both elected and appointed, but once a jurisdiction adopts an appointive system, it cannot return to an elective one. A number of states offer continuing-education courses or related programs in community colleges and conduct certification procedures—the latter of which is often conducted in conjunction with the International Association of Assessing Officers (IAAO).

Ohio's system of contracting out virtually all of its assessment functions to the private sector engendered some discussion on the relative merits of such practices. One participant, whose state has been moving away from the use of private appraisal firms, mentioned local hostility to "outsiders" as a significant force to reckon with in the sensitive area of assessment. The opinions held by some participants that private concerns are unable to provide the quality of service provided by a professional, in-house staff were directly countered by other participants. Lastly, there was noticeable sentiment that assessors should be appointed, and not elected, owing to the increasingly technical nature of their work. "We don't elect city engineers," one participant stated.

Assessment Districts

If diversity was a catchword of the conference, in few places was this better exhibited than in the numbers of assessment districts in various states. In a number of states, there is one assessment district per county, giving Arizona a total of 14. In states where much more localized assessment districts are in existence, the numbers reach seemingly staggering levels. New Jersey has 567 assessment districts. Topping the list were New York, which has, legally, some 1,500 assessment districts and 8,700 taxing jurisdictions, and Minnesota, which has some 2,600 assesssment districts.

The figures for New York and Minnesota prompted Roundtable Chairman H. Clyde Reeves to inquire whether it was possible for the assessment function to be performed in a professional manner with such a plethora of assessment districts—to which he received generally negative replies. The reason for the large numbers, according to the states' representatives, concerned a still-prevailing home-rule mentality that affects, for example, the large number of fire departments in the region just as much as it impacts on property-tax assessment. From another region of the country, Kenneth Graeber gave an update on the attempt being made in Texas to decrease its number of assessment districts (through the creation of *appraisal districts*), something that one state legislator has gloomily referred to as a "noble experiment that the public won't accept."

Classification for Assessment Responsibility

A final topic discussed by conference participants under the general heading of assessment practice concerned classification for assessment responsibility.

Specifically, what is assessed by the state, what is assessed locally, and how are such classifications determined? The four participants selected to provide information on these practices in their states also revealed something of the range of such practices nationwide.

Arizona has central authority for the assessment of railroads, pipelines, and other *complex properties* that often cross county lines. Utilizing a unit-value approach, the taxes on such properties are then collected at the county level. In Ohio, the assessment of railroad and utility property is performed at the state level (as is the assessment of some personal property relative to such concerns), while the assessment of most other real estate is a local function. A similar system is at work in Minnesota, where the state plays a major role in the assessment of railroads and airport property, with the districts collecting the taxes. Texas, on the other hand, is in Kenneth Graeber's words "probably the only state in the Union which has a constitutional prohibition against the statewide appraisal of property." In the cases of the assessment of railroads, pipelines, and mineral properties that cross county boundaries, he reported that these have been contracted out to some five major firms for some time.

For a number of participants, the issue of what is a proper mix of state and local assessment responsibilities is very much a central item in any discussion of the property tax. While acknowledging that state assessment is preferable in certain situations, F. Ted Hebert of the University of Oklahoma asserted that "there are some places where the issue of local assessment is extremely strong and it would not be easy to change." Will S. Myers, executive director of the Advisory Panel on Financing Elementary and Secondary Education, felt that it is necessary to "tie the property tax to the area served . . . It can't be a global tax." Whatever their particular prescription, however, most participants agreed with Will Knedlik who stated that, "The question whether the property tax is a state tax or a local tax has to be addressed more fully."

Costs and Policy Leadership

Two other topics discussed at the conference were costs and policy leadership. Concerning the former, comparative data was provided for several states on average costs per parcel for assessment and on the salary ranges of assessment officers. Considerable speculation also occurred regarding what determines costs per parcel and whether such figures can be adequately assessed. The last topic addressed by the participants was policy leadership—a subject that, once again, yielded a diversity of experiences and concerns.

Costs

Considerable variance existed in the cost-per-parcel data provided by con-ference participants—at least between the U.S. representatives and their sole Canadian counterpart. The figures provided from the United States were fairly uniform: Florida averages out at about $8.50; Maine at around $9; the range in Texas is between $7 and $9; and in Ohio, where the assess-ment function is almost completely contracted out, costs-per-parcel average out at about $10.

In British Columbia, however, where the assessment authority is a government corporation, the average cost per parcel is about twenty-four dollars (in Canadian dollars). J.T. Gwartney gave four major reasons for this seemingly high rate: the province has a large number of industrial prop-erties (including sawmills, pipelines, and oil refineries) that are difficult to value; there is an annual evaluation of all property; the assessment authority is staffed with highly competent, and relatively well-paid, personnel; and the authority virtually pays for everything that it does, including its own data processing. This testimony led to some speculation by participants that the actual costs per parcel in the United States must be considerably higher, owing to the fact that costs such as office space (the assessment authority in British Columbia rents private office space, unlike its U.S. counterparts, which are normally housed in public buildings) are rarely, if ever, figured in.

Information on the salaries paid to assessors was also given by a number of participants. In British Columbia, the heads of its twenty-seven assess-ment regions are paid between $40,000 and $55,000 annually (Canadian dollars). Salaries for full-time assessors in Florida range from $20,000 for smaller counties to upward of $55,000 in larger ones. Texas has a similar spread, ranging from $18,000 to $70,000. In New York state, which has a number of extremely small jurisdictions, annual salaries go from $200 to $20,000 (the latter for the state's larger cities, excluding New York City).

Policy Leadership

Policy leadership in property taxation was, again, a topic of considerably diverse experiences. Two participants stated that there was very little strong policy leadership within their state government, and that they each had "Jarvis-like" individuals (or various taxpayers' associations) that were cur-rently exerting the most power. Two other participants, on the other hand, stated that their own assessment offices were undeniably the leaders in property-tax policy.

Most participants related experiences that were somewhere in the mid-dle; that is, that policy leadership was a shared responsibility and one in which the predominant players were in government service. A representative from a smaller state said that leadership in his state was shared between the governor's office and the legislature and that they set policy generally without the urging of assessment-related personnel. Another participant stated that in his state the head of the state bureaucracy concerned with property assessment plays a major role in setting property-tax policy with the governor's office, even though the legislature feels that it has *the* predominant role. "They think our job is only to carry out policy," he said, "not make it." The testimony of one final participant, an officer in his state's assessment office, well underlined the political nature of policy leadership. In his state, the leadership is supposed to rest with both the legislature and the executive, but neither group has ever taken an active interest in the subject, leaving his office as the primary source. When questioned as to how his office exerted its leadership role, he replied that they "very quietly find someone in the legislature whose idea it then becomes."

Conference participants also highlighted certain political components impacting on the functioning of policy leadership in property taxation. One former state official asserted that in his state, senior citizens wield an immense amount of power in property-tax matters and argued that this situation will be detrimental to the system. "We're not going to have a property-tax system with any integrity left in twenty years," he said, "given the political power that they (senior citizens) have and given the fact that they are being encouraged to remain homeowners at the same time the younger people can't come into the home-ownership category." Other participants argued that the "nature" of most elected officials in dealing with the property tax had to be remembered. One corporate official claimed that "most of the political people whom you have to deal with on these matters don't want to face up to any problems in the current system."

Although there was a considerable divergence of opinion on what the state's (and its component parts) overall role should be in property-tax-policy leadership, there was a general agreement that this area needed better definition. "One obligation of the state," Gene Burner stated, "and here I primarily refer to the state legislature, is clear state laws, and clear public-policy statements in the laws, with respect to how assessment processes should be performed, and not left up to some administrator's or bureaucrat's interpretation."

**The Role
of the State
in Property
Taxation**

1 The Role of the State in Property Taxation in Arizona

Seth L. Franzman

Legal Framework

The Arizona Constitution and the Arizona Revised Statutes provide for a property-tax system that is based upon coordinated state- and local-government efforts. The state's administrative responsibilities are vested primarily in the Department of Revenue, and carried out through the Division of Property and Special Taxes and the county assessors.

The property-tax system has evolved from the first Arizona State General Property Tax adopted at the time of statehood (1912). A territorial property tax was assessed prior to 1913. Under early territorial law, the county sheriff appraised property, assessed taxes, and collected taxes. In 1912, the legislature established a state tax commission to supervise the county assessors and to assess properties of express companies and private-car companies. A board of equalization was created at the same time, with responsibility for setting the state tax rates. From these fundamental concepts, a modern, productive, and complex property-tax system has been developed. Most of the changes introduced into that system have been installed in the period since 1967, when the results of a property-reappraisal program became known. This program was made necesssary by a 1963 Arizona Supreme Court ruling in the Southern Pacific case requiring that the legislature set classes of property and percentage of relationships of assessment to full value, or assess all property at full value.

The current property-tax system incorporates *dual* values (full cash value and limited value) as bases for assessing and levying property taxes. Limited property value was implemented as a means of restricting property-tax increases and was adopted by a special election in June 1980. Another important part of the program to restrict property-tax increases was limitation of increases of the property-tax levy to 2 percent over the prior year (with exceptions for new or annexed property). In general, primary taxes, those approved by referendum or for debts so approved, are levied on full value, and all discretionary rates are levied on limited values. Limited property values had been established equal to the 1979 full cash value. Then, for 1980, 1981, and 1982 the limited assessed value for property could be increased to the current year's full cash value or by 10 percent over the prior year's limited value, whichever is less.

1

A catch-up procedure intended to close the difference between full cash value and limited property value is effective for 1983 and following years, according to current statutory provisions. Under that procedure, limited property value for the prior year may be increased by the *greater* of (a) 10 percent, or (b) 25 percent of the difference between the full cash value for the current year and the limited value of the property for the prior year.

Residential Property-Tax Limitation

By a 1980 amendment to the state constitution, primary property taxes on residential property may not exceed 1 percent of the limited value of that property. If primary property taxes levied on a residential parcel exceed 1 percent of the limited value, the levy will be reduced to the 1-percent level by reduction of the school-district taxes on that parcel. The reduced school taxes are then paid to the school district through additional state aid to school districts. The Homeowner Property Tax Reduction Program (1973) and the program of Additional State Aid to School Districts (1980) have transferred significant funding from the state to school districts for the purpose of reducing the property-tax burden on residential property.

Other Limitation Provisions

Statutory exceptions to the market-value standard for determination of full cash value pertain to agricultural land and to gas- and electric-utilities property. Agricultural land is valued using an income approach. The rate of capitalization established by statute is based upon federal-land-bank interest rates. Specifically, that rate is defined as "one-and-one-half percentage points higher than the average long-term annual effective interest rate for all new federal-land-bank loans for the five-year period prior to the year for which the valuation is being determined." The capitalization rate for 1981 was approximately 10.5 percent.

A special statutory procedure was also prescribed for the valuation of gas- and electric-utilities property, effective for the 1980 tax year. In very simple terms, that procedure provides for valuation of gas- and electric-utilities property on the basis of: (a) depreciated cost of plant in service (with certain adjustments); plus (b) cost of materials and supplies on hand; and (c) 50 percent of the cost of construction work in progress.

Property Classification

Arizona's property-tax system is based upon statutory property classes and variable assessment ratios applicable to those classes. Currently, there are eight legal classes of property, which, with their 1981 assessment ratios, are as follows:

Class One	Airline-flight property, producing mines, standing timber (52 percent).
Class Two	Telephone and telegraph property, gas, electric, and water utilities, pipelines (44 percent).
Class Three	Commercial and industrial property (25 percent).
Class Four	Agricultural property (16 percent).
Class Five	Residential property, nonprofit residential housing facilities for handicapped or elderly persons, licensed nursing-care institutions for handicapped or elderly persons (10 percent).
Class Six	Leased or rented residential property (18 percent).
Class Seven	Railroad-operating property, private-car-company property (to be determined annually by director (35 percent).
Class Eight	Historic property (8 percent).

Prior to 1967, only one class of property legally existed in Arizona. De facto property classes, however, had evolved over many years from assessment practices. Upon completion of a statewide property-reappraisal program in 1967, the legislature adopted four property classes with assessment ratios ranging from 18 percent to 60 percent of full cash value.

The number of property classes has doubled since 1967. Statutory provisions have been adopted, however, which are designed to reduce gradually the assessment ratios for *Class One* and *Class Two* from 1981 levels of 52 percent and 44 percent, respectively, to 25 percent in 1992.

Administration

Administrative Changes

The property-tax program developed by the legislature in 1967 also revised the administration of the Arizona property-tax system. That program contained several significant features. Most of them helped to strengthen the state's role in administering the property-tax system. The most important change was the creation of the Department of Property Valuation, an independent agency, which was created from the Division of Appraisal and Assessment Standards. This department was assigned all the duties of the tax commission with respect to the property tax. In 1974, the department was merged into a newly created Department of Revenue, headed by a director appointed by the governor (with the approval of the Arizona Senate).

Functions of the State Board of Equalization were assigned to a newly created Board of Property Tax Appeals, which was authorized to hear appeals and to equalize property values. The three board members were appointed by the governor and served in a part-time capacity.

Legislation also established that appeals for locally assessed property were to originate at the county-assessor level and could then be carried on to the County Board of Equalization and the State Board of Property Tax Appeals. After levy of taxes, appeals could be carried into the county superior court (trial court). Centrally valued properties could be appealed to the Department of Property Valuation, which had jurisdiction for valuation, then to the state board and the superior court.

A real-estate transfer fee was also adopted that required filing of an affidavit of value of real property. Although the fees (collected by county recorders) are relatively small as a revenue producer, the affidavit is an important source of market data for appraisal purposes. Property-value data from those affidavits became the basis for a computer-assisted market-appraisal model (installed in 1973) and for a sales-ratio-analysis system.

County Assessors

Local-government duties in the property-tax system are primarily the responsibility of elected assessors in each of the fourteen counties. Locally assessed properties include residential, commercial and industrial, agricultural, and other general-property categories. Each county assessor has responsibility for annually ascertaining all property in his county that is subject to taxation (but not otherwise valued by the department), and for valuing that property through use of manuals and procedures prescribed by the Department of Revenue.

Each county assessor is designated by statute as a deputy director of the Department of Revenue. That designation was made for the legal purpose of determining the valuation of property within each county for *state* property-tax purposes. The Department of Revenue has statutory duty to levy the *state* tax rates on real and personal property in the various counties subject to taxation. The county boards of supervisors are then required to levy property taxes for all *county* purposes upon the same property and upon the same valuation. Therefore, assessment of property taxes for state- and local-government purposes is made upon the same property, using the same values, and is a coordinated effort between state and local government agencies.

Department of Revenue

Although most types of taxable property are appraised by the county assessors, several classes of special-use property are appraised at the state level by the Department of Revenue through the Division of Property and Special Taxes.

Such centrally valued property includes railroads; telephone and telegraph properties; gas and electric utilities; pipelines; water utilities; microwave systems; mines; and producing oil, gas, and geothermal interests. Private rail cars and airline-flight property (aircraft) are also appraised by the state, which also collects the property taxes.

The department has the statutory responsibility to adopt standard appraisal methods and techniques for use by the department and the county assessors in determining the valuation of property. The department also has responsibility for preparing and maintaining manuals and guidelines reflecting those methods and techniques; standardization of property-tax information, maps, and records; and insuring the compatability of data-processing systems.

The Department of Revenue is required to furnish assistance to county assessors to implement placement of property values on the tax rolls and to ensure uniform valuation of all property for state property-tax purposes. Department personnel and other resources may be used in furnishing such assistance, and statutory provision is made for counties to be charged for such assistance.

Departmental Organization

Since 1 July 1980, all persons who exercise authority of an assessor or appraiser of property on behalf of any county must be certified by the Department of Revenue to be competent to perform that work. Although exempted from provisions of that statutory requirement, most county assessors have sought to achieve the basic certification required of others.

Performance audits of county assessors' offices are intended to ensure uniformity of assessment practices among the various counties and to determine compliance with department policies, manuals, and guidelines.

The Central Information Services Unit of the department coordinates and administers performance of contractual data-processing services provided by the department to several counties. Those services include all data-processing requirements for preparing and maintaining assessment records and preparing tax rolls, tax bills, and abstracts of the assessment rolls. Other information and assistance are also provided to assessors, county treasures, and the department by this unit.

Data-processing services for the Division of Property and Special Taxes of the Department of Revenue are provided by the Division of Administration. That division also provides data-processing services under contract to several counties for maintaining and processing property-tax records.

Maintaining Appraisals

Estimates of resources required by county assessors for maintaining annual valuations and adequate assessment records were staggering—particularly in the heavily populated Maricopa and Pima counties. Therefore, an alternative to annual property valuations by assessors' personnel was sought by the director of the Department of Property Valuation. Based upon consultation and advice from the attorney general, a three-year appraisal cycle was initiated in Maricopa and Pima counties. Appeals alleging discrimination in that plan were lodged.

A 1974 superior-court decision in Pima County did indeed rule the three-year cycle of appraisal to be discriminatory. Therefore, a technique to permit mass appraisal of locally assessed property was required for the county assessors to comply with the law. Anticipating this need, a computer-assisted appraisal system utilizing the statistical technique of multiple-regression analysis was developed by the Department of Property Valuation and employed in 1973. That technique was adapted to appraisal of residential property because that property class was characterized by a large volume of sales.

Computer-Assisted Appraisal

The Mass Appraisal System, developed at the state level, employs computerized processing of large volumes of appraisal data to project values for residential properties on an annual basis. While not applicable in all counties, or for all residential properties in some counties to which it is applied, the Mass Appraisal System is a major breakthrough in addressing the problem of maintaining annual property-value updates.

Implementation of the system has not been without some problems, however. A report by the Legislative Research Staff of the House of Representatives reported:

> Mass Appraisal System (MAS) valuation runs were made for the 1973 tax year. The values produced by the system were generally 25 percent higher than the values produced by the county assessors. The assessors initially balked at the idea of using such a system, but the Department ordered that the MAS values be used, and the assessors, as deputies of the Department, complied.

Ironically, the Pima County Superior Court decision that found the three-year appraisal cycle discriminatory was subsequently overturned. However, the practical need for an effective computer-assisted appraisal system has remained.

Fiscal Importance

1980 Property Tax

In Arizona the property tax is a major revenue source for schools and local governments. In 1980 only about 12 percent of the total property tax levied in the state was for state purposes. Over 50 percent of that tax was levied for schools and community colleges. In 1980 property taxes levied for all purposes totaled over $821 million. Approximately $3 million more was levied on airline-flight property and private-care companies.

When compared with three other major taxes administered by the Department of Revenue, the property tax, measured by total revenue production (state and local), was the leading revenue producer by a slight margin. For the fiscal year 1979-80, combined state and local property taxes were about 37 percent of the total for sales and use taxes, property tax, income tax, and luxury and estate taxes.

As the Arizona population has grown in recent years, so has the demand upon property tax as a revenue source. Stabilization of the per-capita property-tax burden has been noted recently. That trend should continue under the new limitations on value and levy increases that have been built into the system. The 1980 per-capita property tax was approximately $307.

Assessment Costs

Comparisons of the costs of operating the property-tax system and of assessment results are difficult to make in Arizona. The state is characterized geographically by large open spaces wherein only about 18 percent of the total land area is in private ownership—ranging from a low of 3 percent (Gila County) to a high of 41 percent (Cochise). There is also a wide variety of property conditions scattered throughout the state, with few urbanized areas and generally light population density. Budgets provide the only applicable data available and should be used carefully and considered only as rough indicators due to the limitations inherent in them. (Although these data can be utilized in a number of ways, only per-parcel and percent-of-revenue analyses are summarized here).

Amounts budgeted by the county assessors and the Division of Property and Special Taxes of the Department of Revenue for 1980-81 are likely more than actual costs, because the budgeted amounts represent the *maximum* expenditure (They do not, however, include certain costs involved in the appeals process). Budgeted cost per parcel based upon budgets of county assessors averaged $5.90 per parcel for 1980-81. That expenditure ranged from $2.28 (Apache) to $11.18 (Graham) per parcel. Budgeted expenditure by the Division of Property and Special Taxes for 1980-81 was $1.45 per parcel, based upon a total of 1,616,000 parcels in the state. The total budgeted expenditure by county assessors and the division, then, was $7.35 per parcel.

When analyzed on the basis of a proportion of property tax attributed to locally assessed property, the weighted mean of budgeted expenditures by assessors as a percentage of estimated property tax from locally assessed property averaged 1.73 percent, and ranged from 1.26 percent (Maricopa) to 12.96 percent (Greenlee). The mean of data for individual counties was 3.92 percent; the median was 3.17 percent. Due to distortions in the weighted and unweighted means by Maricopa, Pima, and Greenlee counties the median statistic is a better measure of budgeted expenditures in this case.

No extensive effort is known to have been made in Arizona to estimate the total public cost, including billing and collection, of administering the state's property-tax system.

Policy Framework

Policy Development

In recent years property-tax policies in Arizona have been developed by the legislature and codified in statutes that have given those policies a clear definition of direction. As has been the case in many other states, those policies have frequently been forged in response to events that have placed substantial stresses upon that system.

The 1963 property-reappraisal program was ordered by the legislature in response to the Arizona Supreme Court's decision in the Southern Pacific case. The 1973 Homeowner Property Tax Reduction Program was adopted by the legislature to provide relief to homeowners from increased tax burdens, brought about by increased property values. Those increased values had been charted by a new computer-assisted mass-appraisal system that is better able to keep up with market conditions than previously used methods. Further legislative adjustments to that program have been made in subsequent years to deal with the effects of inflation and changed economic conditions upon property values.

In 1980, major changes in the property-tax program were developed by the legislature in response to expressions of public attitudes toward property-tax burdens and government spending levels. The primary features of that program were referred to the electorate for approval of amendments to the constitution in June 1980. Similar expressions of public opinion in California had brought about adoption of Proposition 13. With prospects of a nearly identical proposition on the general-election ballot in November 1980, the legislature acted quickly to avoid many of the problems inherent in the California response. The new Arizona program is based in large part upon the policies of limiting property taxes by limiting value increases, limiting increases in tax levies, and shifting some of the cost of government away from the property tax.

Administrative policy has been developed with the objectives of improving appraisal and assessment practices throughout the state. Refinement of existing elements of the property-tax system and development of new measures to improve the system are objectives of the agencies that administer the public policy as defined in the law. In the final analysis, however, it is the interested and concerned citizens who shape policy of the property tax and define direction of that system.

Recommendations

The property tax has long been a vital revenue source for state and local government in Arizona. That role will likely be continued, because it would be difficult to replace the property tax with other revenue sources without major shifts and disruptions. Several recommendations have been noted below in the spirit of maintaining the vitality of the property tax as a significant component of state and local government finance:

The market-value standard should be preserved and reinforced as the basis for determining taxable property value. The property tax historically has been a tax upon wealth as represented by property and measured in the marketplace. Market value of property historically has been the standard for measuring the share of government costs to be paid by each property owner in the ad valorem property-tax system. Departure from the market-value standard undermines a basic philosophy of the ad valorem property tax and, thereby, its role in government finance.

Any limitations upon property tax burdens should be imposed upon expenditures and tax levies—rather than by constraining changes in taxable property values. Such practice would help preserve the concept of equity among properties in the same class.

Features of the property tax system such as exemptions and special procedures for treatment of selected properties add to the complexity and cost of administration and should be minimized or avoided. Unless adequate funding is made available to administer added duties, resources will probably be diverted away from the appraisal and assessment functions to accomplish the additional duties. The result is likely to be a deterioration of the quality of appraisal and assessment performance, which may call for more special treatment.

Continued development of appraisal and assessment staff proficiency is essential to maintenance of a competent property-tax system. Training of personnel in the performance of their job tasks is required on a continuing basis to improve upon efficiency of the system. Education in the technical aspects of appraisal, assessment, and related topics is required on a continuing basis to permit improvements in the quality of production of the system. The property-tax system is too valuable to the functioning of state and local governments to be entrusted to personnel who are inadequately trained in its operations or uneducated in its philosophies and principles.

Of the total property tax levied in Arizona in 1980, about 53 percent was levied for education purposes. Another 35 percent of the total was levied for other local-government purposes. Thus, about 88 percent of that total property tax levied was for expenditure by governmental units *at home.*

It is noteworthy that public awareness and concern for property-tax burdens may arise in large part due to that local, at-home character. While there may be a sense of hopelessness among taxpayers about exercising control over other forms of taxation, there may be a sense that the property tax is still within the grasp of those who pay it. If so, that sense is a major, positive commentary on the role of the property tax in government finance. The role of the state in administering that tax should be tempered by understanding that a healthy characteristic of the property tax is that taxpayers *do* feel that they can have a part in property-tax policy.

2 The Role of the Province in Property Taxation in British Columbia

J.T. Gwartney

The functioning of the property tax in British Columbia has undergone substantial change during the past three decades. In 1953 the Assessment Equalization Act was enacted to equalize assessments for school purposes throughout the province at a uniform percentage (50 percent) of actual value. As a result of large increases in real-estate prices beginning in the late 1960s, however, there were restrictions placed upon the amount by which individual assessments could be increased. This policy caused distortions and inequities in relationships within and between the classes of properties and between juiisdictions.

In the early 1970s the proposition of returning to assessments based upon actual (market) value was widely supported by both the provincial and municipal governments. The restrictions on assessment increases had weakened the local assessment function and produced an opportunity for change.

Legal Framework

The British Columbia Assessment Authority

In 1974, an all-party committee of the legislature completed a comprehensive review of assessments in British Columbia and concluded "that legislation be introduced at the current session to create a province-wide assessment authority. This authority must be independent of taxing function (either municipal or provincial) and its control must be such as will result unmistakably in complete independence." This recommendation was acted upon expeditiously and the Assessment Authority of British Columbia Act, which established the British Columbia Assessment Authority, was proclaimed on 2 July 1974.

Section 9 of the act states that the purpose of the authority "is to establish and maintain assessments that are uniform in the whole of the Province in accordance with the Assessment Act." The authority is governed by a board of directors in a manner similar to a public-utility company. The present board comprises six-members appointed by the lieutenant-governor in council for a three-year term, with the terms of two directors expiring each year.

The melding of 140 individual municipal assessment offices and 23 offices that came within the jurisdiction of the surveyor of taxes—who was responsible for assessments in the rural areas—into one organization was achieved, and the authority produced its first assessment rolls for the province in December 1974. The 27 new area offices, with support staff in Victoria, now exclusively carry out the entire process of assessment in the province.

Actual-Value Assessment

The first assessment roll using actual value as the basis for assessing real property was produced in December 1977. Assessments are based on uniform percentages of the actual value for each class of property. For the 1981 assessment roll, assessment was based on the actual value of property at 31 December 1980.

The assessed values on which the 1981 taxes for school and hospital taxation purposes are based have been determined using the percentages of actual value set out to table 2-1. In rural areas the same percentages of actual value are used in determining assessed values for general provincial taxation purposes.

For general municipal taxation purposes, however, municipalities have a choice: they may use the same assessment standard used for school and hospital taxation purposes, or they may choose another assessment standard. A number of municipalities uniformly assess all classes of property for general municipal taxation purposes at their full actual value (100 percent).

All property is valued, whether taxable or exempt. Both the federal and provincial governments pay grants-in-lieu of taxes, equivalent to full taxes in most cases.

Table 2-1
Actual-Value Assessment Table, British Columbia, 1981

Property	Percentage
Farm	10.0
Residential	11.0
Seasonal resort, recreational, and fraternal organizations	11.0
Business	24.5
Machinery and Equipment	25.0
Industries	28.6
Utilities	30.0
Forestry	30.0
Tree farms	60.0

Statutory Framework

Currently, the British North America Act assigns the right to tax property to the provinces. Provincial legislation and regulations govern the application and administration of assessments. The Assessment Act provides the statutory authority by requiring that all property be valued each year at actual value. In the court system, an appellant generally argues against actual value or classification.

Assessment Equity

The courts have held that uniformity of assessment is assured when all property is valued at actual value. If a property is valued at 100 percent of actual value, but others are valued at a lower level, the remedy is to appeal to have the other values raised.

Use-Value Assessments

Farms are assessed at 10 percent of their actual value *for farming purposes*. The assessed values are derived from farm-land-value schedules prescribed by the assessment commissioner. These schedules reflect the actual value of the land for farming purposes without regard to its value for any other purpose.

Agricultural lands may be classified as farm if used for farming purposes and provided the use meets the standards prescribed by the assessment commissioner. In general, these standards are that the primary agricultural production on the land by the owner or lessee sold in a twelve-month period must have a gross value of production at farm-gate prices of: (a) at least $1,600 on the first four hectares (ten acres), and (b) an amount equal to 5 percent of the actual value of the land for farm purposes that exceeds four hectares.

Land classified as a tree farm is valued by capitalizing the income from the perpetual harvest of trees.

The assessment commissioner annually prescribes rates (standard unit values) for railway trackage, telegraph lines, and oil and gas transmission pipelines. These rates are subject to appeal.

Tax-Relief Measures

The percentage levels of actual value used for assessment are determined annually by the government cabinet in an attempt to reduce tax-burden shift from one class of property to another. Tax-rate increases generally are not limited—except in rural areas where they are fixed by statute for general-revenue purposes.

A tax credit of up to $380 is available to eligible homeowners under sixty-five years of age, under the Home Owner Grant Act. Homeowners who reach age sixty-five or more in the current calendar year are eligible for an additional grant of $250. There is a minimum tax amount payable of $75 (or the total tax amount if less than $75) for homeowners under sixty-five years. For homeowners over sixty-five, and others qualifying for the maximum homeowner grant such as disabled homeowners, the minimum tax payable is $1.

Conditions covering the general eligibility for the Home Owner Grant include: the property must the owner's principal place of residence; the owner must annually complete the application form for the Home Owner Grant, set out on the tax notice; and, an owner may not apply for or receive a Home Owner Grant on more than one residence within British Columbia in any one calendar year.

It is possible to defer payment of property taxes on your ordinary place of residence if you are in one of several categories of property owner who may participate under the Land Tax Deferment Act. These categories include those who are sixty-five or over; a widow or widower; or, handicapped as defined in the Guaranteed Available Income for Need Act. Homeowners who qualify may defer taxes on their home until such time as the property is sold or otherwise transferred to another owner. Under the tax deferment program, interest is charged at 8 percent, compounded annually on taxes deferred.

There is no provision for circuit breakers in British Columbia. Renters are allowed to claim an income-tax credit of up to $150 in respect of the taxes they indirectly pay as part of their rent.

Administration

Assessment Authority

The responsibility for providing all assessments throughout British Columbia is the mandate and monopoly given to the British Columbia Assessment Authority, a public corporation. Local and provincial officials have no authority for making assessments. The components of one system function as follows:

> *Provincial government*—exercises the legislative function and can amend the governing acts. The cabinet has an annual responsibility to establish classes of property and percentage levels for assessed values.

Assessment authority—records ownership and property details, annually values all properties in the province, produces the assessment roll, and mails the assessment notices.

Municipalities and collection districts—levy and collect their own taxes and, for administrative economy, collect nearly all the taxes levied against property within their boundaries on behalf of other bodies such as schools, hospitals, the assessment authority, or regional districts.

The authority is governed by a six-member board of directors. The board appoints the assessment commissioner, who is charged with the overall responsibility for the administration of the Assessment Act.

Field Operations

The deputy assessment commissioner is responsible for managing field operations, including the area-assessors and head-office support functions. The authority has divided the province into twenty-seven assessment areas. The assessors and all staff are selected by employment competition, which is advertised throughout the province. The responsibility for the values on the assessment roll is that of the area assessors who each generally service three or more municipalities and rural districts. Support for area offices is provided by support services and appraisal services. Research, experimentation, and development of systems as well as the provision of expertise, ensures a progressive improvement in field operations.

Support Services: The prime mission of support services is to design, build, install, and maintain efficient systems and procedures required to produce assessment rolls in accordance with authority objectives. Its divisions include:

Appraisal and Office-Systems Division: Responsible for the design and maintenance of the actual-value calculation system and regarded as the user representative in head office for these systems.

Technical-Services Division: Responsible for mapping, microfilm, and statutory reporting systems (assessment rolls, notices, assessed-value calculations, reports, and studies).

Computer-Services Division: Responsible for designing, building, and operating the various computer systems to the specifications generated by the other support-services divisions.

Appraisal Services: The functions of appraisal services can be described under three broad headings: appraisal duties, training and research projects, and advice and counsel on unitary type of property. Under statute, the assessment commissioner prescribes the rates for the assessment of farmland, railways, gas and oil transmission lines, and telegraph lines. Technical and specialist appraisers assist with those properties. Four sections comprise appraisal services:

Agricultural Section: Provides farm-valuation schedules to achieve equitable farmland assessments, training so that field personnel can remain knowledgeable in farm valuation, and research in areas of productivity and new farmland creation.

Industrial Section: Provides support in the appraisal and maintenance of major industrial complexes, (for example, paper, pulp, and sawmills; mines; refineries; canneries; and industrial plants), as well as interarea complexes such as pipelines, electrical-power transmission lines, communications, and data-exchange systems.

General-Appraisal Section: Provides support in training, research, and coordination to ensure high quality of appraisals throughout the province. Emphasis is placed upon major office towers shopping complexes, hotels, and like structures that tend to be investments of broad appeal that require information on a provincial, rather than local, basis. Expertise is also provided on frontage tax rolls as well as specified and defined areas for municipalities and regional districts.

Timber-Appraisal Section: Deals with the valuation of both managed and unmanaged forest areas throughout the province.

Administrative Services

The authority, being an independent public body, provides its own adminstrative services. No services are received from other levels of government. The services include:

Financial Services: Charged with the responsibility of controlling the financial matters of the authority.

Personnel: Responsible for staffing, training, labor relations, personnel policies, and procedures for recruitment, selection, position classification, compensation (including benefit plans), staff education, and development.

Field Audit: Provides the assessment commissioner with the findings from an independent, systematic, and unbiased audit of each area office's performance with respect to the quality of the actual values on the current and proposed assessment rolls. Reviews the procedures, documentation, and coding used in the appraisal processes. Findings include cause and effect of various procedures and recommendations for corrective action where necessary.

Information and Legal: Reviews all court cases for possible further action; determines need for legal assistance; reviews and interprets legislation, regulations, and court decisions; replies to public inquiries and complaints; and provides statutory interpretations for field offices.

Staff Relations: Is jointly funded by the employer and the union. Assists any staff member in overcoming difficulties when dealing with personal and interpersonal problems within the working environment. Acts as an information contact point for all staff in areas of general interest such as employee benefits, retirement, and education—while identifying problems in communication, structure, policy, or procedure within the authority.

Assessment Appeals

There is a court of revision appointed for each school district (which often includes several municipalities) to review assessment rolls, hear appeals, make changes, and certify the rolls. The courts are appointed and funded by the provincial government and have no connection with the authority.

Appeals of the court decisions are heard by the Assessment Appeal Board. There are now four appeal boards comprised of lawyers and professional appraisers who are appointed and funded by the provincial government.

Frequency of Assessment

The Assessment Act requires all property to be reassessed annually to reflect actual value. Sales analysis is performed throughout the year. Prior to roll preparation in December, all the values from the previous year's roll are adjusted by a series of market factors. Since it is not possible to physically enter all property each year, the authority has been working on a five-year reinspection program. This plan has allowed time to implement a standardized field card with standard format and data. The program of data capture will be completed at the end of 1981. Then, a six-year program will involve the reinspection of all residential property once and the reinspection of all nonresidential property twice. The purpose will be to improve and consolidate the information we have gathered and to prepare the data for computer-assisted appraisal programs.

Assessment Quality

The legal standard of quality is that all property must be valued at actual value as of December 31 of the year preceding the year in which the assessment roll is used for taxation purposes. This task is difficult to accomplish in a rapidly rising market, as our final computer factoring and updating must be performed in October well ahead of the December 31 valuation date. As a result, a valuation date of July 1 has been proposed as being more practical.

Assessment level is measured in the standard manner by comparing assessments to selling prices. Dispersion is measured by the coefficient of dispersion (C.O.D.). The standards that have been established for the assessment areas are as shown in table 2-2.

The majority of area offices have been able to achieve these standards; however, in 1981, rapid property-value increases may reduce the number of offices able to achieve the standard.

Local Review

In addition to the central computerized sale-ratio studies, area assessors produce their own manual sales studies. Many of our assessment area offices assign work on a geographic basis, where a single appraiser is responsible for approximately three thousand properties. This system enables monitoring of appraisal performance, uniformity of approach within the area, and the furtherance of pride taken in the work by the individual.

Table 2-2
Current British Columbia Assessment Authority Coefficient of Dispersion (C.O.D.) Standards

	Maximum Desirable C.O.D.	
Classification	*1980*	*1982*
Homogeneous—urban (cities, towns, urban districts)	7.5	6.0
Homogeneous—heterogeneous mix (rural, rural districts, urban periphery villages)	10.0	7.5
Heterogeneous—rural (farms, outlying land)	15.0	12.5

Municipalities and individuals have a right to appeal the assessment rolls. Municipalities will bring to the attention of the assessment appeal board any faults in assessment practice.

Reporting to the assessment commissioner is the field-audit section, which periodically reviews the method and success of work performed in each area office and also reviews the sales-ratio studies.

Facilities—Expertise

The area assessors' offices are separate from the municipal buildings, and are generally located with convenient access for the public. Currently, these offices process ownership and value changes on minicomputers. During 1982, an on-line centralized data-processing system will be installed province-wide.

Appraisal staff hired at the appraiser-trainee level have completed substantial classroom work in real-estate and appraisal subjects. To advance to the level of working appraiser, a person must continue with the more advanced appraisal subjects. A record of on-the-job training and proficiency is maintained centrally for each individual.

Supervising appraisers are required to be professional appraisers. Accreditations from the Appraisal Institute of Canada and the Real Estate Institute of British Columbia are currently acceptable as professional designations. Management and supervisory staff are professionally designated—as well as a large number of working-level appraisers.

Current staff compliment (763 total) includes 407 appraisal; 209 clerical; 60 head-office support; 87 management-excluded.

Direct Assessments

The authority has adopted uniform record systems that allow collection of data in a standardized format. Date-base files containing information required for assessment and valuation purposes have been planned. Currently there are subsystems that assist appraisers in valuing land, machinery, and equipment. The most generally used are Replacement Cost New Less Depreciation and Multiple Regression Analyses.

Public-service companies are valued on an ad valorem basis as opposed to a unit-valuation concept.

Direction to Local Assessors

The assessors have statutory responsibility for the production of the assessment roll, and the head-office staff provides advice and assistance to the assessor. This aid consists largely of training, lectures, development of manuals, field-car procedures, data-processing systems, office systems, appraisal systems, personnel procedures, and financial procedures. The assessors report to the commissioner through regional directors and the deputy assessment commissioner.

Fiscal Importance

Actual values have experienced rapid growth since the authority was created in 1974, and property-tax revenues have increased sharply as is shown by tables 2-3 and 2-4.

Assessment Cost

The assessment authority derives its revenue from three principal sources: tax levy on property, 62 percent; provincial grant, 26 percent; other income, 12 percent.

The tax levy is applied to all property taxable. For 1980, the millage rate was set at 1.295.

The provinical government grant is fixed by regulation. For the 1980 budget, it was set at 33 percent of the 1979 operating expenditures or 26 per cent of budgeted revenue.

Other income is derived from the sale of services and supplies. Services include the production of business tax rolls and frontage rolls for some municipalities. Sales of maps, sales listings, assessment-roll copies, land-title plans, microfiche, computer printouts, and interest on total operating expenditures have been increasing steadily—from $18 million in 1975 to $26.8 million in 1980.

The authority expends 74 percent of its budget on the salaries of employees. The balance of expenditures include such items as accommodations, travel, office supplies and equipment, and data-processing services.

Table 2-3
Gross Yield Comparisons, British Columbia

Gross Yield	1960	1970	1979
School property tax	58,946,466	199,713,818	668,060,286
Percentage of total expenditure	58.58%	65.99%	70.51%
Municipal property tax	58,904,114	134,008,334	407,759,000
Percentage of total expenditure	84.79%	77.83%	85.32%
Total property tax	123,837,770	351,249,731	1,097,329,562
Percentage of all government expenditures	25.11%	19.94%	18.31%

Table 2-4
Distribution of Property Tax, British Columbia, 1979

Distribution	Amount
Municipal	$ 507,505,050
School	668,060,286
Rural	21,510,276
Hospital	23,031,219
Assessment authority	17,940,052
Regional districts	16,470,894
Other	4,213,658
Federal and provincial grants-in-lieu	31,082,232
Total property taxes	$1,289,813,667

The cost of assessment and other services provided by the authority in 1980 amounted to twenty-four dollars per parcel.

Policy Framework

Since the real-property tax forms a significant source of revenue for the provincial government, municipalities, school boards and, to a lesser extent, various other bodies that are permitted to levy a tax upon real property, it can be assumed safely that it is under constant surveillance and review to ensure that any defects are remedied and that amendments are made to legislation in order to improve the system.

In April 1975, a Commission of Inquiry on Property Assessment and Taxation was appointed to inquire into all ramifications of an assessment system based on actual value and to view all aspects of property-taxation procedures. A report was submitted in April 1976. The committee made seventy-five recommendations, many of which have been implemented.

The present system of property taxation—which was first implemented for the 1978 assessment rolls—ensures equity and uniformity within the various classes of property throughout the province for school purposes, and also for general purposes in the rural areas. The system also ensures equity and uniformity within the various classes of property within individual municipalities, although each municipality has some choice as to the percentage of actual value at which each class of property shall be assessed.

The introduction of the new assessment system for the 1978 roll naturally caused some significant shifts in the tax burden and, in some cases, substantial increases and decreases in tax liability. However, a phase-in provision was included in the legislation, and a high degree of equity was achieved for the 1981 assessment roll when the phase-in provision was terminated. The substantial increases in assessments experienced by some taxpayers (because of the previously inequitable state of assessment) naturally generated some adverse public reaction, but this result was not unexpected and was less than had been anticipated.

Normally, it is possible to ensure that there is no substantial shift in tax burden from one class of property to another, because the percentage of actual value at which each class of property is assessed is used for school purposes and for general purposes in the majority of municipalities.

Some difficulty was experienced for the 1981 assessment roll since, in some parts of the province, there had been an unprecedented escalation in market values of residential property (with some values increasing by as much as 100 percent in one year). Because the market movement was by no means consistent, it did create some problems in terms of the shift in tax burden as between classes. However, the rapid escalation in values appears to have ceased and, in some areas, to have reversed itself.

The large amount of revenue derived from the real-property tax for municipal purposes (and also for school purposes) would seem to make it extremely unlikely that this source of revenue would not be maintained. However, it is possible that changes may be made to the formula whereby the province's contribution toward the cost of education is calculated, and this change, in turn, would affect the amount of school taxes levied.

3

The Role of the State
in Property Taxation
in Florida

Rodney S. Nedeau

Legal Framework

The Florida Constitution allows local governments to levy ad valorem taxes on real and tangible personal property but specifically excludes their levying ad valorem taxes on intangible personal property. The intangible-personal-property tax is a state tax, even though the bulk of the proceeds finds its way back into local-goverment treasuries by way of state revenue sharing and the Local Goverment Exemption Trust Fund. Although the state is constitutionally prohibited from levying ad valorem taxes on real and tangible personal property, nowhere is either real property (or real estate) or tangible personal property defined in the state constitution. That undertaking is left to Section 192.001, Florida Statutes, which defines real property as simply land, buildings, fixtures, and all other improvements to land. Personal property, on the other hand, is divided into four categories: (1) house goods; (2) intangible personal property, not taxed locally and not within the scope of this chapter; (3) inventory, goods held for sale or lease, including livestock, and; (4) tangible personal property, all goods, chattels, and other articles of value (not including motor vehicles, boats, and airplanes) capable of manual possession, whose chief value is intrinsic to the article itself. Household goods of residents are not taxable. Only tangible personal property and inventory, as defined, as subject to the ad valorem tax.

The constitution provides that municipally owned property used for public purposes is exempt. Further, any property used predominately for educational, literary, scientific, religious, or charitable purposes may be exempted by general law from taxation. The constitution also allows for the exemption of homesteads up to a value of $25,000, subject to the provisions of general law. The Florida Statutes currently allow homesteads to be exempt up to that value for all school levies for each permanent resident who has been a resident of Florida for five or more years. The same residents are eligible for a homestead exemption for all other levies up to $20,000 on the 1981 assessment rolls. This exemption will increase to $25,000 on the 1982 assessment rolls. Both of these increased exemptions were the result of referendums passed in 1980. The homestead exemption was originally enacted in 1934, when the constitution was amended to provide a $5,000 exemption. Under current law, residents of less than five years who qualify otherwise for the homestead exemption receive the $5,000 exemption. Further exemptions of not less than $500 are allowed for property owned by widows or any person who is blind or totally and permanently disabled.

The constitutional standard of valuation for ad valorem tax purposes in Florida is *just value,* a requirement that dates back to the 1868 constitution. The current Florida Constitution (1968) states in Article VII, Section 4: "By general law regulation shall be prescribed which shall secure a just valuation of all property for ad valorem taxation."

The regulations required by the constitution are contained in Section 193.011, Florida Statutes. This section contains eight factors to be considered by property appraisers to arrive at a determination of just value. They are, briefly: the present cash value of the property, exclusive of reasonable fees and costs of purchase, in an arms-length transaction; the highest and best use, and the present use of the property; location; quantity or size; cost; condition; the income from said property; and, the net proceeds of the sale of the property, as received by the seller, after deduction of all of the usual and reasonable fees and costs of the sale.

The courts of the state have defined just value as *fair market value,* or the price a purchaser, willing but not obligated to buy, would pay to one willing but not obligated to sell.

There are two notable exceptions to the just-value concept provided for in the constitution: (a) "agricultural land or land used exclusively for non-commercial recreational purposes may be classified by general law and assessed solely on the basis of character and use"; and, (b) "pursuant to general law tangible personal property held for sale as stock in trade and livestock may be valued for taxation at a specified percentage of its value."

The legislature passed the standard by which parcels of land receiving the agricultural classification would be assessed. Upon the filing of an application by March 1 of each year, the owner of land granted the classification may have his or her land valued with consideration for the following factors: quantity and size; condition; present market value as agricultural land; the income produced by said property; the productivity of land in its present use; the economic merchantability of the agricultural product; and, such other agricultural factors as may from time to time become applicable.

Any land on which an application for classification has either been denied, or not filed in a timely fashion, will be assessed according to the just-value principle.

Pursuant to the provisions of the constitution, inventory has long been assessed at a percentage of its value. For many years, all inventory was assessed at 25 percent of its just value. In 1977, a distinction was made between (1) normal inventory, or inventory held for resale or lease, and (2) goods in the process of manufacture and raw materials held for physical incorporation into the goods to be sold. Livestock were deemed to be in the former class, while fuels used in the production of electricity were put into the latter. So-called normal inventory was made to be taxable at 10 percent of its just value. The raw-materials inventory was made taxable at 1 percent of its just value. It was further provided that the state would replace revenues that local governments lost due to this reduction in taxable value. The 1981 legislature, as part of an economic-development program, removed inventory from assessment and taxation, beginning with the 1982 assessment rolls.

Where ad valorem tax rates are concerned, the constitution makes several requirements. Article VII, Section 2 requires that "all ad valorem tax rates shall be uniform within each taxing unit." There are also millage caps of ten mills for county and municipal governments and school districts. Schools have a lower cap of eight mills specified in the statues if the districts wish "to participate in the state allocation of funds for current operation." An affirmative vote of the qualified electorate is required for the caps to be exceeded for a period of no more than two years. Further, upon an approving referendum, taxes may be levied to service bonded indebtedness by any local government with the power to tax.

Tax-levy and millage-rate limitations have been attempted twice in recent years. In 1979, the legislature passed a 105-percent cap on tax levies on the 1979 tax rolls, based upon the tax levy for each taxing authority in the previous year. Under that one-year law, there was no way for the cap to be exceeded. There were, however, several loosely defined exclusions to the definition of what levies counted in the tax increase. As a result, the law was less than effective. In 1980, the legislature passed a 108-percent threshold on millages in excess of the rolled-back rate (a revenue-equivalent millage based upon previous-year levies and current-year values). There were fewer exclusions in this one-year law. Also provided was a severe penalty for its violation, namely a loss of state revenue-sharing funds. The threshold, could, however, be exceeded by being adopted by an extraordinary majority of each board. This law seemed more effective than the previous year's limitation, although extraordinary majorities did not prove difficult to achieve. There was no millage limitation passed by the 1981 legislature.

In another referendum issue in 1980, voters approved an amendment to the constitution that allows voters of individual counties or municipalities to grant, by separate referendum, to the governing board of the counties or municipalities the authority to grant exemptions for up to ten years from certain levies for improvements to real property and tangible personal property of new or expanded qualified businesses.

Two reforms passed in recent years having to do with the tax-collection side of this tax allow the installment payment of ad valorem taxes, and the deferral of the amount of the tax on a homestead that exceeds 5 percent of the applicant's household's income for the prior year. These plans are designed to make the ad valorem tax less burdensome to pay. Attempts in the past few years to put a circuit-breaker program into the statutes consistently have fallen short. Likewise, a plan by some of the property appraisers to put a fractional-assessment amendment before the voters for referendum failed when the required number of petition signatures could not be gathered in time.

Administration

Local Officials

As in all states, there are three basic functions performed by local officials in administering the ad valorem tax: the determination of the amount of tax revenue required by the governing boards of the taxing authorities; the assessment of property and preparation of the tax roll by the property appraiser; and the preparation and mailing of tax bills and collection of taxes by the tax collector. An additional local official, the clerk of the circuit court, plays a supporting role. In Florida, these officials are, for the most part, elected officials, serving four-year terms. The local officials of primary interest in this chapter are the property appraiser and the tax collector.

The main task facing the property appraiser is the preparation of an assessment roll each year. Florida statutes require that all property is to be assessed regardless of whether the property is taxable, exempt, or subject to classification on January 1 of each year. Another section of the statutes requires that in the course of making his assessment, the property appraiser is required to physically inspect all property every three years. This requirement does not mean that property appraisers reassess their rolls every three years; it is instead a minimum inspection requirement to insure the new improvements are picked up on the roll.

Taxpayer returns of tangible personal property, including inventory, must be filed by April 1 of each year. The property appraiser and his staff must check each return and make a determination of the value of the indicated property. When possible, they must also uncover any tangible personal property that might have escaped attention previously.

The third, and smallest, element of the overall assessment roll is the property assessed by the Department of Revenue. It consists of railroad-operating property and private-car-line rolling stock.

The basic information the property appraiser is required by law to carry on the tax roll includes some reference to the tax return on the property, or a legal description thereof; the just value; applicable exemptions; any appropriate classification and classified value; the owner's name and address; applicable millage; and the tax levied. The property appraiser, in fact, carries much more information on computer files.

The property appraiser and his staff must administer the annual application for exemptions granted to qualified taxpayers. Most exemptions require an annual application. In the second subsequent year of most such exemptions, a short form is mailed to the taxpayer and returned by mail in completed form to the property appraiser. Most institutional and governmental exemptions do not require an annual application.

The property appraiser must also assign a code indicating the predominate use of all real property. A similar code is required to be placed on each personal-property account.

The statutes require that the property appraiser complete the assessment roll by July 1 and certify taxable values to each taxing authority on that date. An extension of time to complete the roll can be obtained from the executive director of the Department of Revenue if circumstances have prevented its timely completion. The certification of value begins an involved budget-adoption process that each taxing authority must go through. On the first Monday in July, the assessment rolls must be submitted to the executive director for approval/disapproval consideration.

Once the property appraiser's roll is submitted, his involvement with the roll is not complete. He gathers certain millage-rate and budget-hearing information from each local authority. With this information, he mails a "Notice of Proposed Property Taxes" to each taxpayer. He also attempts to resolve taxpayer disputes regarding values on his new roll and corrects any errors found. He makes available petition forms to be filed with the clerk's office when taxpayers wish a hearing before the Property Appraisal Adjustment Board because their complaint was not satisfied by the property appraiser. The property appraiser participates in the hearings of the board by presenting his basis for assessments being appealed or for exemption or classifications denied.

Following the conclusion of the adjustment-board hearings, the appraiser's staff makes the changes to the roll that are mandated by board action. When these changes are made and all taxing authorities have completed their budget-adoption procedures, the property appraiser extends the millage rates against the revised values to compute taxes levied and certifies the roll to the tax collector for the mailing of tax bills. Taxes are due and payable on November 1. There is a 4-percent discount granted for payments received in the first thirty days following the mailing of the bills. For each succeeding thirty-day period, the discount rate decreases by 1 percent. The tax bills become delinquent on April 1 of the following year.

The tax collector is also responsible for the advertisement of delinquent taxes as specified in the statutes and the subsequent sale of tax certificates on real property, should the taxes remain delinquent beyond June 1. Tax warrants are issued for the collection of delinquent taxes on tangible personal property. Eventually, tax deeds are issued on real property where the taxes have not been collected. Tangible personal property is seized and sold at public auction.

In addition to these duties of property appraisers and tax collectors, there are several other lesser requirements. They can sign service contracts only with companies and individuals on the *approved bidders list* maintained by the Department of Revenue. In addition, all property appraisers and forty-four of the tax collectors annually must submit their office budgets to the department for approval. After the budgets are approved by the department, they are submitted to the county commissions for final adoption. The budgets of the property appraisers and tax collectors are paid in the form of commissions by the county commissions and municipalities of their counties. The property appraisers must also cooperate with the department in the exchange of information required in the conduct of studies of their assessment rolls by the department.

The clerks of the circuit courts, as indicated above, have a supporting role in the administration of the ad valorem tax system in Florida. They maintain the official record books in their offices. In these books are posted all conveyances that individuals must record as part of the official record. Real-estate transactions are posted to these books in the form of deeds and mortgages and contracts for deeds. These records are valuable sources of market information for the property appraisers. The clerks of the counties regularly make this information available to the property appraisers. The appraisers update their records for parcels of property that have recently sold, including the sales price. The clerk is also the clerk of the Property Appraisal Adjustment Board and, as such, handles all clerical functions for that body.

The county commissioners and members of the school board have a duty in addition to the determination of policy and their annual budgets. Each year, three county commissioners, one of whom will be elected chairman, and two members of the school board, serve on the Property Appraisal Adjustment Board. Petitions may be filed with the clerk anytime on or before the thirtieth day following the mailing of the "Notice of Proposed Property Taxes." The adjustment board begins its hearings between thirty and forty-five days following that mailing. Each petitioner is notified of his scheduled appearance. Each petitioner may be represented by an attorney or agent. All petitions must be heard by the board.

The power of the Property Appraisal Adjustment Board is limited to granting relief to taxpayers whose properties are assessed in excess of constituional standards and to granting lawful exemptions or classifications in cases where the property appraiser erred. The board is bound by the same standards as the property appraiser in determining values and granting exemptions. The county property appraiser's determination of value is entitled to a presumption of correctness before the board as well as in the courts.

Therefore, the petitioner has the burden to prove that the property appraiser's value was incorrect. Every decision of the board must be in written form and must contain findings of fact, the nature of the change, and the values of the parcel in question before and after the change. The board may hire special masters to act in the board's place. The special masters must be a member of the Florida bar and knowledgeable in ad valorem taxation or be a member of a professional real-estate-appraisal organization with at least five years of experience.

The State

The leading state employer in property taxation in Florida is the Department of Revenue. One of the most important divisions within the Department of Revenue, in turn, is the Division of Ad Valorem Tax, which operates under the following statutory mandate: "The responsibilities of the Division of Ad Valorem Tax shall be to carry out the relevant provisions of ad valorem tax law and other department responsibilities involving local governments. The functions of this division shall include, but not be limited to, ad valorem administration, assessment standards and review, central property evaluation, and field operations."

The cornerstone of the involvement of the state government in the administration of the ad valorem tax in Florida is Section 195.022, Florida Statutes. It states:

> The Department of Revenue shall have general supervision of the assessment and valuation of property so that all property will be placed on the tax rolls and shall be valued according to its just valuation as required by the Constitution. It shall also have supervision over tax collection and all other aspects of the administration of such taxes. The supervision of the department shall consist primarily of aiding and assisting county officers in the assessing and collection functions, with particular emphasis on the more technical aspects. In this regard, the department shall conduct schools to upgrade assessment skills of both state and local assessment personnel.

This provision of general law clearly involves the department in every aspect of this local tax source. There are, however, several other provisions of the statutes that contain specific requirements as to the roll of the state in the ad valorem tax. For instance, the department is required to prescribe and furnish all forms to be used by the property appraisers, tax collectors, clerks of the circuit court, and property-appraisal adjustment boards in the administration of this tax. Local officials can use forms of their own design, at their own expense, provided they have written permission from the department and the local form does not differ in substantive content with the corresponding state form. The department also is required to provide to the property appraisers, upon written request—or at least every three years—aerial photographs and nonproperty ownership maps.

The department is also required to promulgate reasonable rules and regulations for the assessing and collecting of taxes. The rules were adopted according to the provisions of the Administrative Procedure Act, a very precise procedure requiring public hearings preceded by advertisements, economic-impact statements for each rule, and final adoption by the governor and cabinet sitting as the Department of Revenue.

The chapter of the Florida Administrative Code containing ad valorem tax rules and regulations, promulgated by the department in 1976 is currently under review.

The department is also required by law to establish and promulgate standard measures of value to be used by the property appraisers to aid and assist them in arriving at assessments of all property. These standard measures of value constitute guidelines and do not have the full force of law that the rules or statutes carry. These guidelines are adopted using a process similar to that used to adopt the rules. There are four sections to the guidelines: general real property, classified-use real property, tangible personal property, and mapping. Finally, the department is required to prepare and maintain a current manual of instructions for the use of officials connected with the administration of property taxes. The manual is required to contain the rules and regulations, standard measures of value, and the forms and their instructions.

The primary responsibilities of the department in the administration of the ad valorem tax are to determine the condition of the assessment rolls with respect to just value and equity and to assure that the rolls are in compliance with the requirements of law. These two responsibilities are accomplished by two interrelated processes. The primary tool used to determine the condition of the assessment rolls is the in-depth study. The primary enforcement mechanism is the roll approval/disapproval process. A secondary enforcement method is the authority, given the department by the statutes, to bring and maintain lawsuits, including mandamus and injunction.

The Division of Ad Valorem Tax is required to study the assessment roll of each county no less often than every two years. This in-depth study is currently performed only on the real-property rolls. Beginning in the near future, the studies will include the tangible-personal-property rolls. The study is based upon a stratified random sample of parcels on the roll. There are a minimum of eight strata required to be studied as defined in the statute. Most strata are studied using appraisals performed by the division's field staff. Classified-use parcels are appraised according to their classified-use value. All other parcels are appraised according to their just value. In counties where an active real-property market exists, certain strata can be studied using sales. The use of sales is restricted to owner-occupied residential and vacant-land parcels. The sales sampled are selected randomly from each stratum where sufficient sales are present. All sales are qualified as arms-length transactions and verified as to correct cash-equivalent price by contacting the grantee. When the new roll is available, the assessed value that was determined by the property appraiser is picked up, and ratios are calculated for each parcel. Finally, the ratio statistics are computed for each stratum and for the roll as a whole.

Should the in-depth study indicate that the roll, or a portion thereof, is deficient in some respect, a notice of defect is issued to the property appraiser. The property appraiser can either request a conference or notify the executive director in writing of his intention to correct the deficiency. In either case, the executive director must issue an administrative order requiring the necessary remedial action to be taken to correct the problem on the next assessment roll submitted to the department for approval consideration.

On the first Monday in July each year, the property appraisers must submit their assessment rolls to the executive director for review and possible approval. This submission is in the form of recapitulations of the roll and computer tapes of the real-property roll. Analyses are performed on the recapitulations and the tape, including a sales-ratio study, in an effort to ascertain the condition of the roll. The statutes specify that the executive director shall disapprove any roll, or part thereof, not in substantial compliance with the law, or not in full compliance with any administrative orders that may have been issued previously against the current roll.

Another important function the department performs is the assessment of all operating property of railroads and rolling stock of private-car lines operating in Florida. Each company operating in the state must annually file a return with the department by April 1. The statutes require that these companies be assessed using the unit-rule method and that the assessed value of these companies be apportioned to individual counties based upon track miles. The department must submit the apportioned values to the appraisers by June 1 of each year. The department's central assessment staff of three utilizes four computer jobstreams to perform their function.

As previously mentioned, the property appraisers and forty-four of the sixty-seven tax collectors submit their office budgets to the department for approval. This requirement is intended to insure that these officials have sufficient resources to perform their duties adequately. The department also is given the responsibility to conduct research and maintain accurate tabulations of data and conditions existing as to ad valorem taxation. Further, the department administers two trust funds to replace revenues lost due to exemptions required by statutes. The department also maintains and administers the Property Assessment Loan Fund. This fund is used to make loans to appraisers to assist the counties' fund-reassessment programs that might not be adequately covered by existing resources.

The final formal function performed by the department toward the ad valorem tax is the coordination of an educational program for the benefit of personnel in local appraisers' offices and at the state level. Twice a year, classes are conducted by the International Association of Assessing Officers and the department. Individuals completing a basic curriculum receive a certification signifying an accepted level of appraisal ability. Property appraisers thus receiving the designation of certified Florida appraiser qualify for an additional $2,000 per year in salary.

Fiscal Importance

Fiscal data on the ad valorem tax in Florida from even the recent past is difficult to locate. The 1968 constitution moved the responsibility for supervision of the tax from the comptroller's office to the Department of Revenue. This move, coupled with very weak reporting requirements up until just a few years ago, makes performance comparisons with even ten years ago difficult at best. In addition, the most recent year for which data should be complete does not yet have complete data. The governor, in 1979, announced a statewide reappraisal for the 1980 assessment rolls. Most counties' tax rolls were late due to the tremendous amount of work required to bring the rolls up to acceptable quality. Several of the rolls were disapproved by the executive director, requiring additional work to be accomplished before they were finally acceptable. As such, comparisons can only be made using data for the six years from 1974 to 1979, and estimates for 1980. Table 3-1 shows tax levies, parcel counts, average millages and taxable values for the years indicated.

The distribution of the ad valorem tax among property classes is shown on table 3-2. Unfortunately, a breakdown of the burden is not available for the 1980 tax rolls. Note that the burden of residential property has been steadily increasing in recent years. The increased homestead exemption was intended to restore the relative burden of this type of property achieved when the original homestead exemption was passed in 1934.

Table 3-3 shows the distribution of ad valorem taxes levied by type of taxing authority.

Table 3-4 shows assessment cost, in terms of total property-appraisers' budgets, cost per parcel, and as a percentage of total tax levies. These years are the only ones for which data is available.

Table 3-1
Tax Levies, Taxable Values, Parcel Counts, and Average Millages in Florida

Year	Total Taxes Levied	Total Taxable Value	Parcel Count[a]	Average Millage
1974	$1,488,642,100[b]	$ 81,277,982,885	d	18.32
1975	1,747,814,709	91,843,425,302	4,562,027	19.03
1976	1,918,834,390	98,472,436,723	4,744,870	19.49
1977	2,156,794,922	107,774,941,095	5,002,169	20.01
1978	2,295,648,969	117,596,657,106	5,210,054	19.52
1979	2,349,081,616	217,558,180,383	5,426,402	18.41
1980	2,986,000,000[b]	c	5,650,002[b]	d

[a]Real property only.
[b]Estimate.
[c]For 1980 and 1981 there was a split tax base. Estimated 1980 taxable values: schools, $159. billion and all other, $171. billion.
[d]Not available.

Policy Framework

There is no tax in Florida that is more controversial, or receives more public scrutiny, than the property tax. Taxpayers, associations representing taxpayers, property appraisers, tax collectors, the Department of Revenue, the legislature, and the governor's office all take a keen interest in the various aspects of this tax source. This interest occurs in spite of the fact that Florida has a relatively light burden in ad valorem taxes and in total

Table 3-2
Distribution of Ad Valorem Tax among Property Classes in Florida, 1976-1979
(in percentage)

Class	1976	1977	1978	1979
Residential	48.73	49.31	49.95	50.57
Vacant land	11.47	10.95	11.05	10.71
Commercial	12.90	12.75	12.83	12.64
Industrial	3.41	3.45	3.36	3.33
Agricultural	4.36	4.10	3.98	3.81
Miscellaneous real property	2.74	2.77	3.02	3.06
Tangible personal property and central assessment	16.39	16.67	15.81	15.88

Table 3-3
Distribution of Ad Valorem Taxes Levied by Type of Taxing Authority,
Florida, 1975-1979
(in percentage)

Taxing Authority	1975	1976	1977	1978	1979
Counties	35.35	34.80	36.74	35.90	40.60
Municipalities	16.94	17.23	16.57	16.51	17.16
School districts	43.65	43.14	41.82	42.06	38.04
Independent districts	4.06	4.83	4.87	5.53	4.20

state and local taxes. Each legislative session sees the introduction of many proposals that would address some perceived problem with ad valorem tax. Whatever the language of the proposals, they are subject to spirited debate by all interested parties. Taxpayers are justifiably concerned about the fairness and burden of the tax. Taxing authorities are concerned about its viability as a revenue source and the amount of local discretion left to them in its use. Property appraisers, tax collectors, and the department are concerned about its fairness, burden, and ease of administration. Each session, the governor, who is concerned about every aspect of this tax, has a legislative proposal prepared for introduction that addresses the most pressing ad valorem tax issues of the past year.

In 1980, the far reaching Trim Bill was passed by the legislature and signed into law by the Governor. This bill has many different provisions. The primary feature, however, is a new budget-adoption procedure that better informs each taxpayer or proposed tax changes they will face in the next year. There are new notices and advertisements provided in this new law as well as two mandatory public budget hearings for each taxing authority.

The main proposal introduced in the 1981 session was a very large and detailed bill designed to strengthen the budget-adoption requirements of the Trim Bill. This bill did not pass in 1981 but will no doubt be reintroduced in 1982. Current concern has also centered around the ability of local govern-

Table 3-4
Assessment Costs in Florida, 1977-1980

Terms	1977	1978	1979	1980
Total budgets	$39,231,739	$41,863,758	$44,145,853	$48,981,866
Cost per parcel	$7.84	$8.03	$8.13	$8.67
Percentage of tax levies	1.82%	1.82%	1.88%	1.64%

ments to raise additional revenues to offset cutbacks taking place in Washington. Balancing the taxing authorities' need for additional revenue with the taxpayers need for reasonable taxes will provide for a lively debate in future legislative sessions.

4 Hawaii's Constitutional Mandate on Decentralization of Property-Tax Functions

Stanley T. Ooka

The Real-Property Tax in Hawaii

The real-property tax has been condemned widely for being regressive, inequitable, and a burden to taxpayers. The obvious underlying reason is that the tax is determined mainly by the valuation of property, a judgmental process readily open to challenge by the taxpayers. Therefore, even under the most ideal properly managed statewide system, criticism and demand for fiscal change would occur. In Hawaii, this criticism resulted in the transfer of all the real-property-tax functions from the state to the four counties by a state constitutional amendment. But, before discussing the activities relating to this transfer, it would be appropriate to first review recent events concerning the transfer and some of the problems relating to its administration.

Hawaii's centrally administered property-tax system, although efficient, was not without problems—particularly for the counties. In 1933, the territorial legislature set dollar limits on the amount each county could raise as revenue from property tax. The result was that the quantity and quality of services and capital improvements suffered, especially in the face of inflation and population growth. In 1957, some relief was provided by changing the real-property-tax limitation from an absolute-dollar ceiling to a rate ceiling. The territorial legislature provided for a statutory maximum on the rate for each county, ranging from $16 to $18 per $1,000 of assessed value. The counties could set their rates within their respective ceilings but had no control over the establishment of the assessment base that directly influenced their revenue source. The state legislature was finally convinced of the lack of need for such controls when it abolished the rate ceiling in 1963. Also, over the years, liberal enactments of exemptions by territorial and state legislatures had effectively reduced the counties' real-property tax base so that by 1980, the exemption came to nearly 50 percent of the taxable value in aggregate of the four counties. To compensate for the reduction in the tax base, the counties increased their tax rates—shifting the burden of the increased tax onto the remaining taxable properties. To further focus

Printed by permission of the International Association of Assessing Officers (IAAO) and the author. This chapter was originally presented at the 1981 IAAO Washington Forum.

the responsibility for the increasing property tax on the counties, the legislature enacted, in 1976, what is commonly referred to as the Florida Plan, reducing the legal ratio from 70 percent to 60 percent of market value. Under the Florida Plan, the state director of taxation certifies the tax rate that will produce the same revenue as the previous tax year. This rate stands unless it is increased or decreased by the action of the county councils.

Activities Relating to the Transfer

Over a period of several years prior to the 1978 transfer, there were numerous proposals before the state legislature to transfer all or part of the real-property tax functions to the counties. There appeared to be no consensus, however, among the advocates who wished to effect the transfer of this responsibility. Some wanted to transfer all of the responsibilities, while others wanted to transfer only a limited portion of the real-property tax functions, such as the assessment and collection of the tax with the legislative powers retained by the state. In 1958 and 1962, the Public Administration Service (PAS) was contracted as consultant to the state to make recommendations on assessment improvements and to survey the financial relationship between the state and the four counties. In the studies, the consultant advised against transferring the assessment function to the counties and recommended no change in the state-managed system. Echoing the PAS study findings, the State Department of Taxation and the Tax Foundation of Hawaii supported the state-managed system with the argument that it is more efficient, economical, and equitable. Nevertheless, as the taxpayers' protests about the rising property assessment became more concerted, the state's resistance to the transfer correspondingly decreased. This feeling finally led to a constitutional amendment in which the Constitutional Convention of 1978, with the affirmative vote of the people of Hawaii, transferred the property-tax program to each of the four county governments effective 1 July 1981.

Arguments presented for and against the transfer were as follows:

1. *For the transfer:*
    a. The real-property tax is the counties' most important source of revenue; therefore, each county should be able to tailor the tax to serve its revenue needs.
    b. Assessment uniformity among counties in Hawaii is not as important as equalization within each county, since the counties are noncontiguous and have only one level of assessment.
    c. The county councils, not the legislature, are better able to understand local conditions and determine whether an exemption is warranted in the county or a tax-reform measure is desired.

   d. The expected cost increase from decentralization can be kept to a
       minimum by continuing the existing central services under a con-
       tractual agreement among the four counties.
2. *Against the transfer:*
   a. The state ultimately is responsible for the economic health of the
       counties and, therefore, should have some control over the coun-
       ties' taxing policies and powers.
   b. Similar classes of property would be treated differently among
       counties, and an inequitable condition would result with serious
       economic and social consequences. Furthermore, the inequities
       may be magnified by more political interference at the local level.
   c. Statewide interests cannot be pursued if legislative control is cur-
       tailed. Each county would use exemptions to serve its own local in-
       terest, and such interest may not be consistent with overall state
       goals and objectives.
   d. Tax assessment should be placed in the unit that can perform the
       function most efficiently and economically. Decentralization of the
       assessment function would require an expensive duplication of the
       central services such as mapping, technical assistance, and data
       processing.

   In adopting its proposal to transfer the real-property tax powers to the
counties, the constitutional convention offered the following reasons:

1. County governments are completely responsible and accountable for
   the administration of their local affairs. Accordingly, they should have
   complete authority over their finances, including all administrative and
   legislative powers on property tax.
2. By placing total responsibility for the real-property tax program with
   the counties, public confusion as to who or which level of government
   is responsible for the tax increase will be eliminated.
3. County administration of the real-property tax is consistent with home
   rule.
4. There are different economic bases and needs of the counties that cannot be addressed by a single statewide solution.

   Several property owners' associations testified strongly against the
transfer at the convention hearings. They argued that exemption and assessment policies will differ for each county, making it difficult for taxpayers to
evaluate the fairness of the distribution of tax burden, and present exemptions and preferential assessments may be reduced or eliminated. To eliminate such fears, the convention made the transfer subject to the following
transitional mandates:

1. For eleven years after ratification (that is, until 6 November 1989), all four counties must agree on uniform exemptions and assessment policies.
2. Exemptions and dedications (preferential assessments) cannot be eliminated or diminished during the eleven-year period after ratification. New or increased exemptions and dedications may be made by the counties during the eleven-year period after ratification, provided they are uniform among all four counties.
3. Policies and methods shall be adopted by county ordinances before 1 July 1981 to supersede state laws. If the counties fail to adopt uniform ordinances by that date, the existing state law will continue in effect on a statewide basis.

Outlook

The property transfer was one of the more narrowly decided issues in the 1978 Constitutional Convention, with a small majority of only 51.9 percent voting for passage. This narrow majority no doubt has put the burden on the counties to prove to the people of Hawaii in the coming years that they are better able to administer the program than the state. This public support is vital to the counties, since the transfer was made with certain restrictions or transitional mandates to make the program returnable to the state if the people so desire. Accordingly, the people of Hawaii will have another opportunity to assess the wisdom of this transfer when the next constitutional convention meets by 1989, before the expiration of the transitional mandates.

5 The Role of the State in Property Taxation in Iowa

Steven D. Gold

The Iowa property tax underwent major changes during the past fifteen years, with the state expanding its role in both tax administration and the provision of property-tax relief. Reliance on the property tax has been considerably reduced at the same time that the average quality of administration has improved. Nevertheless, tension still remains in the division of responsibilities between the Iowa Department of Revenue and local assessors. The quality of assessment administration is still highly uneven, varying from excellent performance in some jurisdictions to poor performance in others. On the other hand, property-tax-relief programs instituted in the late 1970s have defused the property tax as a political issue.

Legal Framework

The property tax has been an enduring source of controversy in Iowa, spawning major upheavals in the 1930s and 1940s. One major result of the tax revolt during the Depression was the creation of a homestead credit, which paid up to $62.50 of each homeowner's property-tax bill. State taxes on individual and corporation income and on general sales were also enacted, with property-tax relief being one of their main selling points.

Another round of reform occurred in the late 1940s. The number of assessment jurisdictions was reduced from over 1,500 to 119. (Each of ninety-nine counties have a single assessor and cities larger than 10,000 have the option of having their own assessor.) Today the number of jurisdictions is 117, since two cities have elected to consolidate their assessment offices with the county in which they are located.

The last half of the 1940s was also a period of extensive school consolidation. Since the combination of urban and rural school districts often resulted in significantly higher property taxes for owners of farmland, a new form of property-tax relief was provided, the agricultural-land tax credit. Like the homestead credit, this program was state funded, with the state appropriation raised gradually over the years until it reached $18 million in the early 1970s.

The year 1967 began a decade of turmoil for the property tax in Iowa. One fundamental change was that the state began to administer the property tax energetically. Previously, all property was supposed to be assessed at 60

41

percent of market value, but in fact the true assessment ratio was closer to 25 percent, with significant variations from county to county. The legislature formally enacted 27 percent as the de jure assessment level for all property, because it was close to the average level in effect. As part of the reform, a Department of Revenue was created, and it began to conduct annual assessment-ratio studies and to issue periodic equalization orders to bring the average assessment ratio for homes, farmland, and commercial property in each jurisdiction to the legal standard.

Because farmland had been assessed de facto at an even lower proportion of market value than other types of property, the 1967 tax reform provided that half of its assessment would henceforth be determined by its use value, with the other half being based on market value. Use value was based on a five-year average of net income per acre capitalized at a *fair* rate as determined by the State Board of Tax Review, which will be discussed below. Initially, the capitalization rate was set at 6 percent, although it was later raised to 6 1/2 percent and ultimately to 7 percent in the early 1970s.

Another major 1967 initiative was to provide property-tax relief by increasing substantially the state role in school finance. With funds from higher state income and sales taxes, state aid to school districts tripled between 1967 and 1969. The state share of elementary- and secondary-school budgets rose from 14.6 percent in 1966-1967 to 32.1 percent in 1968-1969, and the property tax's share fell from 82.4 percent to 61.7 percent.

The final major property-tax legislation of 1967 was creation of a personal-property tax credit. Since it provided for the state to pay a portion of personal-property-tax liability, it relieved the tax of owners of farm machinery, livestock, and business inventories, which were the main types of personal property still subject to taxation. Most household personal property had been exempted in previous years.

Several of the 1967 reforms contained the seeds of future trouble, however, and by 1971 it was necessary to reconsider school finance. Between 1969 and 1971, property taxes had jumped 20 percent, with school taxes a leading factor. Therefore, when the state once again raised income-tax rates to boost school aid, it also placed strict limits on school spending, guaranteeing that the gradually rising state aid would result in property-tax relief rather than higher school spending. Barring major increases of assessments, the 1971 school-finance reform removed schools as a future source of sharply higher property taxes.

The 1971 school program worked as a means of keeping a lid on property taxes. In the following four years, state aid to schools increased $147 million, while school property taxes fell more than $4 million.

In 1973, the state expanded two of its other property-tax-relief programs. First, the complete elimination of the personal-property tax was decided upon, with the personal-property tax credit scheduled to rise gradually over a ten-year period until it covered all personal-property-tax liability. This phase out is considerably behind schedule, however, due to postponements in the late 1970s and early 1980s when the state budget was under pressure.

A second 1973 action was enactment of a circuit breaker for senior-citizen homeowners and renters. This circuit breaker replaced a double homestead exemption for households with income under $4,000, which had been begun in 1969. Originally limited to households with income below $6,000, the circuit breaker has been gradually expanded so that its income ceiling is now $10,000.

A relatively inconsequential change introduced at this time was to raise the de jure assessment ratio from 27 percent to 100 percent, with corresponding adjustments in millage limits and other provisions of the tax law.

The inflation of the 1970s had a particularly dramatic impact in Iowa. Not only did homes rise rapidly in value, as they did throughout the country, but farm values soared even faster. Between 1972 and 1976, the average value of an acre of Iowa farmland jumped from $82 to $1,368. Since over 40 percent of assessed valuation in Iowa is agricultural, this inflation promised more controversy for the property tax.

In August 1975, the revenue department issued an equalization order raising the average value of home assessments by 29 percent, and farm assessments by 52 percent. Following an appeals process, which generally upheld the legality of the orders, assessors had to raise assessments for each class of property by the amounts ordered by the revenue department. Many assessors applied the orders across-the-board, while others adjusted assessments on a parcel-by-parcel basis. These new values were for 1 January 1975 and represented the basis for taxes in fiscal year 1977 (1 July 1976 to 30 June 1977).

The state mitigated the effects of the revaluation of property in a two-step process. In 1976, the state built upon its system of credits. The homestead credit was made equal to the property tax on the first $4,500 of assessed valuation of a home—in effect, approximately doubling its value. The funding for the agricultural-land tax credit was raised from $18 million to $42 million. The state was able to bear the higher cost of these credits because the bill for state aid to school districts was sharply reduced, due to the provision that made the amount of aid vary inversely with assessed valuations. If the legislature simply had adjusted the school-aid formula to offset this windfall to the state, a major increase in the proportion of property taxes impacting on homeowners and owners of farmland would have taken place. The rise of the property-tax credits by the state prevented or mitigated such shifts.

In 1977, a more long-term solution to the property-tax dilemma was developed, as the state limited the annual increases of assessed valuation (excluding new construction) for homes and farms to 6 percent per year. This limitation applies to the aggregate statewide valuation of each type of property, not to individual parcels. It is implemented through promulgation by the revenue department of a factor that must be multiplied by each assessed valuation to obtain the figure used in computing tax bills. For example, 1978 residential valuations were multiplied by .78; 1979 values by .64; and 1980 values by .68. The virtue of this system is that it prevents large shifts in the proportion of taxes impacting on each class of property. One of its questionable aspects on the other hand, is that it freezes the distribution of tax burdens as of a certain date.

The overall impact of these changes has been fundamental. Iowa's system of assessment limitations amounts to a new form of classification, one in which the relative assessment ratios among classes of property change each year.

The system of assessment limitations has been modified in relatively minor ways since 1977. The annual valuation increase was lowered to 4 percent. Limitations were extended to other classes of real property, such as commercial, industrial, railroads, and utilities other than railroads.

Another change introduced in 1977 was to base the assessment of farmland 100 percent on use value. While this measure would have been very consequential if adopted by itself, with the limitation on assessment increases it was, in effect, relatively unimportant. It could have a bearing in the future if use value rises by less than 4 percent per year or declines, because other classes of property are not allowed to rise by more than the amount that farmland rises.

There are other limitations on the property tax in Iowa. For at least half a century, cities and counties have been subject to millage or tax-rate limits. These limits have been binding on a relatively small number of local governments, particularly ones with abnormally small tax bases in relation to their population. They will become increasingly restrictive in the future if the 4-percent-assessment growth limitation is maintained, because it does not adequately reflect inflation.

Iowa also imposed levy limitations on cities and counties for three fiscal years—that is, from July 1976 to June 1979. These 9-percent annual limitations were dropped when the assessment limitations became effective. Like the millage limitations, certain major expenditures were exempted from them. The levy limitations were not particularly restrictive on most cities or counties.

School-district spending limits have remained in effect since 1971, and the legislature has raised or lowered them nearly every year. Unlike the millage and levy limits, the school spending limits have certainly restricted school-district spending and indirectly moderated property-tax increases.

Administration

The Role of the State

As noted above, the role of state government in property-tax administration changed substantially after the Department of Revenue was created in 1967, replacing a three-member tax commission that previously had responsibility for supervising the property tax. Under the leadership of three able directors, the department has expanded the state role and substantially improved the quality of administration.

Among the duties of the department in relation to property taxation are:

Administration of an examination that would-be assessors must pass to be eligible for appointment. Selection of assessors is the responsibility of local conference boards.

Biennial issuance of equalization orders designed to assure that property is treated uniformly in all jurisdictions.

Assessment of utility property.

Providing technical assistance to assessors and conducting an education program for them.

Publication of annual statistical reports including an assessment-ratio study, a summary of assessed valuation by class of property for each assessment jurisdiction, and a description of tax levies by assessment jurisdiction.

Administration of tax credits and exemptions.

Promulgation of regulations on assessment procedure.

All of these activities are performed by a unit of the Revenue Department, its Property Tax Division, which in turn is divided into four sections: equalization, central assessments, credits and exemptions, and appraisals. The division has fifty-six authorized positions, although it seldom has attained its full complement of staff.

The department has become more aggressive in recent years, availing itself of powers it had not employed previously. For example, it was not until 1979 that it began to issue orders requiring assessors to revalue property on a parcel-by-parcel basis. That year it issued more than thirty orders in jurisdictions where it believed that the quality of assessment administration was particularly bad. Among the factors considered in deciding where to issue the orders were coefficients of dispersion and indexes of regressivity derived from assessment-ratio studies, the quality of records kept by assessors, the history of past equalization orders, and the length of time since an outside firm had last been brought in to help with a reassessment.

The department has also devoted increasing attention to industrial property (which has never been covered by equalization orders). A special study conducted in 1977 revealed serious irregularities in the treatment of industrial properties in certain jurisdictions. As a result, the department began to do appraisals of all industrial properties in certain selected jurisdictions each year. The results of these appraisals are turned over to assessors, who use them subsequently in determining new assessed valuations for these properties.

An important unit that is independent of the revenue department is the State Board of Tax Review, whose three members are appointed by the governor and confirmed by the state senate. Members are appointed for six-year terms and may not be reappointed. The Board of Tax Review hears appeals from assessors concerning decisions of local boards of review and the Department of Revenue.

Another agency is the Assessor Education Commission, which must approve all courses assessors take to fulfill their continuing-education obligations. The commission consists of two assessors, the director of the Department of Revenue, one person from the State Board of Tax Review, and three other persons appointed by the governor.

The state comptroller also plays a role in property-tax matters. Most importantly, the comptroller compiles information on taxes levied in each taxing jurisdiction in the state. In this context, a taxing jurisdiction is an area served by a particular school district, city, and county. With more than 440 school districts and 950 cities, there are many thousands of taxing jurisdictions. This information was demanded by the legislature in 1976 when it was concerned about shifting property-tax burdens. The state comptroller is also the agency that receives information on the budgets of assessment jurisdictions.

Most of the state's activism in the period since 1967 does not stem from new legislation but rather from enforcement of statutes already on the books. The initiatives would not have been possible without increased budget support provided by the legislature and governor.

The Local Role

Assessors are appointed for six-year terms by a local conference board, which consists of county supervisors and representatives of all school districts and cities within the assessment jurisdiction. Although the membership of the conference board may exceed two dozen, only three votes are cast in it—one for the county, one for the school boards, and one for the cities. The conference board also sets the salaries of the assessor and his or her employees and the budget.

Salaries for assessors in Iowa are rather low. A 1977 survey reported the average salary of assessors to be slightly less than $15,300.

By law, as of 1981, assessors are supposed to revalue all properties every two years. Prior to 1978, the period between reassessments supposedly had been four years, but in many jurisdictions revaluation occurred much less often. For example, in Polk County, the largest county in the state, no parcel-by-parcel revaluation occurred for nearly fifteen years. Other jurisdictions, however, have revalued relatively frequently, often with the assistance of professional appraisal firms.

Assessors are required to participate in a continuing-education program consisting of at least 150 hours during their six-year term. At least 90 of these hours must be in courses that have an examination at their conclusion.

Property owners who wish to protest the assessment of their property may appeal to a local board of review. This board consists of three or five members, who are appointed by the conference board, and meets for a few weeks each year. The board of review has the power to review assessments even if they are not appealed and may raise or lower them. While some boards actively pursue this course, most do not.

Evaluation

Iowa has done a good job of coping with the property tax in two respects, but it falls short of satisfactory in two other ways.

The state has been successful in providing property-tax relief. Prior to the 1970s, Iowa had long been characterized by unusually high levels of property taxation. Iowa took massive strides away from overreliance on the property tax during the past decade, avoiding a potentially explosive property-tax revolt. Between 1971 and 1980, the property tax fell from 6.1 percent to 4.1 percent of personal income; the effective tax rate on homes decreased from more than 2.6 percent to less than 1.4 percent. Few states provided as much property-tax relief as did Iowa. Its tax is now close to the national average (which itself dropped substantially during the 1970s).

A second success has come in equalizing assessment ratios throughout the state. According to U.S. Advisory Commission on Intergovernmental Relations calculations based on 1976 Census Bureau data, only three states had achieved a greater degree of uniformity among jurisdictions in assessment ratios for homes. Few states also have greater conformity between the legal assessment standard and the actual average assessment level. Property tends to be underassessed in Iowa, as it does everywhere, but Iowa comes closer to what the law stipulates than most other states do.

These successes involve areas where the state exercises maximum influence. The situation in Iowa is less satisfactory in terms of intrajurisdictional uniformity than interjurisdictional. The Department of Revenue's annual assessment-ratio studies consistently have shown that most jurisdictions have coefficients of dispersion above 20, a degree of nonuniformity that implies large inequities.

Even in this area, the picture is not all dark. Census Bureau data suggests that, as bad as it is, the typical coefficient of dispersion in Iowa is much lower than in the typical state; this result is of dubious significance because the Census Bureau samples only a small percentage of jurisdictions in Iowa, and they are mostly urban ones where the degree of assessment uniformity tends to be relatively high. Another positive indication is that the coefficient of dispersion reported by the Department of Revenue has tended to decline over the years. Here again, a caveat is necessary: assessors apparently are more careful to point out abnormal transactions than they were formerly, so a smaller proportion of "bad" sales are included in Department of Revenue calculations. This increased "purity of the data base" would alone account for greater apparent uniformity of assessment ratios.

A second blemish on the property tax is more within the power of the state to rectify. Iowa has been rather parsimonious in granting relief to low-income nonelderly households because its circuit breaker does not cover them. Nonelderly renters in particular are excluded from relief programs.

Overall, the Iowa property tax has been greatly improved over the past fifteen years. Most of the improvements have resulted from enlightened state policies, but there has apparently been improvement at the local level as well. It appears that Iowa has one of the better property-tax systems in the United States.

6

The Role of the State in Property Taxation in Kansas

Lyle W. Clark

The only statewide property-tax levies in Kansas are a total of 1.5 mills for state educational and institutional building funds, estimated to total $15,300,000 for fiscal year (FY) 1983. However, the property tax is still the predominant source of revenues for most subdivisions of government in Kansas.

Legal Framework

All property in Kansas, not otherwise exempt—with the exception of certain types of personal property—must be taxed at a "uniform and equal rate of assessment and taxation." This mandate is contained in Article 11, Section 1 of the Kansas Constitution. It states:

> The legislature shall provide for a uniform and equal rate of assessment and taxation, except that the legislature may provide for the classification and the taxation uniformly as to class of motor vehicles, mineral products, money, mortgages, notes and other evidence of debt or may exempt any of such classes of property from property taxation and impose taxes upon another basis in lieu thereof. All property used exclusively for state, county, municipal, literary, educational, scientific, religious, benevolent, and charitable purposes, and all household goods and personal effects not used for the production of income, shall be exempted from property taxation.

All property, other than constitutionally exempted properties, must file for original exempt-status authorization to the State Board of Tax Appeals. So long as the property does not change ownership or use, a claim need be filed with the county annually on or before March 1. (The legislature has classified motor vehicles and intangibles separately and has applied special taxes to such property in lieu of the general property tax.)

A 1976 amendment to the Kansas Constitution authorizes use valuation of land devoted to agricultural use, but no statutes implementing this amendment have been enacted by the legislature. The amendment provides, in part, that, "land devoted to agricultural use may be defined by law and valued for ad valorem tax purposes upon the basis of its agricultural income or agricultural productivity, actual or potential, and when so valued such land shall be assessed at the same percent of value and taxed at the same rate as real property."

In accordance with the constitutional mandates, statutes have been enacted providing rules for valuing and taxing property. All real and tangible personal property shall be appraised at its fair market value in money. Following appraisal at 100 percent of fair market value in money, property is to be assessed at 30 percent of such value. A general definition of *fair market value in money* is provided for in a statute, which states, in part, that, "fair market value in money shall mean the amount of money that a well-informed buyer is justified in paying and a well-informed seller is justified in accepting, assuming that the parties thereto are acting without undue compulsion and that the property has been offered at the market place for a reasonable length of time."

Property-Tax-Relief Measures

The Kansas Homestead Property Tax Refund Act (the homestead program) was first proposed in Kansas in 1969 and was enacted the next year. In form, the Kansas homestead program is a circuit breaker—that is, property taxes in excess of a certain proportion of household income are refunded (up to a limit).

Refunds are currently available to claimants with household incomes of less than $12,800 who are fifty-seven years of age or older, widows fifty-three years of age or older, disabled or blind, or who have one or more dependent children under eighteen residing at home the entire year. Meeting these qualifications does not, however, guarantee a refund. Two factors—total household income and property tax paid (or 15 percent of rent paid for occupancy)—determine the amount of refund, if any. The maximum refund is $400. Actual expenditures for homestead refunds for the last four years have been as follows:

Fiscal Year	Expenditures
1981	$ 9,439,385
1980	$10,559,562
1979	$ 8,726,901
1978	$ 8,221,678

Kansas presently does not have a homestead exemption.

There exist provisions in Kansas for the refund of property taxes for homes with solar energy. However, these refunds are intended more as incentives for alternative-energy development than as property-tax-relief measures. Classification is discussed later.

Quality of Existing Appraisals

Although the law, as stated above, requires that property be assessed at 30 percent of fair market value, the 1980 assessment sales-ratio study shows that, statewide, urban real estate was assessed at 9 percent and rural real estate at 6 percent. These figures have declined from ratios of 26 percent for urban realty and 19 percent for rural realty in 1955.

The Division of Property Valuation also computes the coefficients of deviation for various subclasses of urban and rural real estate in each of the 105 counties in Kansas. The coefficient of deviation is the percentage by which the various individual-assessment sales ratios differ, on the average, from the median ratio. In 1980, only three counties had coefficients of deviation for urban property of 20 percent or less; 70 counties had coefficients of 41 or over for urban property. For rural property, two counties had coefficients of 20 or below; 80 coefficients were over 40.

Reappraisal Legislation

During the 1978 and 1979 interims, the Special Committees on Assessment and Taxation recommended enactment of legislation that would have initiated a program of statewide data collection to be completed in approximately three-and-one-half years. In addition to market-value data for all property, data would have been gathered to permit use-value appraisal of farmland; however, neither the new appraised market values nor any values based on use-valuation could have been used for the levy of taxes without further legislative action.

The governor threatened to veto this bill unless a system of classification was enacted to protect homeowners and farmers from the shift in property taxes that would result from reappraisal. Consequently, the bill was withdrawn from the house calendar and referred to the House Committee on Assessment and Taxation in 1979. The bill remained in committee during the 1980 session, and died at the end of that session.

Classification

The term *classified property tax* is generally used to describe a system of taxing property by segregating it into groups to which different effective rates of taxation are applied. While a form of classification results from exempting some property and thus creating two classes (taxable and nontaxable), legal classification more properly is based on constitutional or statutes provisions that specify that different classes of property shall be taxed at different effective rates. Extralegal, or de facto, classification can result from administrative procedures or rulings of a central administrative agency or from practices developed within or among local jurisdictions by local assessors.

As noted above, Article 11, Section 1 of the Kansas Constitution requires a uniform and equal rate of taxation. Thus, Kansas is not among the states having either constitutional or statutory classification.

Tax Lid

The 1970 *tax lid-budget lid law* applied to tax levies made and budgets adopted in 1970, 1971, and 1972. Counties, cities, unified school districts, and community colleges were subject to that law. A 1973 law extended the tax lid indefinitely and discontinued the budget lid. The present law applies to counties and cities. (Budgetary controls were imposed on unified school districts under the 1973 School District Equalization Act and on junior colleges by another 1973 law. The 1977 legislature removed community colleges from the lid, and, in 1981, budget controls were eliminated.)

There are numerous types of tax levies that are exempt from the lid. There are about a dozen exemptions carried over from the original law enacted in 1970. Four exemptions were added in 1971, four more in 1972, three in 1973, fifteen in 1974 (including two for junior colleges), five in 1975, three in 1976, seven in 1977, three in 1978, and three more in 1979. Some of the exemptions have broad application (for example, levies for payment of principal and interest on bonds and for payment of employer contributions for employee benefits such as social security, retirement programs, workmen's compensation, and unemployment insurance), other exemptions apply only to a type of taxing subdivision—such as all counties or all cities—and still other exemptions are applicable only to a specified county or city. Most of the exempt levies added in the last few years require voter approval or are subject to a petition for an election.

In August 1977, the attorney general ruled that, because the tax-lid law is not uniformly applicable to all cities (or to all cities within each of not to exceed four classes) or to all counties, they may exercise their home-rule powers to exempt themselves from the lid. Many have done so, either entirely or in part.

The basic property-tax limitation under the 1973 law is essentially the same as under the 1970 law, namely, taxing subdivisions covered by the law cannot levy an amount *in dollars* greater than the amount levied in 1968 or 1970. This limitation is on the aggregate of nonexempt levies and not on levies for individual funds.

While the tax lid has provided a restraint, it has not prevented total property-tax revenue from rising (nor was it intended to). There are several reasons for this fact. One is that the lid does not apply to all types of taxing units. Also, a number of special-purpose levies made by counties and cities are exempt from the lid by law even if home-rule authority is not used. Furthermore, property-tax revenue may rise because the millage rate computed under the lid can be applied to increased valuations of new improvements on real estate and of personal property. In other words, *natural growth* in assessed valuation within a taxing subdivision can produce more tax dollars, even if the tax rates under the lid were not changed or even if they were reduced slightly.

Administration

Most of the responsibility for administering the property tax in Kansas falls on local officials, but the state also has a major role. Officials involved include county appraisers, county clerks, county treasurers, county boards of equalization, the Division of Property Valuation, Department of Revenue; and the State Board of Tax Appeals (which serves as the State Board of Equalization). County appraisers are responsible for discovering, valuing, and listing all taxable tangible property within the county. Although the state values some property (utilities), the major part of this important function is done at the local level.

Prior to 1968, county clerks, treasurers, and appraisers were elective offices. In most of the smaller counties, the county clerk served as the ex officio county assessor. The 1968 session of the Kansas legislature passed laws permitting the appointment of a county assessor if certified by the director of property valuation as being qualified. That session of the legislature provided that from and after 1 January 1979, no person shall be appointed to or serve as county assessor unless such person shall have been certified as being qualified. The director of property valuation was also required to prescribe standards for—and to institute training courses for—assessment personnel, with the objective of raising the professional standards and qualifications of assessing personnel.

The 1974 session of the Kansas legislature passed a law requiring that all county appraisers (assessors) be appointed for a four-year term from and after 1977. All appointments have to be made by the Board of County Commissioners from an eligibility list certified by the director of property valuation. To appear on the eligibility list, one must pass the state-appraiser examination, after which time he or she must pass progressive courses of appraisal each year as maintenance of eligibility. At this point, one progressive course each year is required. The major problem experienced in this plan has been the maintenance of an adequate list from which appointments are to be made.

County clerks and treasurers are responsible for the process of calculating, mailing, and collecting property taxes.

The director of property valuation administers the Division of Property Valuation within the Kansas Department of Revenue. The director is to exercise general supervision over the administration of the assessment and tax laws of the state to ensure that assessments of property be made relatively just and uniform and at true and full market values, and to require all local appraisers to "assess all property of every kind and character at its actual and full cash market value." Another statute specifically requires that the director devise forms, records, and other assessment tools that will help assure uniform assessments throughout the state. That statute also requires the director to prescribe guides showing the fair market value in money of personal property. Local appraisers, in setting values for personal property are required to conform to the values shown in the personal-property-assessment guides. While compliance with the property-assessment guides is mandated by statutes, the guides usually state that local appraisers are to deviate from the guides when necessary to assess at 30 percent of fair market value.

The Division of Property Valuation appraises public-utility and railroad property. The unit-value concept is employed—the property of each company is appraised as an operating unit. The market value of each company is determined after analyzing the several applicable indicators of value that are developed within the three standard appraisal approaches: cost, market, and income. Value indicators are calculated whenever feasible, and the director of property valuation determines the correlated unit value after reviewing the indicators of value and any other relevant material. After the unit market valuation of each company is determined, the value is allocated to Kansas and assessed at 30 percent. The assessed value of the utility is then distributed to the taxing districts in which the property is located and is included in the base for levying of ad valorem taxes.

Motor-carrier over-the-road equipment is appraised by the Division of Property Valuation on the basis of a personal-property vehicle and equipment guide. After the equipment valuation is determined, a factor, which is established by miles in Kansas to miles everywhere, is utilized to allocate value to Kansas. The allocated value is then assessed at 30 percent, and taxes are levied by use of an aggregate statewide levy of the preceding year for all levied taxes statewide. The Division of Property Valuation collects the resulting taxes. Receipts originally were used for school finance but presently are deposited in the State General Fund. An amount equal to the tax collected is later transferred from the State General Fund to the Special City and County Highway Fund.

The Board of County Commissioners in each county sits ex officio as the Board of Equalization. County Boards of Equalization hear *appeals* from appraisals made by the County Appraisers. Appeals from this board, as well as tax-protest cases, may be made to the State Board of Tax Appeals, which serves as the State Board of Equalization in appeals of appraisals. Members of the State Board of Tax Appeals are appointed by the governor with confirmation by the senate. No more than three of its five members may be from the same party. Appeals from decisions of the board are taken to the courts.

Fiscal Importance

Property taxes levied in Kansas in 1980 (for 1981) totaled $903.4 million, an increase of 79.0 percent over the $504.6 million levied in 1970 and a 221.6-percent increase over the 1969 levies of $280.9 million. Nevertheless, the property tax has accounted for a decreasing percentage of total state and local taxes in Kansas over the last half century. The property tax decreased from over 82 percent of the total in FY 1930 to less than 40 percent in FY 1980. However, most of this decrease took place in the 1930s, 1940s, and 1970s, as shown in table 6-1.

While property taxes declined relative to all state and local taxes in Kansas between 1960 and 1980, they remain a large share of the total relative to the national average and to most of our neighbors. In FY 1979, the latest year for which comparable data are available, property taxes were 40.7 percent of the total state and local tax mix in Kansas, while the U.S. average was only 31.6 percent. (Among our neighbors, only Nebraska placed greater reliance on the property tax). An advisory Commission on Intergovernmental Relations (ACIR) report indicates that property taxes made up 79.7 percent of local taxes, nationwide, in FY 1978. In Kansas the percentage was 93.5.

Table 6-1
Ratio of Property Tax to Total Kansas State and Local Taxes
(in percentage)

Fiscal Year	Ratio
1930	82.02
1940	62.95
1950	52.19
1960	56.44
1970	53.06
1980	39.20

Of course, the dependence on the general property tax varies among the levels of local government. For instance, 1980 general property taxes made up 84.2 percent of county taxes, 85.3 percent of city taxes, 100.0 percent of school taxes, 80.3 percent of township taxes, and 100.0 percent of special-district taxes. In 1980, general property taxes were 92.9 percent of all local taxes in Kansas.

Nationally, the property tax as a percentage of local tax collections increased from the turn of the century until the Great Depression but has decreased since, as is shown in table 6-2 (data are ACIR computations based on Bureau of Census reports).

The percentage distribution of 1930 through 1980 property taxes by type of taxing units is presented in table 6-3. More than half (54.9 percent) of all property taxes were for schools, including community colleges, municipal universities, and unified school districts in 1980. The state's share of 1.7 percent is the result of its 1.5 mill levy for education and institutional building funds.

The average *cost per parcel* for assessment in Kansas in 1979 was $5.77. Statewide, this cost ranged (by county) from $1.52 to $13.22.

The 1981 Special Committee on Assessment and Taxation has been instructed to: "Study real and personal property taxation in Kansas, including a review of the present method of unit valuation of state-assessed properties, the need for statewide reappraisal of property, alternative methods of reappraisal, and ways to mitigate the effects of reappraisal, such as alternatives to the *fair market value* concept, partial property tax exemptions, and temporary or permanent classification systems."

The committee was unable to report its findings in December 1981 as expected, and when a final report may be released is uncertain.

Table 6-2
Property Taxes as Percentage of Local Tax Collections, Kansas

Fiscal Year	Percentage
1902	88.6
1913	91.1
1922	96.9
1927	97.3
1932	97.3
1936	94.7
1940	92.7
1948	88.6
1956	86.8
1964	87.2
1972	83.5
1976	81.2
1978	79.7
1980 estimate	77.2

Table 6-3
Distribution of Property Taxes by Type of Taxing Units, Kansas, 1930-1980

Unit	1930 Taxes	Percentage of Total Tax	1940 Taxes	Percentage of Total Tax	1950 Taxes	Percentage of Total Tax	1960 Taxes	Percentage of Total Tax	1970 Taxes	Percentage of Total Tax	1980 Taxes	Percentage of Total Tax
State	7,367,986	840	4,735,790	7.64	6,631,053	4.99	7,748,185.27	2.76	9,147,188.43	1.81	15,228,934.13	1.69
County	20,883,306	23.80	17,557,083	28.33	35,795,546	26.93	61,671,871.70	21.96	104,273,745.16	20.66	193,338,242.20	21.40
City	14,771,577	16.83	10,682,592	17.24	19,574,389	14.73	40,313,463.14	14.35	83,979,809.38	16.64	152,893,423.76	16.92
Township	6,630,527	7.55	2,621,691	4.23	6,244,123	4.70	8,381,852.10	2.98	8,414,439.20	1.67	14,077,210.47	1.56
School	37,793,556	43.06	26,199,960	42.28	64,116,393	48.24	160,170,480.06	57.03	288,901,328.89	57.25	496,499,988.25	54.96
All other districts	317,179	.36	171,395	.28	544,007	.41	2,591,600.77	.92	9,917,520.12	1.97	31,344,389.30	3.47
Total	87,764,135	100.00	61,968,511	100.00	132,905,511	100.00	280,877,453.04	100.00	504,634,031.18	100.00	903,382,188.11	100.00

7 The Role of the State in Property Taxation in Kentucky

Robert H. Allphin,
Richard Thalheimer, and
Virgil O. Barnard

Legal Framework

The Kentucky legislature met in special session in 1949 to enact a series of laws aimed at improving the overall quality of assessments. For the first time, serious attempts at scientific reappraisals were undertaken. Funding was provided to begin collection of the necessary information, such as parcel maps, and the working relationship between the department and the tax commissioners was more clearly defined.

The primary responsibility for making assessments was left with the tax commissioners. The Department of Revenue was given supervisory powers over the methods and procedures by which the tax commissioners were to operate. As a result, the department began to build the staff expertise necessary to aid the commissioners in planning and executing valuation programs to promote equity within the counties. Manuals were written for field-valuation use, office procedures were suggested, maps prepared, and direct valuation assistance given in many counties.

By 1954, after several years of promoting equalization within each county, the department used its strengthened supervisory powers to require equalization between counties at full-value levels. This requirement created a difficult political situation, as large tax increases would result. After a seemingly successful battle for statewide equalization, it seemed the war was lost, however, when a change in administrations resulted in a policy of benign neglect with regard to county levels of assessment. The department staff suffered heavy attrition, and the counties were allowed to revert to a system allowing levels of assessment far below the constitutionally mandated fair cash value.

This period lasted for a decade—until 1965, when a group of taxpayers challenged the department for permitting such inequalities to exist. The courts agreed with the taxpayers, and in *Russman* v. *Luckett,* the Kentucky Court of Appeals (now the supreme court) directed that the Department of Revenue and the tax commissioners (now called property-valuation administrators) adhere to the full-value standard. This ruling caused great consternation throughout the state, as blanket assessment increases would be required to raise county assessment levels ranging from 15 percent to 40 percent up to full value. The resulting increases in taxes would have been tremendous, as most districts levied the same maximum statutory rate each year.

As a result, the legislature met in special session to reduce the state general-property tax rate from five cents to one-and-one-half cents per one hundred dollars and to establish a rollback procedure for all local rates, limiting overall tax increases to 10 percent for 1966 and 1967, excluding revenue from new property. After that time, the tax rates would remain unchanged, except to increase for any loss in tax base due to exemptions in any year.

While the *Russman* case served to require a full-value assessment in all counties, the language was not specific with respect to clarifying the position of the department in supervising the property valuation administrators (PVAs). Thus, the same caution that prevailed in the department following the push for full value in 1954 continued after this decision.

The requirement for full value was clearly established, but the precise responsibilities were left unclear in achieving the goal. Neither the elected PVAs nor the politically sensitive Department of Revenue wanted to engage in a full dispute over the issue.

There was another trend during the period from the late 1940s to the present that directly affected the administration of the property tax. This trend was the fragmentation of the tax base, caused by creation of a large number of special classes of property subject to separate rates. Originally, there were very few distinctions made as to the amount of tax levied against different kinds of property, but now there are about forty separate classes established by the legislature. Table 7-1 lists the various classes as of 1980, together with the applicable tax rates. Some of these classifications appear to have a legitimate basis; others, however, seem to be merely responses to powerful interest groups. The legislature cannot exempt property from taxation; a constitutional amendment is required. The legislature can, however, set such a low rate of tax on a class of property that it becomes uneconomical to collect any single bill. Any tax levied on a class must be uniform within that class, and classes must have a reasonable basis in distinctions of property type rather than form of ownership. The various classifications shown in table 7-1 at a one-tenth of a cent per one hundred dollars rate are results of such legislative "exemptions."

These actions complicate the task of administering the tax in several ways. First, each new classification leads to a more complex recordkeeping and valuation system. Second, as new property classifications are established at reduced tax rates, the burden of taxation becomes greater on the remaining properties. This raising of the tax burden increases the taxpayers' sensitivity to the tax. Finally, a system that legislates inequities between

Table 7-1
Classified Property-Tax-Rate Structure, Kentucky

| Class of Property | Statute | Cents per One-Hundred Dollars of Assessed Valuation | | | |
		State	County	City	School
Agricultural products					
Tobacco in hands of producer or agent	132.020(1)	1.5	None	None	None
Tobacco not at manufacturer's plant	132.020(1)				
(storage)	132.200(6)	1.5	1.5	1.5	None
Other agricultural products not at manufacturer's plant	132.020(1)				
(storage)	132.200(6)	1.5	4.5	4.5	None
Alcohol production facilities	132.020(1)	.1	None	None	None
Annuities (see Rights to receive income)	132.215(2)	.1	None	None	None
Bank deposits					
Domestic	132.030(1)	.1	None	None	None
Out-of-state (also see Intangibles)	132.020(1)	25.0	None	None	None
Bank for cooperatives					
Capital stock	136.300(1)	10.0	None	None	None
Bank shares	136.270	85.5	19.0	19.0	None
Brokers' accounts receivable (also see Margin accounts)	132.050	10.0	None	None	None
Car lines	136.120(4)	100.0	None	None	None
Coal (see Unmined coal)					
Common-carrier truck lines (rolling stock)					
Regular route	136.120(2)	45.0	Full	Full	Full
Irregular route	136.120(4)	100.0	None	None	None
Credit-union accounts	132.047	.1	None	None	None
Distilled spirits	132.160	45.0	Full	Full	Full
Farm machinery used in farming	132.020(1)	.1	None	None	None
Goods in transit (See Public warehouses)					
House trailers (mobile homes)	132.260(2)	45.0	Full	Full	Full
Intangibles					
Money in hand, shares of stock, notes, bonds, accounts, and other credits, except those arising from out-of-state business, shares of stock in affiliated companies, and others not specified elsewhere	132.020(1)	25.0	None	None	None
Accounts receivable, notes, bonds, credits, nondomestic bank deposits, and other intangibles arising from out-of-state business, patents, copyrights, and shares of stock in affiliated companies	132.020(2)	1.5	None	None	None
Public service company (nonoperating)	136.120(2)	25.0	None	None	None
Leasehold interests (owned by tax-exempt governmental unit)	132.020(1)	1.5	None	None	None
Life insurance companies (domestic)	136.320				
Capital		70.0	15.0	15.0	None
Reserves		.1	None	None	None
Policy proceeds on deposit (individual)	132.216	25.0	None	None	None
Livestock and poultry	132.020(1)	.1	None	None	None

Table 7-1 *(continued)*

| Class of Property | Statute | Cents per One-Hundred Dollars of Assessed Valuation | | | |
		State	County	City	School
Manufacturing machinery	132.020(1)				
(owned and used by manufacturers)	132.200(4)	15.0	None	None	None
Margin accounts (see Brokers' accounts)	132.060	25.0	None	None	None
Pollution-control facilities	132.020(1)	15.0	None	None	None
Production-credit association	136.300(1)	10.0	None	None	None
Public warehouses					
Property in storage except goods in transit	132.260(1)	45.0	Full	Full	Full
Goods in transit	132.095	1.5	None	None	None
Radio, television, and telephonic equipment	132.020(1)	15.0	None	None	None
Raw materials and products in	132.020(1)				
course of manufacture	132.200(4)	15.0	None	None	None
Retirement plans	132.043	.1	None	None	None
Real estate	132.020(1)	24.1[a]	Full[a]	Full[a]	Full[a]
Rights to receive income (see Annuities)	132.215(2)	.1	None	None	None
Savings and loan associations (domestic)	136.300(1)	10.0	None	None	None
Stocks and bonds (see Intangibles)					
Tangible property not elsewhere specified	132.020(1)	45.0	Full[a]	Full[a]	Full[a]
Truck lines (see Common carriers)					
Unmined coal	132.020(5)	.1	Subject only to taxation for local bond levies voted before 1 January 1977		
Watercraft (commercial)	136.181	45.0	Full	Full	Full

[a]Subject to compensating rate adjusted annually.

some classes of properties complicates the goal of reaching equality between others.

There were two amendments to the constitution, in 1969 and 1971, that dealt with lessening the tax burden on certain types of property owners. These were the Agricultural Deferred Value Amendment and the Homestead Exemption Amendment. The first was passed to shield farms located in areas subject to speculative value increases from taxation on the portion of fair market value of the land that exceeded the value in use as a farm. To qualify for this exemption, land has to meet certain minimal guidelines designed to ensure that only land in use as a farm receives the benefits. These requirements call for a certain level of farm income each year, depending upon the number of acres in the parcel. For example, a ten-acre parcel would be required to earn at least $500 annually from farm operations before qualifying. The deferred taxes become payable for the current year—and the immediately preceding two years when the land is converted to a use not eligible for special treatment.

Over the period 1975 through 1980, the full fair-cash-value assessment of farms in Kentucky rose by more than 110 percent, while the taxable portion of value rose by only about 40 percent. Shown below is a tabulation that indicates the total potential deferred taxes resulting from the implementation of this act as of 1 January 1980 (in millions):

	1978	1979	1980	Total
State	$13.2	$15.6	$17.1	$ 45.9
County	8.4	10.4	13.7	32.5
School	12.2	15.5	17.1	44.8
Other	1.2	1.5	1.6	4.3
Total	$35.0	$43.0	$49.5	$127.5

Because only a small portion of farmland actually changes use in any one year, it is unlikely that any substantial portion of this amount will ever be collected. The result has been a decided shift in tax burden away from farms and toward other types of taxable property.

The second amendment, the Homestead Exemption, was passed in 1971 and provided partial tax relief to homeowners over sixty-five years of age. A maximum amount of $6,500 (in terms of 1972 purchasing power) was to be exempted from taxation. By 1980, the exemption was adjusted to $10,200, and slightly more than $1.9 billion in valuation was exempted from taxation. About 195,000 individuals utilized this exemption in 1980, for a savings in state taxes of about $4.6 million and a savings of over twice that amount in local taxes. Again, however, the tax savings to the elderly were offset by increased taxes to all property owners to ensure no "real" loss to the taxing districts.

The state general-real-property tax rate, reduced to 1.5 cents per one hundred dollars after the *Russman* full-value case, was raised to 31.5 cents in 1977. The rate applying to tangible personal property was also raised at that time from 15 cents to 45 cents per one hundred dollars. This increase in state rates of thirty cents was directly offset by a decrease of thirty cents in the maximum allowable school rates. The purpose of these actions was to provide for a system of funding for schools that would ensure that the poorer counties had access to funds equal to the rich counties. For the initial year, the additional funds collected by the state under this program were directly redistributed to all school districts on the basis of a formula to equalize the potential tax base per pupil. Since that time, the revenues have gone into the general fund without allocation to a particular program, and funding for the *power equalization program* is no longer specifically tied to state-property-tax revenues. This action greatly reduced the importance of the property tax to school districts, although it is still a principal source of revenue to most.

The period of 1970 to the present saw a rapid yearly increase in property values in general. This increase led to pressures for higher assessed values, and with tax rates fixed at one level by most taxing districts, a corresponding increase in taxes came about. This situation continued until 1979, when the highly contagious California Proposition 13 was answered in Kentucky by a special legislative session with its House Bill 44. This bill was a tax-relief measure based on providing more taxpayer control over establishment of local rates that would produce any increases in aggregate revenues from real estate from one year to the next, excluding new property increases. Any rate that produced up to a 4-percent increase was subjeced to a public hearing to explain the need. A rate that exceeded this 4-percent limit was subjeced not only to a public hearing but also could be put to a general vote if certain petition requirements were met. Maximum rate limitations were left in place. The state rate on real property was limited to that producing no more than a 4-percent increase in total revenue each year.

The result of House Bill 44 has been a declining trend in tax rates as property values and assessments have skyrocketed and taxpayers have resisted increased levies. The following tabulation helps reveal its impact:

	Average 1978	*Average 1979*	*Percentage of Change*	*Average 1980*	*Percentage of Change*
State: real	31.5	27.90	−11.4%	24.10	−13.6%
County	22.0	20.58	− 6.5%	19.01	− 7.6%
School: common	22.1	20.60	− 6.8%	19.56	− 5.0%
independent	51.3	47.40	− 7.6%	44.07	− 7.0%

The declining trend in tax rates can be expected to continue under House Bill 44, if property values continue to rise at an annual rate exceeding 4 percent. A major and positive impact of this bill, aside from obvious taxpayer savings, is the fact that it served to focus the attention of the taxpayers on the tax-levying authorities as the source of increased taxes. Before this act, an official could state that he had not raised the tax rate, while raising taxes through levying the same rate on higher assessed valuations. With House Bill 44, the property-valuation administrator (PVA) could begin to distance himself from the amount of tax collected. An increase in assessment no longer automatically meant a corresponding increase in taxes due. The law appears to have accomplished the intent of the legislature at the time of passage—to slow the rate of increase in taxes caused by the rapid rise in property values and to allow taxpayers themselves a greater voice in the determination of the tax rates. Theoretically, the PVAs could now pursue the goal of full-value assessments in a time of property-value inflation without causing undue hardships on taxpayers. To an elected official, this ability is extremely important.

Administration

The department and the PVAs were still, in 1979, unsure of their working relationship. The Kentucky constitution required full fair-cash-value assessments: "All property, not exempted from taxation by this Constitution, shall be assessed for taxation at its fair cash value, estimated at the price it would bring, at a fair voluntary sale."

Russman v. *Luckett* reaffirmed this point. The legislature, however, had enacted statutes that could be interpreted to require either party to bear the responsibilities. Both the PVAs and the department were charged with achieving full fair cash value, with the department given general supervisory powers. The question was, Did these supervisory powers extend to requiring the PVAs to reach full value themselves or did the department bear the major burden?

This issue was avoided up until 1980, and instead the department attempted to rely on persuasion and implied authority, rather than direct orders, in shaping property-tax policy. Administrative and valuation manuals were still provided to the PVAs. A staff was again in place to provide help in local administration. Mapping projects were continuing, with increased effort to gather property—characteristic data to improve the information base available to the PVAs. Over the years, little effort had been made by the PVAs to collect such information needed for professional valuation. Their major effort in valuing real estate was to ensure that sales were recorded on the tax rolls under the new owners' names. If any increases in assessments were needed, blanket percentages were usually applied without attempts at individual equalization. Very little tax-roll information existed; usually the name and address of the owner, type of property, value, and perhaps the number of acres and a brief sales history. A few PVAs collected additional information, but most preferred to avoid the controversies caused by beginning a complete data-collection program. Even in counties where mapping projects were completed by the department and given to the county offices, little was done to maintain them and they quickly became outdated. Through the political process, PVAs came and went, with varying degrees of professionalism. A qualifying exam required of all new candidates for the office did little to ensure that a qualified PVA would take office.

The mixed loyalties of the PVAs led to natural problems. Raising assessments to the required full value was perceived as not being helpful to one's chances of reelection. The department itself was not immune to political pressures against raising assessments, as most administrations did not wish to undertake the unpopular task of raising property taxes. So the stalemate over final authority continued from the 1954 revaluation effort to the present, with a brief court-ordered effort at equalization in 1966-1967.

Assessment-sales ratio studies for each county have been conducted annually since 1937 by the department and, for the whole state, are based on 20,000 to 25,000 actual transactions each year. The sales are screened for validity, analyzed and adjusted for price-level trends to represent market value as of the assessment date, and compared to the assessment effort to arrive at a percentage relationship. The ratios from 1967 showed a general decline through 1979, especially in the residential class.

This trend was reversed dramatically in 1980, as another change in the state's administration led to a more active role being taken by the department to achieve full value. Under its statutory powers as supervisor of the PVAs, the department required that counties be within 5 percent of full value in 1980 (as indicated by the assessment-sales-ratio studies). This requirement was met by 103 of the 120 counties. There was resistance in the courts from many PVAs to this unaccustomed push from the department. Basically, the PVAs contended that the department had the responsibility for increasing any county's assessments that it felt were below full value. The department countered that while the ultimate responsibility was indeed its own, the primary repsonsibility lay with the PVAs. The department, as the PVAs' statutory supervisor, had a duty to require the PVAs to perform properly the function for which they were elected. Seventeen counties were ordered by the court of appeals to be certified at less than the department's standard, to avoid local taxing problems while the matter was being resolved. The case was decided in favor of the PVAs in both the circuit court and court of appeals, but the Kentucky Supreme Court ruled in favor of the department's position. Basically, the supreme court defined the relationship between the department and the PVAs as that of a team, with the department as team leader. The PVAs the court found, while elected, serve subject to the "direction, instruction, and supervision" of the department.

The decision by the supreme court is a landmark one, since it deals so specifically with the relationship of the elected PVAs to the department. It appears that the delineation of responsibility and authority for administration of the property tax has at last been clarified.

At the present time, most types of property are valued locally by the PVAs under the general guidance of the department. Property belonging to public-service companies is valued directly by the department, however, due to its special nature. The unit-value approach forms the basis for appraising the property of such companies. This approach calls for an appraisal of the entire company as a unit, using the income, cost, and market approaches to the extent applicable, and allocating value to the various taxing districts on the basis of physical location of the property and contribution to the unit value indicated by usage. A professional staff has been developed to administer this program. It has been hampered in the past by a lack of communication with both the PVAs and the department personnel concerned with local valuations. The allocation of portions of the unit value to specific properties owned by public-service companies has not been done with great efficiency. The small staff available to the department is capable of making unit appraisals with proficiency but is incapable of physically inspecting and placing appropriate values on all the component parcels of the companies each year.

At the local level, the perception of the department's success in valuing large concerns such as railroads or utilities rests almost totally on values placed on actual real-estate parcels in the counties. If adequate values are not placed on such properties, the appearance is one of underassessment even though it is more a problem of allocation of value between real, tangible, and intangible properties than one of making a correct unit appraisal. The PVAs, however, point to obvious errors in value allocations on public-service-company properties and use such examples to counter department pressures on them to achieve full market value.

House Bill 44 has highlighted the problem of public-service-company valuations. The unit values of these regulated firms tend to rise at a slower rate each year than typical residential properties. This lag is due to the restricted nature of their earnings, coupled with ever-rising investor demands for returns—but to the average taxpayer it appears inequitable. As public-service-company assessments grow at a lesser rate than other types of property, they make up an ever-decreasing percentage of the total tax base. This fact, coupled with the general decline in tax rates outlined earlier, leads to decreasing tax bills in many cases for public-service companies and increasing bills for other property taxpayers. This shift in the tax burden is not new, but House Bill 44 has focused attention on the various components of the tax base and how they interrelate in producing revenue totals.

The legislature, through committee hearings, is responding now to local criticism of the taxation of public-service companies. At the present time, the problems of shifting tax burdens and allocation of values are being studied. Alternatives to alleviate the shift in burden are limited, since public-service companies must be taxed equitably with other properties under the Kentucky Constitution. The problem of allocation of values is more amendable to correction, as this situation can be improved through greater reliance by the department on the PVAs and other local valuation staff with their greater numbers and more detailed knowledge of the counties.

So, the department and the PVAs are now wrestling with the problems of who should play what role in the administration of the property tax. For most of the history of the tax the department has pretty much left local administration alone, preferring to offer advice and criticism from the sidelines. At the same time, the department has not attempted to utilize the field resources available to it in the valuation of public-service properties. The PVAs, on the other hand, have held the department at a distance with regard to seeking the stabilizing influence of centralized information and assistance. The politics of confrontation with the department have been chosen more often than not in attempts to win favor at the polls at the expense of efficient tax administration.

The current dispute may well signal the beginning of the establishment of a working relationship between the parties. From history, it seems obvious that a locally elected official has no real incentive on his own to strive for a full-value assessment each year. At the same time, the department cannot hope to assess all property in the state without a great amount of input from the local level.

Both the department and the PVAs have qualities that are needed in an overall system of property-tax administration. Neither can do the job effectively on his own. The department can establish methods and policies that can provide a standard of equalization throughout the state. It has the ability to employ professionals who could assist in any county, while most counties would be unable to employ such individuals. The department may also be able to maintain greater objectivity in dealing with local issues, thus promoting more equal overall tax administration.

The department can also bring greater resources to bear in the development and administration of more modern valuation procedures, such as computer-assisted mass-appraisal programs. In the 1974-1975 fiscal-year period, the department received a grant from the National Science Foundation for a two-phase research project aimed at evaluating then-existing computer programs and developing, testing, and evaluating alternative approaches and techniques for computerized-valuation and land-records systems. The first phase was carried out in Fayette County (Lexington), while the second phase was never begun due to a shift of resources within the department. There are still personnel in the department who participated in the project, and data collection is currently under way in several counties in anticipation of an effort to pick up the development of such a program where phase one left off.

The PVAs also provide functions needed for proper administration of the tax. They are familiar with local markets and, through the elective process, are sensitive to local needs. Given adequate training and compensation, they and their staffs can serve as indispensable sources of information for the overall valuation system. The department has encouraged attendance at various appraisal courses for both its own staff and the PVAs.

It would appear that history has shown us in Kentucky that there is a need for a central authority at the state level in administering the property tax. Whether or not the local assessing official should be elected is open for debate, but perhaps it would not matter if an adequate system of operating controls exists. Here in Kentucky, we are moving on a path that, it is hoped, will demonstrate the desirability of such controls.

Fiscal Importance

The property tax represented over 86 percent of all state receipts in 1793 and made up over 60 percent of receipts as late as 1920. Currently, it represents less than 10 percent. Counties, schools, cities, and various other taxing districts still rely on the property tax as a major source of revenue, although they too are beginning to develop alternate sources of funds.

8

The Role of the State in Property Taxation in Maine

R.L. Halperin with
R.W. Meskers and *A.J. Neves*

Legal Framework

The original constitutional provision (1820) providing for equal apportionment and assessment of real estate based on just value was amended in 1876 to include personal property. The just-value standard has been excepted only twice. The voters at General Election in 1970 provided that the legislature could establish current-use-valuation laws for farm, forest, open-space, game-management, and wildlife-sanctuary lands. Again in 1978, the electorate allowed the legislature by law to approve a cost-sharing formula for school districts that apportioned tax burden between jurisdictions on other than just value.

These special cases aside, the concept of *just value* is the key to property-tax equity. The courts have interpreted just value to mean market value, and the legislature has enacted a statutory definition that attempts to identify important elements to be considered in determining just value.

The administratively significant exception to just value is current-use valuation in the case of certain lands. The Maine Tree Growth Tax Law provides for the valuation of qualifying forest land on a productivity basis. These values are determined by the state tax assessor in accordance with statutory guidelines. Reimbursements have been provided municipalities that the legislature determines to be entitled to assistance because of the valuation limitations.

The other classes of land provided the benefits of current-use valuation are covered under the Farm and Open Space Land Law, which has evolved from its original enactment in 1971. Valuations for land classified under this law are determined by the local tax assessor utilizing established guidelines. In both the Tree Growth and Farm and Open Space laws, the assessor must decide if land is eligible for classification. Each law levies a penalty for the withdrawal or change of use of land.

Although the exceptions to just value are limited, Maine law does allow for exemptions. The Maine Supreme Court in a 1945 advisory opinion explained the legislature's latitude concerning the constitutional requirement of equal apportionment and assessment:

> The full power over taxation is vested in the Legislature including power of determining upon what kind and classes of property taxes shall be imposed, and what shall be exempt from taxation and is limited only by the positive requirements and prohibitions of the Constitution. (141 Me. 442)

Thus, property-tax exemptions are provided by statute except those few required by federal law or the Articles of Separation (from Massachusetts in 1820). It is interesting to note that until 1845, Maine law merely listed those categories of property to be taxed. Subsequently the law has required more or less general taxation, with enumerated exemptions.

Section 8 of the constitution was amended in 1915 to allow the legislature to fix a rate on intangible personal property. In 1961, the legislature amended the definition of personal property so that it no longer included intangibles, thus excluding them from taxation. The long troublesome issue of accurate listing and valuation of intangibles was therefore ended.

Article IX, Section 8 of the Maine Constitution, which establishes the standard of just value for real and personal property, has been reviewed along with the exceptions:

1. Current-use valuation
2. Allocation of school-district costs
3. Exemptions
4. Statutory exclusion of intangibles

Another related constitutional provision was approved by the voters in November 1978. Article IV, Section 23, reads:

> *Section 23. Municipalities reimbursed annually.* The Legislature shall annually reimburse each municipality from state tax sources for 50% of the property tax revenue loss suffered by that municipality during the previous calendar year because of statutory property tax exemptions or credits enacted after April 1, 1978. The Legislature shall enact appropriate legislation to carry out the intent of this section.

The driving force behind this amendment was the Maine Municipal Association. Since its enactment, it would seem that neither the municipalities nor the state have found it to be entirely satisfactory. Because reimbursement is fixed at 50 percent, both the state and the municipalities must share equally the burden of exemption.

Although Article IX, Section 7 deals with a general valuation at least once in ten years, current-day standards of equity have significantly eclipsed this requirement, and there is now an annual state valuation.

Two other provisions dealing specifically with taxation are worthy of mention in setting the constitutional framework. Article I, Section 22 and Article IX, Section 9, provide:

Section 22. No tax or duty shall be imposed without the consent of the people or their representatives in the Legislature. (Contained in the Constitution as originally enacted.)

Section 9. The Legislature shall never, in any manner, suspend or surrender the power of taxation. (Added in 1876 by Amendment XVII.)

These two somewhat complementary mandates have insured that property-tax statutes remain the province of the people, either by statewide referendum or through the legislature.

A final comment concerning constitutional impact on property-tax law relates to the assessment appeal process. An appeal process is guaranteed by the equal-protection and due-process requirements of the Maine Constitution. The state has in turn established specific statutory guidelines.

Beyond this system of just value and its exceptions is a statutory property-tax circuit-breaker system for the elderly. The Elderly Householders Tax and Rent Refund Act provides a limited measure of tax relief. Qualifying individuals with income in the case of single-member households up to $6,200, or multimember households up to $7,400, receive a rebate on their property tax or its equivalent for renters. The amount of rebate is limited to $400. The program is state administered.

Administration

To describe the operation of the property tax in Maine, it is necessary to explain governmental organization. There are three basic levels of government; state, county, and municipal. The county's only involvement with the property tax is the apportionment of its expenses against municipalities and the unorganized territory. Municipalities assess, levy, and collect all property-tax revenue (except in the unorganized territory, which, lacking local government, has its property-tax responsibilities administered by the state).

Currently, Maine is comprised of 497 municipalities, of which 22 are cities, 432 are towns, and 43 are plantations. Plantations are a rudimentary form of town government consisting, in part, of three assessors and a tax collector elected by majority vote at a town meeting.

Towns or cities may establish a single assessor or board of three, five, or seven members. The selection of board members and the tax collector is accomplished by vote of the electorate. The single assessor, if this option is selected, is appointed by the selectmen, or council, for a term not to exceed five years. Boards of assessors usually are selected annually and consist of the town's elected selectmen with one member designated as chairman. Assessors must be at least eighteen years of age, and except in the case of those appointed on a full-time basis, citizens of the United States. The municipalities establish the compensation for assessors. The municipal assessor is an agent of the state tax assessor when performing the assessment function.

The state tax assessor is appointed by, and serves at the pleasure of, the commissioner of finance and administration. The state tax assessor administers the Unorgnized Territory Educational and Services Tax along with the county tax in the unorganized territory. In addition, the state tax assessor, as director of the Bureau of Taxation, is responsible for supervising municipal administration of the property tax and for establishing an equalized valuation of municipalities (which will be discussed later).

From 1820 until 1891, the duties associated with state administration of the property tax were performed by the state treasurer. A committee of the legislature, based on a valuation taken every ten years, equalized the assessments among counties and annually apportioned the state tax among the municipalities. In 1932, a reorganization of state government led to the replacement of the State Board of Assessors. The Bureau of Taxation, headed by the state tax assessor, was vested with the responsibilities of the board along with the administration of the gasoline tax. A Board of Equalization was created consisting of the state tax assessor and two members appointed by the governor and council. The Board of Equalization was abolished in 1970 when full equalization responsibility was transferred to the state tax assessor. A five-member Municipal Valuation Appeals Board was established to hear municipal appeals on state equalization.

The supervision of municipal tax administration includes several responsibilities. The Bureau of Taxation is responsible for investigating and adjudicating complaints of improper assessment of property. Statutory authority permits the state tax assessor, either on his own initiative or upon complaint, to investigate assessment practices. Furthermore, he is empowered to insure the reassessment of property when necessary, and request legal action of the attorney general when appropriate. Historically, the supremacy of the state in the municipal assessment of property has been exercised infrequently.

During the past decade, a significant effort has been made to provide for the utilization of improved assessment technology. Since the linchpin of quality assessment administration is a well-trained assessor, statutory provisions have been enacted that allow the state tax assessor to establish an assessor training program. The Bureau of Taxation currently coordinates a series of basic courses conducted through various adult-education programs and an annual week-long training seminar, offering advanced studies, in conjunction with the Maine Chapter of the International Association of Assessing Officers and the Maine Association of Assessing Officers.

The law provides for the certification of assessors by the state tax assessor based upon qualifying examinations and recertification through a continuing-education requirement. The certification can be revoked for cause. Certified Maine Assessor (CMA) designations are held by 264 persons. A less-demanding program is offered for assessors in small municipalities; the Certified Assessment Technician (CAT) designation has been awarded to 62 persons. Certification is required for full-time professional assessors, and those serving municipalities with a population exceeding 3000 must be a CMA.

Beyond the role of the state tax assessor, the statutes establish the operational guideposts of local tax administrative requirements relating to assessment, appeals, and enforcement. Local assessors establish the value of all taxable real and personal property within their jurisdiction as of April 1 annually. Property owners must, upon the request of the assessor, provide a list of estates. Failure to comply results in the forfeiture of appeal rights.

Assessors determine the ratio, or percentage of just value, at which they assess property, subject to a 70-percent minimum limitation. The local-valuation book is the public record of assessments and is available for public inspection. If a taxpayer can establish that his valuation does not have the same relation to just value that the average valuation of other properties bear, or that an error of law exists, then there is a basis for an abatement request to the assessor. The assessors, within one year from commitment, or the municipal officers thereafter but within three years from commitment, may make abatements to correct any illegality, error, or irregularity in assessment. The assessor's decision may be appealed to a board-of-assessment review, or, if there is no board, to the county commissioners. Decisions concerning the valuation of land (relative to its classification under current-use provisions) are appealed to the Land Classification Appeals Board. Requests for abatements due to poverty or infirmity are filed with the municipal officers. In all cases, ultimate recourse is to the court system. Maine does not have a tax court, but the appeal is heard in superior court rather than district court.

Although the state tax assessor is not authorized to abate taxes assessed in municipalities, assessment-ratio studies performed by the Bureau of Taxation are prima facie evidence of the local ratio. Few taxpayers request abatements due to a general lack of understanding of the property tax. Appeals to the county commissioners too often produce unsatisfactory results since they generally are more politically oriented than local officials.

Maine municipalities enjoy significant latitude in specifying property-tax due dates, interest rates, and early-payment discounts. The usual legal-enforcement tools are tax liens against real estate, and civil action against personal property.

The *state valuation* is a process and record of the equalized full value of all taxable property in the state. It consists of a gross valuation of property in each municipality and the individual valuation of each parcel in the unorganized territory. This process is de facto an assessment review program. The state valuation filed with the secretary of state prior to February 1 of each year is based upon the local valuations for April 1 two years prior. This lag in equalization results from a lengthy process, which begins with the accumulation of sales data reported in real-estate transfer-tax declarations of value that must be filed prior to deed recording in the county Registry of Deeds. All transactions occurring in one-year period that surrounds the April 1 assessment date are reviewed by state and local officials to assure that the basis for all assessment-ratio determinations consists of only arms-length transactions.

Although uniform property-classification systems are not required, field personnel separate the local-valuation base into broad categories that include land under current-use classification; undeveloped land; electric-utility property; commercial, industrial, recreational, residential, and personal property. Each property class is projected to full value based upon assessment-ratio studies or state appraisals. In those instances where insufficient sales activity precludes reliable assessment-level analysis, the sales period is extended or field appraisals are conducted by field staff using an assessment manual published by the Bureau of Taxation.

Preliminary state valuations for each municipality are published, hearings are held, and a municipality may formally appeal remaining disagreements to the Municipal Valuation Appeals Board. The major purpose of the state valuation is its use as an equalization factor in the formulas for determining the distribution of financial assistance to municipalities based on property valuation. Its principal use is in determining the local share of education costs.

Two by-products of the equalization process are used as measures of assessment performance: the assessment ratio, or level of assessment, and the assessment-quality rating (which provides a measure of assessment uniformity or equity). In 1975, the legislature enacted assessing standards to insure just assessing practices without mandating specific means to achieve this objective. A minimum assessment ratio (that is, the ratio of local assessment to market value) of 70 percent was established, as well as a maximum rating of assessment quality of 20 percent. A quality rating of 20, or less, requires assessments to deviate, on the average, less than 20 percent from the average level of assessment.

Table 8-1 reflects the substantial improvement in local assessing practices that has resulted from local efforts to improve assessments. The Bureau of Taxation continues to assist municipalities in their efforts to achieve or maintain these ratings through advisory and limited staff involvement; however, the majority of improvement was the direct result of professional revaluation contracts initiated as a result of the enforcement, or threatened enforcement, of the assessing standards.

Enforcement of assessing standards, to date, has been limited to cases involving failure to achieve the minimum assessment ratio. Depending upon

Table 8-1
Local Assessment Improvement, Maine Counties, 1965 and 1980

County	Average Assessment Ratio		Average Quality Rating	
	1965	1980	1965	1980
Androscoggin	55	83	30	13
Aroostook	44	78	35	15
Cumberland	62	75	26	13
Franklin	46	89	33	17
Hancock	45	78	34	20
Kennebec	58	86	30	14
Knox	53	85	30	14
Lincoln	33	75	29	18
Oxford	47	86	34	13
Penobscot	40	86	37	14
Piscataquis	37	79	41	17
Sagadahoc	48	75	30	16
Somerset	43	84	34	15
Waldo	41	78	35	16
Washington	43	73	31	24
York	41	73	32	15

Note: Although a 1965 base year is used here for comparison purposes, it bears notation that the assessing performance remained relatively unchanged until the mid-1970s.

the circumstances, several corrective measures have been mandated: acquisition of tax maps, professional revaluation, professionally assisted revaluation, or local revaluation. Compliance with state mandates has generally been satisfactory, however, several civil actions in the courts have been necessary.

Municipalities that do not attain the minimum level of assessment are prohibited, by statute, from receiving reimbursement for taxes lost as a result of the current-use valuations of the Tree Growth Tax Law. Thirty-nine municipalities were denied reimbursements totaling about $34,000 for the 1980 tax year.

In 1980, seventy-four municipalities failed to achieve the minimum assessment ratio, and eighty-six failed to achieve the maximum quality-rating standard. Pressure from the state and responsible local administrative action continues to correct these discrepancies.

The property-record systems in Maine have, in many cases, evolved from a mass appraisal by an equalization firm. Needless to say, the standards legislation spurred the growth of the appraisal industry, including tax-mapping firms. Unfortunately, contracts for equalization services entered into by inexperienced boards of assessors may deteriorate for lack of expertise or funds to maintain them. Local part-time assessors generally cannot maintain the equalization process and often are unable to obtain the funds to contract their maintenance. The reluctance of small municipalities to contract for revaluations is based upon cost and a widespread belief that revaluations lead to higher taxes—an impression that derives from the confusion that the property tax is somehow related to the ability-to-pay concept as measured by income, not property value. This impression is empirically reinforced by observation of the level of taxation in the urban communities that attempt to maintain accurate valuation levels.

Clearly, state equalization is heavily dependent on accuracy achieved at the local level. In 1973 only 30 percent of Maine's municipalities had property-record cards. This figure had increased to 62 percent in 1980.

Until the mid-1960s, few municipalities had tax maps. Maps generally were utilized by larger cities with more sophisticated management and full-time assessors. Momentum for tax maps increased during the next decade due to escalating property values and tax rates, as well as base-map production for many related uses. A 1973 law required municipalities to acquire tax maps by 1980, but local pressures forced repeal in the next legislature. In 1973, more than 200 municipalities (40 percent) were without formal maps; in 1980, this figure had dropped to 69 (13 percent).

An *assessment district law* was enacted in 1974 that required all assessing jurisdictions to have a certified assessor by 1980. However, this provision was relaxed subsequently and now applies only to jurisdictions with full-time assessors, of which there are about 70.

It is unlikely that the number of full-time assessors in Maine will increase greatly in the near future. Most municipalities cannot afford and do not need—at least in their perception—full-time, trained assessors. In addition, reversals of legislative attempts to mandate larger, more efficient assessment districts clearly demonstrate that change will not likely result from voluntary, cooperative efforts by municipalities seeking to balance equitable tax administration against scarce revenue.

The state does not directly assess any property for local-valuation purposes except in the unorganized territory. However, several types of property may be valued by state personnel in the process of state equalization; these include major industrial facilities, electric-utility property, and other special-use property that comprise a substantial portion of the local tax base.

Assistance is made available to local assessors in several forms. The equalization field force of ten appraisers assists assessors by analyzing sales, discussing assessment practices, and generally familiarizing them with state assessment procedures. In most cases, this process permits active exchanges of information, and both state and local equalization efforts benefit. At other times, this process suffers from the historical polarization of state-local interaction, and only perfunctory assessment analysis is possible.

Assessment technology varies widely. In the most sophisticated assessor's offices, detailed classification and tax maps, property-record cards, pricing schedules, technical libraries, and computerized ratio-study and update capabilities offer professional assessors and their staff a full complement of tools necessary for efficient and quality tax administration. At the other extreme are the diminishing number of jurisdictions where the valuation book or assessment list, subject to annual adjustment by "windshield appraisal," is the basis for property-tax assessments.

The average parcel inventory is approximately 1,200, but this figure ranges from less than 50 in the sparsely populated areas of the state to over 22,000 in the largest city. Assessor burden is perhaps more accurately reflected by population density rather than parcel count.

Fiscal Importance

Despite the common charge that the property tax is the most poorly administerd of all taxes, it persists as one of the oldest, most productive revenue sources. The property tax accounts for one-third of all state and local governmental revenue from Maine sources and about 45 percent of all revenue available to local governments. School districts receive approximately 58 percent of all local tax revenues.

Although a state property tax was "assessed" by municipalities until 1975, the revenue therefrom was available for local expenditures. The last state property tax that was, in fact, a general state revenue source was repealed in 1952.

The general revenue of local governments derives from two principal sources: intergovernmental transfers and local sources that include the property tax, special-service assessments, interest-income and motor-vehicle excise taxes that are in lieu of the personal-property tax. State and federal revenue-sharing programs have provided payments to local governments that have helped to relieve further burden on the property tax. In 1980, the average effective property-tax rate for Maine was sixteen mills.

The state revenue-sharing program in 1980 transferred about $16 million to municipalities on the basis of population and local tax effort. State revenue-sharing funds are statutorily prescribed to be 4 percent of the general state sales- and income-tax programs. This statute serves to protect this source of local revenue from the impact of inflation—particularly with regard to the unindexed and generally unadjusted progressive-income-tax system.

The relative importance of the property tax to local governments has declined considerably in the last two decades. Local revenue in the 1963 through 1979 period increased almost 400 percent, while the property tax increased only 200 percent. In Maine, the state provides most of the intergovernmental revenue, and state/local transfers increased almost ten-fold during this period.

The property tax is basically a residual tax that raises the amount by which local budget requirements exceed revenue from other sources. Although there are no constitutional or legal restrictions or limitations on property-tax burden, most municipalities recently have exercised considerable restraint in formulating budgets. The relative importance of the property tax in the future will, in large measure, be determined by legislation at the federal and state level, since transfer payments and the availability of new local revenue sources, or expansion of the tax base, are the alternatives to increasing the property-tax burden.

A recent survey of assessment costs in twenty-nine municipalities that enjoy full-time assessing staffs follows:

Average parcel count	5,064
Average cost of assessment administration	$40,826
Average cost as percent of property-tax revenue	1%
Average cost of administration per parcel	$8.06
Average area of jurisdiction	23,040 acres

Assessment costs in most of Maine's smaller taxing jurisdictions are not available, since the assessment function is not a line item in the local budget. Generally, the elected town selectmen serve as the local board of assessors, and data accounting for time, supplies, and, in some cases, professional assistance are not available.

Except for periodic revaluation efforts, which average about twenty dollars per parcel if professionally done, it is estimated that less than 0.5 percent of property-tax revenue is expended in assessment administration in the majority of Maine towns.

The assessment function in the unorganized territory is performed by the state, and the cost of this program is recovered through the tax assessment. The unorganized territory consists of about 8.4 million acres and 15,486 parcels. The average cost of administration is $9.40 per parcel, which represents about 1.9 percent of the property-tax revenue. However, it should be pointed out that the average effective tax rate in the unorganized territory is about ten mills, as compared with sixteen mills in the municipalities. Furthermore, the assessment cost in the unorganized territory includes revaluation charges that are excluded from the municipal costs.

Policy Framework

The Maine property tax and its functioning, while of general concern to property owners, has been the subject of limited legislative improvement. The cast of special-interest groups with an ongoing interest in property-tax law is small. Legislative study committees, the state administrative agency, executive commissions, assessor associations, and the Maine Municipal Association have been the principal players.

Administration of the property tax in Maine has, on the other hand, been principally the domain of the local assessors. To this end, the spirit of Yankee independence and the realities of local government have controlled. Maine has not experienced a public ground swell demanding equity. Neither has there been any concerted attempt to limit property taxes on a statewide basis similar to Proposition 13. The only governmental unit in Maine to attempt a binding limitation was the town of Saco. Its cap on taxes was lifted after the municipality was faced with bankruptcy.

Presently, the executive and legislative branches of Maine government are studying the property tax and alternatives to it with regard to mining property. The discovery of substantial amounts of copper and zinc ore raises the possibility of large-scale mining operations in Maine. The property-tax treatment of such a resource is perceived to be difficult to administer. As a result, alternative taxes that appear to be more administratively efficient and compatible with the state's natural-resource policies are being reviewed.

Maine is a state steeped in the New England tradition of local control. Very limited supervision of local tax administration over the years has resulted in an inertia in the area of state intervention. Local budgets are voted at town meetings. Insufficient funding and staffing of overseeing state agencies, combined with the desire for local autonomy within the state, have resulted in an undeclared detente with regard to tax administration. The inability or disinclination of the legislature to resolve this state-local intervention issue is perhaps inevitable by virtue of the political tension caused by the local-control philosophy, the election process, and the cost of change.

Efforts to improve assessor qualifications are stymied by the high turnover of local assessors. It is difficult to establish rapport with local assessors when they are subject to annual election. The rapid turnover of local assessors likewise makes the maintenance of professional standards difficult.

In 1976, a uniform state property tax was enacted by the legislature. This tax, designed to equalize property-tax effort with regard to educational costs, required certain of the property-rich municipalities to subsidize municipalities with smaller tax bases in relation to educational need. The law was repealed by referendum in 1977, due ostensibly to the fear that the state property tax eroded the local control of education.

Efforts to preserve the property tax as a viable source of local revenue in Maine have revolved around: (1) expanding the local tax base by phasing out certain classes of property exemptions; (2) enabling legislation permitting municipalities the option of imposing service charges on certain classes of exempt property; and, (3) increasing state support for financing public education. Support for these concepts appears to be increasing, but recent legislation in these areas has failed.

The constitutional provision requiring state reimbursement for 50 percent of local revenue losses caused by property-tax exemptions enacted after 1 April 1978, has been an effective deterrent against further erosion of the tax base.

The Role of the State in Property Taxation in Maryland

Gene L. Burner

The property-tax system in Maryland has survived a decade of siege. The attacks were frequent, the battles fought on numerous fronts, the fighting fierce, and now, the war is over. The changes that took place during the 1970s dramatically altered the role of the state government in property taxation.

State law requires that real and personal property be assessed on the basis of its full cash value. Personal property (only business personal property is assessed) is actually valued and assessed at 100 percent of its original cost, less depreciation. Four counties have elected to exempt all personal property from taxation. Real property is actually valued on the basis of its current market value and assessed at a fixed percentage of that value. There are a few exceptions to the market-value approach such as agricultural land and woodland. Such land is assessed according to use, and the assessment ratio is 50 percent. Public utilities are taxed on the basis of the full cash value of the operating property, determined using either the cost or income method, while the real property of the utility is assessed as other real property.

Legal Framework

Constitutional Provisions

The most important constitutional provision in Maryland relating to property taxation is the provision of uniformity. In the early and mid 1970s, property-taxpayer unrest became common throughout the state. Mass assessment-protest meetings were held in the more urban counties. Busloads of angry taxpayers descended upon the State House in Annapolis during the annual sessions of the Maryland General Assembly.

Many state officials reacted to the considerable political pressure being exerted by introducing legislation that would freeze residential assessments at their present level. Other bills were introduced to place restrictions on the allowable percentage increase in the assessment. Based on the mood at the time, it is reasonable to assume that there were sufficient votes available to pass one or more of these measures seeking to place artificial restrictions on the assessment. However, all such attempts were found to violate the uniformity provision of the constitution, and they were defeated. Clearly, the constitutional provision of uniformity serves many important purposes, not the least of which is to deter so-called quick-fix solutions to extremely complex issues.

Statutory Provisions

In 1957, Maryland became the first state to require assessors by law to value farmland, as long as it is actually used in agriculture, on the basis not of market value but of its *value in agriculture*. The statute has survived numerous challenges and has now taken its place as one of the most important statutory provisions in the overall state-property-taxation system. In 1982, land actively devoted to agricultural use is valued throughout the state at a maximum of $400 per acre. The assessment is 50 percent of that value. Because an acre of unimproved land in the more urban areas may sell for as much as $20,000, the use-value assessment is a significant factor in the state's efforts to preserve agricultural land. In 1979, an additional statutory provision was added that imposed a *development tax* when agricultural land is converted to a higher use. In 1981, this tax was modified to an agricultural-transfer tax, with the tax being imposed at the point of sale of agricultural land. The tax is waived if the purchaser signs a declaration of intent to continue to farm. The revenues from this tax are used by the state to purchase development rights to existing agricultural land.

It now appears that the most significant legislative act to occur in recent years was the state assumption of the assessment process. Prior to 1973, assessment personnel were county employees. Although the State Department of Assessments and Taxation had responsibility for issuing rules and regulations to insure uniformity of assessments, local governments were responsible for the actual assessment function. In 1973, the Maryland General Assembly enacted legislation that, over a three-year period, transferred all assessment-office personnel to the state. By 1975, the assessment process was consolidated at the state level.

At the time of the move toward consolidation of the assessment process, taxpayer unrest was increasing. Moreover, there was increasing pressure from the voters for relief from rapidly rising assessments. Although initially not in the form of a statutory provision, one of the first reactions to this public pressure was action by the governor to reduce the assessment ratio. Prior to 1974, the ratio of assessment to market value was established by the governor. The law, at that time, provided that all real property shall be valued at its full cash value and that there shall be an allowance for inflation. In 1973, the allowance for inflation was 40 percent—meaning that assessments were 60 percent of full cash value. In 1974, the governor issued an executive order establishing the allowance for inflation at 50 percent, resulting in a 16.6 percent reduction in the level of assessment.

Yet, property-owner unrest continued. During the spring of 1975, the General Assembly met in special session and enacted the Homeowners' Property Tax Credit Program (commonly referred to as the circuit breaker). The initial program provided benefits only for homeowners age sixty or over or disabled. The formula used to determine a homeowner's maximum tax liability was fairly restrictive. This program has been amended over the years to the extent that in 1981, it provided approximately $36.5 million in state-funded property-tax credits to over 110,000 homeowners, regardless of age.

The 1977 session of the Maryland General Assembly provided two significant statutory provisions that now represent important elements of the overall policy framework of property taxation. A program of mandated local-property-tax credits against real-property taxation for owner-occupied residential properties was established. The credits are granted by local governments at their expense and in an amount attributable to the property taxes generated by an increase in an assessment over 15 percent above the prior year.

Secondly, the Constant Yield Tax Rate, or Florida Plan, was established. This plan provides that in any year in which a county or municipal government wishes to establish a local-property-tax rate at a level that would produce more property-tax revenues than were generated in the prior year, it must advertise its intent and hold a public hearing to explain the reasons for any proposed increase.

At the 1978 session, the acting governor recommended legislation that once again provided for a reduction in the assessment ratio. The legislation added a special homestead allowance for inflation of 5 percent and placed the new ratio of 45 percent in the law. This legislation represented the first, and to date, the last successful attempt to adjust assessments to accomplish a shift in property-tax burden.

During the period of these changes, taxpayers continued to demand other action by the state to relieve the burden of rapidly increasing assessments—while government officials fought among each other. State elected officials blamed local officials for not reducing the property-tax rate. Local officials blamed the state for increasing the assessments. The taxpayer, it seems, was caught in the middle of a full-scale finger-pointing exercise. Consequently, unrest and political pressure continued.

The year 1979 brought with it a legislative proposal and subsequent statute that may represent the beginning of the end of the unrest and turmoil of the 1970s. In that year, the governor proposed, and the legislature enacted with certain amendments, the triennial-assessment law. Prior to

1979, state law required annual assessments. In 1973, a landmark court decision held that if the law said annual assessments, it meant annual assessments and ordered that the state discontinue its practice of only assessing once every three years. Consequently, all real property in the state was reassessed each year. It is, therefore, reasonable to conclude that the shift to annual assessments in 1973 may have been a contributing factor to the increased taxpayer unrest during the 1970s.

The triennial-assessment law has two key features—a three-year assessment cycle, and an automatic indexing of the assessment ratio. The three-year assessment-cycle provisions require that all real property in the state be revalued and reassessed once every three years. Any increase in value resulting from the physical review of the property is phased in over the ensuing three years in equal increments. While the indexing of the assessment-ratio provision is complex from a mechanical point of view, the concept is relatively simple. As the revaluations conducted by the Department of Assessments and Taxation produce an aggregate increase in property values in excess of 6 percent of the prior year's total statewide values, the assessment ratio is adjusted downward. The extent of the downward adjustment is such that the total statewide assessable base will only grow by 6 percent each year.

The triennial-assessment law has been in operation in Maryland for only a short time. While it is too early to predict the real impact of the new law, some observations are possible. First, the level and degree of taxpayer unrest has subsided, as evidenced by a major reduction in the number of assessment appeals and by the marked absence of assessment-reform legislation. Second, the triennial-assessment law has placed the emphasis of property taxation at the local-government level. This observation is based on the loud outcry from local governments that the automatic-indexing portions of the new law be repealed.

There are, of course, numerous other statutory provisions that have been added over the years. Maryland, like other states, has authorized a number of property-tax exemptions and local-property-tax credits. The exemptions are typically for broad classes of property, while the tax credits tend to be for a specific type of property within a particular jurisdiction.

Administration

Prior to 1914, the administrative responsibility for assessments was spread over three levels of government—towns, counties, and the state. Each level assessed independently of the other, and only when additional property taxes were needed. In 1914, the Maryland State Tax Commission was formed and charged with oversight of the assessment function. The most significant change was that only one assessment was made for use by all levels of government. Reassessments were to be conducted once every five years, although only two occurred until the late 1930s.

In 1943, the General Assembly authorized the first full-time permanent staff of assessing officers. Previously, assessors were elected locally—and more for their political skills than for their expertise in the appraisal field. The new group of assessors were county employees, and remained in this category until 1974.

During the late 1940s and early 1950s, the law required that each county be divided into five equal districts, and that one district be reassessed each year. Not long after enforcement of this plan by the State Tax Commission, it was discovered that considerable inequities existed among the five groups, and in 1953 the General Assembly ordered a three-year rotational-assessment law. To prevent the inequities that had existed previously under the five-year plan, the law provided that at the completion of the three-year cycle, the reassessments would be entered on the tax rolls and subject to levy. This change so greatly disrupted local revenues that the General Assembly reacted once again and changed the law to require annual assessments.

Although annual assessments were required by law, the state remained on a three-year assessment cycle with the assessments being entered on the tax rolls as they were reassessed.

The next major administrative development occurred in 1959, when the State Tax Commission was replaced with the State Department of Assessments and Taxation and the Maryland Tax Court. The change was significant because it placed the total administrative responsibility for the assessment function at the state level, although funding was provided by local governments. The change was also important because it placed the responsibility for assessment appeal with an independent review body. The Maryland Tax Court continues to function today as a separate agency within state government.

In the mid- to late-1960s, property-owner groups began comparing assessment levels between jurisdictions. Many complained that assessment practices were not uniform throughout the state—and in most instances these charges were correct. The heart of the problem lay with the funding of the local assessment offices.

Beginning in 1968, proposals were made for the complete state assumption of the assessment process. The initial reaction by local elected officials was negative, because they felt they would be losing control of what appeared to be a local matter. After years of defeat, the General Assembly passed a bill in 1973 authorizing the complete state takeover of the assessment function. The takeover was designated in three steps. First in 1973, all local assessment supervisors became state employees. Then, in 1974, all assessors joined the state. Finally, in 1975, all clerical employees of the local assessment offices became state employees.

In 1982, the State Department of Assessments and Taxation had an annual operating budget of more than $19 million in state general funds. No local-government funding has been provided since 1975. The department employs approximately nine hundred persons, most of whom are involved in the assessment process. The department maintains an assessment office in the county seat of each of the twenty-four counties, and each office is headed by a supervisor of assessments. The supervisor is appointed by the director of the department from a list of five qualified candidates submitted by the governing body of the county. Statewide coordination of the assessment process is handled through a network of regional or area supervisors, who in turn report directly to the state supervisor of assessments, who is appointed by the director. The state supervisor reports to the director of the department, who is appointed by the governor.

One of the most important advantages of state consolidation of the assessment process is the enhancement of statewide uniformity of assessment. A closely related advantage is the ability to better inform the taxpayer regarding assessment practices. This aspect is even more valuable in a state such as Maryland, where there is a fair amount of intrastate taxpayer mobility. Regardless of the county selected, the Maryland taxpayer can expect to be treated the same as far as the assessment process is concerned in all parts of the state. The local property-tax rates may vary significantly; however, the assessment and valuation process will remain the same.

Another important advantage of state consolidation relates to economies of scale. When there is only one large assessment jurisdiction, it is possible to provide centralized, or at least regionalized, services such as data processing, property-map preparation and maintenance, and personnel. Without consolidation, each of these services would have to be provided at the local government level. Also, additional savings can be realized through the standardization of assessment procedures and assessment-office practices. Maryland's experience has been that consolidation has led to the ability to reduce total staff requirements and to save taxpayers' dollars.

Due to consolidation at the state level, Maryland's assessment process is now more responsive to legislative changes. During the unrest of the 1970s, a number of legislative changes were implemented throughout the state within just one or two months. Without proper managerial accountability, it could have taken years to make such major changes. Also, the ability of the assessment process to respond more quickly and efficiently to legislative changes enhances the state's ability to develop and implement programs within an overall policy framework.

While the consolidation of services such as data processing results in dollar savings through economies of scale, it also results in an increased ability to utilize the services of data processing and to further develop those services. Standardized data-processing systems tend to produce standardized management reports. Consequently, data-base maintenance and management is enhanced on a statewide basis. State consolidation opens the door to a more effective use of computer-assisted mass appraisal. At this point, Maryland has not taken this step yet, although it is not far away.

Finally, an important advantage of state consolidation is improved professionalism. A statewide assessment organization offers greater resources for training programs and continuing education. Currently, Maryland conducts an annual assessors' school designed to train an average of seventy-five to one-hundred new employees in the concepts and principles of real-property valuation and assessments. These courses are accredited by the International Association of Assessing Officers.

There are, however, a few disadvantages of state consolidation. The one disadvantage most frequently mentioned in Maryland relates to the problem of differences in the cost of living throughout the state. All assessment personnel are state employees and are paid on a standard pay scale. These state pay scales do not recognize differences in the cost of living that is significantly greater in the Maryland counties adjacent to Washington, D.C. In these counties, retention of assessors is particularly difficult.

Another disadvantage of consolidation in Maryland is closely related to the problems associated with statewide pay scales. Because the entire assessment function is 100-percent state funded, the Department of Assessments and Taxation must compete with other state agencies for available dollars. In times of a recession, the competition becomes tougher. Thus far, the State Department of Assessments and Taxation has received adequate funding to carry out its necessary functions. However, there has been a need to reallocate existing resources among counties, which has resulted in some cutbacks in the more wealthy jurisdictions to aid the less wealthy counties. It is possible that of the twenty-four jurisdictions, two counties may now be providing less services than would be the case without consolidation.

Finally, there is the potential for a lack of accountability at the state level for property taxation. At the present time, I do not view this lack as a serious problem or a disadvantage. However, caution must be exercised in administering a statewide assessment process to avoid adopting a hierarchical attitude. State officials and assessment personnel must be careful to not view their function as superior to that of local government. While assessment personnel must attend to the business of assessing, they must also bear in mind that they are only one part of the overall property-tax structure and that property taxation is a shared responsibility.

Although consolidation has occurred through the state assumption of costs, data-processing systems continue to remain fragmented. Currently, approximately two-thirds of the twenty-four counties are serviced by a standard state data system. The remaining county assessment offices are served by either the local-government data system or by outside vendors. The department is undertaking an aggressive plan to incorporate these remaining data systems into the state system. However, total state control of all county systems is a number of years away.

Another important change that must be initiated by the department is the partial automation of the assessment function. In a fully consolidated environment such as Maryland's, computer-assisted mass appraisals would be an extremely useful tool in improving efficiency and the quality of the assessment.

Finally, full consolidation of the assessment function offers the possibility of some degree of regionalization. Currently, the department maintains an assessment office in each of the twenty-four counties in the state. Frequently, and mostly due to budget restrictions, it is necessary to reassign personnel on a temporary basis to complete assessment work in another county. The department is currently exploring the possibility of hiring regional teams of assessors. These teams would serve under the direction of an area or regional supervisor and would be sent into those counties in most need of assistance at a particular time.

The future of assessment consolidation at the state level in Maryland is reasonably clear for the decade of the 1980s. There does not appear to be any serious threats or proposals that the assessment function should be returned to the control of local governments.

Fiscal Importance

The property tax is an important revenue source in Maryland. The twenty-four counties in the state rely heavily upon the property tax as a major source of revenue to support local governmental services. Generally, the property tax represents approximately 20 to 25 percent of county revenues, and it is the only major revenue source with local-government rate-making authority. Local property-tax rates range from a low of $1.49 to a high of $5.93. Thus far Maryland has resisted Proposition 13 approaches as well as spending limits. Also, it is important to note than the automatic indexing of the assessment ratio, combined with the requirements of the Constant Yield Tax Rate law, represent restrictive measures that help to hold down excessive increases in property tax.

Policy Framework

Delegate Benjamin Cardin, speaker of the Maryland House of Delegates, was probably the first state official to publicly articulate Maryland's policy regarding property taxation. In an address before the annual conference of the Maryland Association of Assessing Officers in the spring of 1980, Speaker Cardin announced four objectives of the property-tax structure. Senator James Clark, Jr., president of the Maryland Senate, who followed, added the fifth. Those five objectives are listed below, along with the appropriate program or statutory provision designed to meet the objective:

1. *Accountability by Government for Property Tax Revenues.* As a result of the taxpayer unrest and government finger-pointing during the 1970s, State elected officials have adopted the philosophy that accountability for taxation should rest with the level of government that receives the revenues. Three approaches have been used to implement this policy.

> *Constant Yield Tax Rate (the Florida Plan)*—requires local governments to disclose their intent to gain additional property-tax revenues.

> *Assessment Ratio Indexing (a part of the triennial assessment law)*—limits assessable base increases to a statewide average of 6 percent per year.

> *Local Property-Tax Credits*—few are mandated from the state. In most instances, the state will grant an authorization to a local government to grant certain property-tax credits. These credits are at the option of the local governing body.

The intended effect of the first and second programs listed above was to place additional emphasis on the local property-tax rate. So far, they appear to have been successful. Fewer and fewer taxpayers are appealing to the state legislature for assessment relief. Also, there has been a dramatic reduction in the number of assessment appeals filed with the state each year. In the past, many of these appeals were not related to the assessment but rather were a protest against higher property taxes. The third program listed above is really more of an informal policy adopted by the General Assembly. It is intended to create more flexibility at the local-government level, and to this extent it has worked.

2. *Relationship of Property Tax to Ability to Pay.* This objective could never be met under the property-tax concept, for if it were, property taxes would be abolished in lieu of an income tax. However, the state-funded circuit-breaker program does move in that direction by limiting the maximum tax liability of a homeowner according to gross income. Generally, the current program appears to be designated to provide a proper level of benefits. It is large enough to provide $38 million in benefits to over 110,000 homeowners, but not so large as to result in a major redistribution of state income and sales-tax revenue. The program appears to be effective and is operating at a reasonable level of efficiency. The administrative costs of the program are about 2.3 percent of the total state grants.

3. *Quality/Uniformity of Assessment.* Two programs have been enacted by the legislature that address this objective. They are:

Consolidation of the Assessment Process at the State Level—all assessment personnel are employees of the State Department of Assessments and Taxation. The director of the department is required by the statute to see that all assessments are based on full cash value and that they are uniform with the assessments of other comparable properties.

Triennial Assessment Law—requires that all properties be physically reviewed, revalued, and reassessed once every three years. Prior to 1979, annual assessments were required. Consequently, additional assessment resources are available to improve quality.

There is some evidence to suggest that the senate assumption of the assessment process has resulted in greater uniformity and improved quality of the assessment. Adequate time has not passed to evaluate accurately the impact of the triennial-assessment law on quality and uniformity. However, initial indications are that some improvements have been made in both areas.

4. *Break the Direct Relationship between Assessment Increases and Inflation.* Prior to 1977, an increase in market value as determined by the Department of Assessments and Taxation meant a corresponding increase in assessment. In 1977, and again in 1979, programs were adopted by the state to break this direct tie with increases in market values. The two programs are:

Credit for Assessment Increase in Excess of 15 Percent—This program represents one of the few instances where the state has mandated a property-tax credit against local taxes, and yet not provided state f·nds. The program requires that a credit be included on the tax bill of owner-occupied residential properties if the assessment increased by more than 15 percent over the prior year. The credit is equal to the additional taxes resulting from the excess increase.

Assessment Ratio Indexing—As the statewide average increase in property values exceed 6 percent, the assessment ratio automatically declines to offset the increase so that the average assessment only increases by 6 percent.

Both of the programs listed above have been successful in breaking the direct relationship of the assessment to market-value increases. However, the first is most suspect in terms of creating equity problems and violating the constitutional provisions of uniformity of taxation. When enacted in

1977, the program was determined to be constitutional as long as it was temporary. It was extended to apply to property-tax bills issued in July 1982. The program is beginning to appear more and more permanent, and its extension has created serious distortions among residential taxable assessments. Moreover, in the first year of the absence of the program, there will be extremely large taxable assessment increases so that the taxable assessment reaches the significantly greater actual assessment.

The second program listed above is perhaps more important in that it represents one of the few mechanisms available to states seeking to limit assessment growth. Also, the concept of indexing the assessment ratio does not bring with it the problems of equity and uniformity that occur when artificial limits or ceilings are imposed on individual assessments. The assessment-ratio-indexing provisions are specified in the law, and the Department of Assessments and Taxation is charged with the responsibility of calculating annually the new assessment ratio according to the formula. Notwithstanding the arguments set forth by local government officials, there is little difference between this approach—which results in steady and predictable declines in the assessment ratio—and the previous adjustments made to the ratio in election years.

There are, however, some policy issues that must be considered carefully before adopting a program of ratio indexing. For example, should the same ratio be applied to the full cash value of all classes of properties, or should there be separate ratios at various levels to create or maintain a desired tax-burden shift? In Maryland, the same ratio (45.6 percent in 1982) is applied to all real property, except that property valued according to use. The assessment ratio for use-value properties is 50 percent of value. Personal property in Maryland is assessed at 100 percent of its full cash value. If separate ratios were used and each was indexed by the same 6-percent limitation, the residential property ratio would decline rapidly, while the commercial and industrial ratio would decline only slightly, if at all.

Another issue or potential problem associated with assessment ratio indexing is that at some point in the future, the ratio will begin to approximate zero. In such an event, the only available solution would be to increase the ratio in one year legislatively and require that all local tax rates be reduced accordingly.

5. *Agricultural-Land Preservation.* For the purposes of this discussion, this objective also includes the preservation of woodland. The two programs are:

Agricultural-Land Use Valuation—If actively devoted to agricultural use, the land is valued based on the soil-productivity capability. The use rates are based on the capitalization of income derived from an average acre of corn.

Agricultural-Land-Preservation Program—The purchasing of develop-ment rights on certain agricultural land is funded by a tax on the sale consideration in the transfer of agricultural land of 5 percent on parcels of twenty acres or more and 4 percent on smaller parcels. As indicated earlier, the tax is waived if the purchaser signs a declaration of intent to continue farming.

There is no accurate method of evaluating the effectiveness of the agricultural-use assessment in meeting the objective of agricultural-land preservation. Clearly, the significantly lower assessments have helped to prevent forced conversion; however, the extent of the assistance is difficult to measure.

In summary, a state policy framework of property taxation does appear to exist in Maryland. That policy consists of at least the five objectives and associated programs mentioned above. In most instances, the individual programs are meeting their intended objective. Overall, policy changes have resulted in improved quality of assessments, better uniformity, increased local-government accountability for property-tax revenues, and a break with high property-value inflation. To some degree, agricultural land has been preserved.

10 The Role of the State in Property Taxation in Minnesota

Lyle H. Ask

Legal Framework and Fiscal Importance

Minnesota's original, 1858 state constitution provided that all taxes on property should be uniform and equal. Difficulties in assessment procedure and inexperienced assessors, however, quickly led to inequities, and in 1860 the State Board of Equalization was created.

Uniform assessment was the major goal throughout the late 1800s. The real impetus for improvements in the assessment of the general property tax, however, came with the passage of the Wide-Open Tax Amendment in 1905. This key amendment removed all restrictions on the legislature's power of taxation, except for the requirements that taxes be uniform on the same classes of subjects, that taxes be for a public purpose, and that certain property be exempt from taxation.

In 1907, the Minnesota State Tax Commission was created. One of its first tasks was to obtain better compliance with, and administration of, the property tax. The members of this first tax commission were strongly in favor of a classification system; one that would differentiate between homesteads, cultivated farms and business property, wild and unimproved lands, mineral and timber lands. There was no question that members of this first tax commission felt that not all property receives the same benefits from government, and not all property has the same capacity to pay.

In 1913, the Minnesota legislature began the process of establishing classes of property, and authorizing the assessor to use different percentages of values for different classes of property. The original classified-property-tax system created four classes:

Class I   Iron ore at 50 percent of value.

Class II   Household goods at 25 percent of value.

Class III   Livestock, agricultural products, inventories, furniture, tools, implements and machinery, unplatted real estate, goods in process or finished goods, at 33⅓ percent of value.

Class IV   All other taxable property at 40 percent of value.

In 1916, the Minnesota Tax Commission, in evaluating the classification system, reported that the new law "legalized the illegal system of under-valuation." However, by fixing the percentages by statute rather than through the "caprice of the assessor," the classification system resulted in uniformity and equality.

The development of *gross-earnings taxation*, especially of railroads, began a year prior to Minnesota statehood. In 1857, the act incorporating the Minnesota and Pacific Railroad Company imposed a gross-earnings tax of 3 percent on the company in lieu of all state and local taxes and assessments. This law was enacted in consideration of land grants to the company that were to be exempt until the land was sold. Other railroads were given similar exemptions. However, railroads incorporated without land grants were required to pay the property tax.

In 1873, the St. Paul, Stillwater, and Taylor Falls Railroad Company was exempted from property taxation and assessments by agreeing to pay a tax of 1 percent of its annual gross earnings for three years, 2 percent for the next seven years, and 3 percent thereafter. Other railroads could elect to come under this law by an act passed in the 1873 session of the legislature.

By 1887, all railroads were required to be taxed on their gross earnings in lieu of other taxes and assessments. The tax rate remained at 3 percent until 1905 when, by a legislative act of 1903, the rate was increased to 4 per-cent. The Minnesota Tax Commission, in 1912, recommended that the rate be increased to 5 percent so that railroad and other property would be taxed on a more equal basis. That increase was enacted in 1913.

Prior to 1921, state aid for highway construction was financed by a small property-tax levy of 1/20 of a mill. The levy was for an internal-improvement fund and was raised to 1 mill by 1911.

In 1920, an amendment to the state constitution was passed that authorized the creation of a trunk-highway system. This system was to receive federal appropriations on the condition that the state raise the re-quired matching funds. To raise the funds, motor vehicles were exempted from the general property tax in favor of a registration tax of 2 percent of the manufacturer's list price.

During the 1920s, there was also growing pressure to levy special taxes on the iron-mining industry. As far back as 1881, a one-cent tonnage tax had existed. While the output of the mines was increasing at a very profit-able rate, total tax collections during the period were very small. By 1897, the inequities were so apparent that the one-cent tonnage tax was repealed and the property tax was imposed on iron ore. Although the 1913 property-classification law assessed ore at a higher ratio than other property, the 1921 legislature proposed a constitutional amendment for an additional occupa-tion tax, and in 1923 a 6-percent royalty tax was imposed.

The Depression, which brought about a decline in the personal income of Minnesotans from $1,593 million to $832 million between 1929 and 1933, imposed severe financial stress on the state and local governments. Not only did state revenues from iron-ore, gross-earnings, motor-vehicle, and gasoline taxes drop dramatically, but the property tax became much more difficult to collect. As tax delinquencies rose and prices fell, market values declined. Tax delinquencies, which in 1929 amounted to $28.6 million, grew to $59.8 million by 1933. These delinquencies represented 22.8 percent of the total taxes levied in 1929 and 55.2 percent in 1933. At the same time, the cost of government, especially of education, could not be reduced proportionately and, together with general relief programs, was becoming a severe burden on the state's treasury.

The situation facing the legislature in 1933 merged the demand for property-tax relief and the need for replacement revenues. In response, the legislature reduced the assessment rate on certain agricultural and homesteaded property, thereby creating three new classes of property under the property-tax-classification system:

Class 3a   Agricultural machinery and horses used by the owner, and agricultural products in the hands of the producer and not for sale at 10 percent of full and true value.

Class 3b   The first $4,000 in value of unplatted real estate used for a homestead at 20 percent of full and true value.

Class 3c   The first $4,000 in value of platted real estate used for a homestead at 25 percent of full and true value.

These classifications provided relief to certain classes of property but increased the burden on the remaining classes. A new source of state revenue was needed. After more than forty years of attempts, the 1933 legislature did enact an income tax on the income of both individuals and corporations. (The property-tax-classification system was further modified in 1937 so that the first $4,000 in value of a homestead was exempt from the levy for state purposes).

During the 1940s, the property-tax-classification system was expanded. *Class 3d,* consisting primarily of livestock and agricultural tools, was assessed at 20 percent of full and true value. Special laws were passed to guarantee that servicemen would not lose homestead status. In 1953, *Class 3c* was created to provide reduced assessments to disabled veterans.

In the early 1960s, property taxes contributed $392 million, or 46 percent of the total state and local tax collections. Personal-property-tax collections provided an additional $93 million. However, while the proportion of state tax revenue generated by the property tax decreased from 50 percent in 1903 to 6 percent in 1962, the property tax still accounted for 97 percent in local tax collections in the early 1960s.

While property-tax relief in Minnesota was a product of the Depression, the trend in the last two decades has been an even more intensive demand for reductions in the burden of property taxes. The sharply rising costs of local governments, primarily in the areas of education and welfare, that prompted legislative action to reduce property taxes in the 1960s, continues today.

The first major reform came in 1967 with the enactment of the Tax Reform and Relief Act as the state took increased fiscal responsibility for local costs. The state reduced property taxes by requiring lower local levies and then reimbursing local governments for lost revenues. The six programs enacted were:

1. *Homestead Property-Tax Credit*
   Property taxes collected on homestead property were reduced 35 percent, up to a maximum credit of $250.
2. *Rent Credit*
   Renters were entitled to receive a credit against their state income tax equal to 3¾ percent of annual rent paid, up to a maximum of $45.
3. *Senior-Citizen Income-Tax Credit*
   Persons sixty-five years of age or older were allowed a credit against state income taxes for property taxes paid, up to a maximum of $300 (depending on the level of their income).
4. *Personal-Property Exemptions*
   Livestock and machinery used for agricultural purposes were completely exempted from the property tax. Manufacturers, wholesalers, retailers, and contractors were given the option of exempting either inventories held for resale or their tools and machinery. The property-tax-relief fund would reimburse taxing districts for the loss of tax base.
5. *Elimination of the State Mill Levy*
   Prior to the 1967 act, the state levied a property tax to finance the State Teachers' Retirement Program and to pay the interest and principal on bonded indebtedness. After 1967, the new property-tax-relief fund was designed to contribute a portion of retirement costs in the state's largest cities: Minneapolis, St. Paul, and Duluth. The contributions were for the purpose of reducing the mill levy.
6. *Local-Government Aids*
   The property-tax-relief fund also provided direct payments to schools and local governments. These payments were to be financed by one-fourth of the sales-tax collections or $37 million whichever was larger. In the case of rural schools, the payment was to be used for reduction of the mill levies.

In fiscal year 1967, Minnesota ranked fifth in the nation with per-capita property-tax payments of $180.02, compared to the U.S. average of $132.81.

by 1969, when the effects of the 1967 act were realized, per-capita property taxes had dropped to $156.02, with Minnesota ranked twenty-second among all states.

Although the 1967 legislature lowered property taxes, the tax continued to rise at a rate of 10 percent to 15 percent a year. By 1971, property taxes exceeded the levels of 1967—due primarily to the growth of county and municipal expenses, as well as the growth of educational costs.

In an effort to insure permanent property-tax relief, the 1971 legislature imposed levy limitations on all units of government in an attempt to restrain the growth of property taxes. It did so by limiting local districts to a 6-percent increase in the levy-limit base per capita over the levy-limit base per capita in the previous levy year. To ease the administration of the property tax, adjusted value (formerly full and true value) was eliminated, and all property was assessed at its market value. Prior to this change, the practice was to take one-third of the market value to arrive at adjusted market value. The classification rates were then applied to the adjusted market value to determine assessed value. With the passage of the 1971 act, total assessed values tripled, and the mill rates were reduced to one-third of their previous level. In addition, reform steps were taken to undergo a certification procedure under the newly created State Board of Assessors.

The 1973 legislature continued the policy of property-tax relief. A 5-percent reassessment limit was placed on residential, farm, and seasonal recreational-residential properties, creating the concept of limited market value. The Homestead credit was increased from 35 percent to 45 percent, up to a maximum of $325. The rent credit, which had been raised in 1971 to 7.5 percent up to a maximum of $90, was again increased in 1973 to 10 percent, up to a maximum of $120. Additional tax relief was also enacted for senior citizens through the *senior-citizen property-tax freeze.*

The 1975 Omnibus Tax Bill provided further property-tax relief through a new program called the *income-adjusted homestead credit* or *circuit breaker.* The theory of the circuit breaker provided that homeowners should pay no more than a specified percentage of their household income in property taxes, and the state would reimburse them for the rest. Under the 1975 act, the refund was a graduated percent of income, from 1 percent up to 4 percent, with a maximum credit of $475, including the homestead credit. The rent credit was repealed, but 20 percent of rent paid was considered to constitute property taxes, thus qualifying renters for the circuit breaker. The senior-citizen property-tax freeze was also revised by the circuit-breaker law. Senior citizens and disabled persons were allowed an additional $200 credit above the maximum of $475. With this additional credit, the freeze was phased out starting at income levels over $10,000 and completely eliminated when incomes reached $19,500.

Changes in 1975 affecting the assessment of property included:

1. *Flexible Homestead Base*

    Prior to the 1975 act, the first $12,000 of market value was assessed at a lower rate. The new law provided an increase of $500 in the base for each 3.5 percent inflationary increase statewide in home values.

2. *Five-Percent Reassessment Limit was Repealed*

    The concept of limited market value, however, continued. Property was to be viewed and reassessed every four years. Any assessment increases of 10 percent or less were added the first year. Increases between 10 percent to 40 percent were added at 10 percent a year until the full value was reached. Increases over 40 percent were added at 25 percent per year over a four-year period.

In 1977, property-tax relief was again an area of concern. The circuit breaker was renamed the *property-tax refund.* Other changes included:

1. Clarifying the household-income definition for the property-tax refund.
2. Excluding the income of dependents from the household income.
3. Increasing the percentage of rent paid that qualified for property-tax refunds from 20 percent to 22 percent.
4. Repealing the senior-citizen property-tax freeze.
5. Providing an additional refund called *co-insurance* for homeowners at a maximum of $475. This co-insurance feature paid up to 35 percent of the excess tax up to $800 and 50 percent of the excess tax up to $800 for seniors and disabled.

Additional property-tax relief came in the form of changes in the classification ratios. Homestead base values were increased to $15,000 for payable 1978 and assessed at 22 percent with the excess value assessed at 36 percent. For payable 1979, the assessment rates were scheduled to be 20 percent and 33⅓ percent. Changes were also made on agricultural homesteads and *Class 3cc* property.

A major tax-court decision in 1979 (*Malcolm A. McCannel and Edward N. Nelson* vs. *State of Minnesota and County of Hennepin.* Minnesota Tax Court, 31 January 1979) had a significant impact on the property tax law. The tax court ruled that the concept of *limited market value* was unconstitutional because it discriminated between property within the same class. The concept of limited market value was designed to mitigate rising property taxes caused by rapidly inflating home values. Limited market value allowed homes to be taxed at a lower valuation than estimated market value. Although the decision affected only the plaintiff in the case, the legislature responded by making substantial changes in the property-tax law designed to cushion the impact of higher property-tax burdens if limited market values were judicially repealed.

The 1979 Omnibus Tax Act provided a two-year phase out of limited market value. In the first year, increases in assessments would be the greater of 10 percent of the value of the preceding assessment or one-half of the total increase in valuation. The excess of this amount plus any additional increase in valuation would be added during the second year. At the end of the two-year phase out, all property would then be assessed at its full market value. the legislature also made four major changes to provide property-tax relief:

1. Increased the homestead credit over a two-year period from 45 percent of the eligible tax to a maximum of $325 to 50 percent up to $550 in the first year and 55 percent to $600 in the second year.
2. Increased the homestead base value to $21,000, with future increases of $1,000 (rather than $500) for every 3.5 points of increase in the homestead base-value index.
3. Made reductions in the classification ratios to be implemented over a two-year period.
4. Increased the maximum circuit breaker to $650, raised the co-insurance percentage to 50 percent to a maximum of $1,000, and increased the percentage of rent qualifying as property taxes from 22 percent to 23 percent.

Another major change affecting property taxes resulted from the Federal Railroad Revitalization and Regulatory Act of 1976. This law prohibited states from placing any tax on railroad property that would be higher than taxes levied against other commercial and industrial property. In addition, states were to cease discriminatory taxation of railroads within three years.

In light of this law, the 1979 legislature was forced to address the gross-earnings tax on railroads, which was viewed as discriminatory. Subsequent legislation contained in the 1979 Omnibus Tax Act provided a two-year phase out of the gross-earnings tax. For two years, the railroad companies were required to pay a 2-percent gross-earnings tax. At the same time, the commissioner of revenue would assess and levy the property tax based on the unit-valuation method of assessing property. If the 2-percent gross-earnings tax was greater than the property tax levied, the railroad company would receive a refund for the difference. If the gross-earnings tax was less than the property tax levied, the railroad company was required to pay the excess. At the end of the two-year period, the gross-earnings tax would no longer apply to railroads.

The decade of the seventies witnessed the shift away from the property tax to a greater reliance on the income tax. Fundamental changes in tax policy regarding school financing, state participation in the welfare system, and aids to local government prompted the legislature to use the income tax as the major source of additional revenues.

Administration

Timetable

The assessment date in Minnesota is January 2. All taxable real and personal property is listed annually with reference to its value on January 2. Also, the classification status is determined by use as of this assessment date. However, midyear homesteads are established as of June 1, and a few other exceptions prevail. Minnesota law makes no provision for prorating either the assessment, the classfication, or the tax obligation.

Local Board of Review

Minnesota statutes provide that the town board, the city council, or an appointed body of each district shall be a board of review. The charter of certain cities may provide for the establishment of a board of equalization.

The statutes state that the county assessor shall fix a date for each board of review, or board of equalization, to meet for the purpose of reviewing the assessment of property in its respective town or city. The county assessor is required to serve written notice to the clerk of each body on or before April 1 of each year.

These meetings are required to be held between April 1 and June 30, and the clerk of the board of review or the board of equalization is required to give published and posted notice at least ten days before the date set for the first meeting.

The board of review or the board of equalization of any city must complete its work and adjourn within twenty days from the time of convening specified in the notice of the clerk, unless a longer period is approved by the commissioner of revenue. No action taken subsequent to such date is valid.

A request for additional time to complete the work of the board of review must be addressed to the commissioner of revenue in writing. The commissioner's approval is necessary to legalize any procedure subsequent to the expiration of the twenty-day period. The commissioner of revenue will not, however, extend the time for local boards of review to meet past June 30, because county boards of equalization convene in July.

Each year, the local board of review has the authority to consider all assessments of both real and personal property. The assessments of each description of real property consisting of land, buildings, structures, and improvements may be reviewed by the board. The assessments of personal property are likewise within the board's jurisdiction. The board may give consideration to both valuation and classification of real and personal property.

The authority of the local board extends over the individual assessments of real and personal property. The board does not have the power to increase or decrease by percentage all of the assessments in the district of a given class of property. Changes in aggregate assessments by classes are made by the county board of equalization.

Although the local board of review has the authority to increase or decrease individual assessments, the total of such adjustments must not reduce the aggregate assessment made by the county assessor by more than 1 percent. This limitation does not apply, however, to the correction of clerical errors, or to the removal of duplicate assessments.

The local board of review or equalization does not have the authority in any year to reopen former assessments on which taxes are due and payable. The board considers only the assessments that are current.

In reviewing the individual assessments, the board may find instances of undervaluation. Before the board raises the market value of property, it must notify the owner. The law does not prescribe any particular form of notice, except that the person whose value is to be increased must be notifed of the intent of the board. The local-board-of-review meetings assure property owners opportunity to contest valuations that have been placed on their property, or to contest or protest any other matters relating to the taxability of their property. The board is required to review each matter and may make any corrections that it deems just.

When a local board of review convenes, the local assessor is required by law to be present with the board's assessment books. The local assessor is also required to take part in the proceedings, but has no vote. In addition to the local assessor, the county assessor or one of the assistants is required to attend. The county assessor is required to have maps and tables relating particularly to land values for the guidance of boards of review.

It is the primary duty of each board of review to examine the assessment record, to see that all taxable property in the assessment district has been properly placed upon the list and valued by the assessor. In case any property, either real or personal, has been omitted, the board has the duty of making the assessment.

A nonresident may file written objections to his or her assessment with the county assessor prior to the meeting of the board of review. Such objections must be presented to the board for consideration while it is in session.

County Board of Equalization

The county board of equalization follows the local board of review in the assessment process. In every county the basic problem of county equalization is essentially the same: it involves the equalization of the assessments of property between the individual assessment districts. The other important part of the work of the county board is to equalize the assessments of the various classes of property within the county.

The county commissioners, or a majority of them, with the county auditor, (or, if the county commissioner cannot be present, the deputy county auditor, or, if there be no such deputy, the clerk of the district court), forms a board for the equalization of the assessment of the property of the county, including the property of all cities whose charters provide for a board of equalization.

Minnesota law allows the county boards to appoint a special board of equalization to which it may delegate all of the powers and duties of equalization. This special board of equalization serves at the direction and discretion of the appointing county board and is subject to the same lawful regulations as the county board of equalization.

Minnesota law allows the county boards to appoint a special board of equalization to which it may delegate all of the powers and duties of equalization. This special board of equalization serves at the direction and discretion of the appointing county board and is subject to the same lawful regulations as the county board of equalization. The appointing board determines the number of members to be appointed to the special board, compensation and expenses to be paid, and the term of office of each member. At least one member of the special board of equalization must be an appraiser, realtor, or other person familiar with property values in the county. The county auditor is a nonvoting member and serves as the recorder for the special board.

The county auditor is to keep a record of the proceedings and orders of the board. This record is to be published in the same manner as other proceedings of the county commissioners.

The county board of equalization may adjourn from time to time but must finalize its work within ten working days. Any action taken subsequent to the allotted time is invalid unless a longer session period is approved by the commissioner of revenue.

If a change in the assessments becomes advisable after the board has adjourned, the change may be recommended by the board of county commissioners to the commissioner of revenue.

The board may make percentage increases on each class of both real and personal property in the entire county—or in any particular city, town, or district in the county when the board believes such property has been valued at less than market value. On real property, such percentage increases may be limited to land or structures alone or may be made on both land and structures. The board is not required to give notices when applying aggregate increases.

The board may make individual increases in the assessments of both real property when they believe such property has been valued at less than market value. In these cases, the board must give notice to the owner of its intentions. The notice must also set a time and place for a hearing.

The board may make percentage decreases and individual decreases in the assessments of both real and personal property when they believe such property has been valued at more than market value. On real property, decreases may be limited to land or structures alone or may be made on both. The board cannot, however, reduce the aggregate value of the real property, or the aggregate value of the personal property by more than 1 percent of the aggregate value as returned by the assessors (including any additions made by the county auditor). The limitations on aggregate reductions must also be separate as to real property and personal property. The limitations apply to the aggregate of the assessments in the county as a whole and not individual districts.

Any complaints or objections made by taxpayers must be considered by the board. Protested assessments must be reviewed in detail, and the board has the authority to make any corrections it believes to be just. In reviewing a protest to an assessment, the board may ask the county assessor to investigate the case.

The county board of equalization does not have the authority in any year to reopen former assessments on which taxes are due and payable. The board considers only the assessments that are in process in the current year. It also may exempt property from taxation.

The county board may not place omitted property on the assessment books. This power is vested only in the local boards of review and in the county auditor.

The county board has no authority to make original assessments. Its duties are restricted to review and equalization of assessments already made.

Property owners may not appear before the county board of equalization to complain about an improper or unequal assessment unless they have first taken the matter before their local board of review.

State Board of Equalization

The commissioner of revenue constitutes the State Board of Equalization. The board meets annually to examine and compare the assessments of the property in the several counties and to equalize the same so that all the taxable property in the state is assessed at its market value, subject to the following rules:

1. The board may increase the aggregate valuation of the real property of every county it believes to be valued below its market value.
2. The board may reduce the aggregate valuation of the real property of every county it believes to be valued above its market value.
3. If the board believes the valuation of the real property of any town or district in any county, or the valuation of the real property of any county not in towns or cities, should be raised or reduced, without raising or reducing the other real property of such county, or without raising or reducing it in the same ratio, *the board may raise or reduce the valuation of any one or more of such towns or cities* or of the property not in towns or cities.
4. *The board may increase the aggregate valuation of any class of personal property* of any county, town, or city the board believes to be valued below the market value.
5. *The board may reduce the aggregate valuation of any class of personal property* in any county, town, or city, the board believes to be valued above the market value.
6. *The board may not reduce the aggregate valuation of all the property of the state,* as returned by the several county auditors, more than 1 percent on the whole valuation thereof; and
7. When it would be of assistance in equalizing values, *the board may require any county auditor to furnish statements* showing assessments of real and personal property of any individuals, firms, or corporations within the county. The board may consider and equalize such assessments and may increase the assessment of individuals, firms, or corporations above the amount returned by the county board of equalization when it shall appear to be undervalued, first giving notice to such persons of the intention of the board so to do, fixing a time and place of a hearing. The board may not decrease any such assessment below the valuation placed by the county board of equalization.

The State Board of Equalization may apportion the levies of a district lying in two or more counties when assessment sales-ratio studies as determined by the Equalization Aid Review Committee show the average level of assessment differs by more than 5 percent.

State Board of Equalization Orders

A certified record of all proceedings of the commissioner of revenue affecting any change in the assessed valuation of any property, as revised by the

State Board of Equalization, is mailed to the auditor of each county on or before November 15 or thirty days after the abstract of assessment has been filed with the commissioner, whichever is later. The law requires each county to file complete abstracts of all real and personal property in the county, as equalized by the county board of equalization, with the commissioner on or before August 1. This certified record specifies the amounts or amount, or both, added to or deducted from the valuation of the real property of each of the several towns and cities, and of the real property not in towns or cities, also the percent or amount of both, added to or deducted from the several classes of personal property in each of the towns and cities. It also specifies the amount added to or deducted from the assessments of individuals, copartnerships, associations, or corporations.

The county assessor enters all changes made by the State Board of Equalization in the assessment books.

Additional Duties of the Commissioner of Revenue

The commissioner of revenue may receive complaints and examine all cases where it is alleged that property subject to taxation has not been assessed, or has been improperly or unequally assessed, or the law in any manner evaded or violated. If cause is found the commissioner may institute such proceedings as will remedy improper or negligent administration of the tax laws of the state.

The commissioner of revenue may raise or lower the valuation of any real or personal property, the valuation of the real or personal property of any individual, copartnership, company, association, or corporation, provided that notice of the intention to raise such valuation and of the time and place at which a hearing thereon will be held is given to such person at least five days before the day of the hearing.

Property owners may not appear before the commissioner to complain about improper or unequal assessments unless they have taken the matter before the county board of equalization. Owners may approach the county board of equalization in person, by counsel, or by a written communication. If property owners have failed to take their complaints before the county board of equalization, they can appeal assessments to the commissioner only if they can establish that they did not receive notice of their market value at least five days before the local-board-of-review meeting.

Orders made by the commissioner of revenue are appealable to the tax court; those made by the State Board of Equalization are not.

11 The Role of the State in Property Taxation in New Jersey

J. Henry Ditmars

Legal Framework

The present-day system of property taxation in New Jersey has roots in the eighteenth century. New Jersey's first constitution (1776) called for the appointment of commissioners of appeal to "hear and finally determine all appeals relative to unjust assessments in public taxation." Appointed on a township basis, the commissioners of appeal were required to issue a transcript of their judgment where the appellant was allowed a reduction. The commissions of appeal were a part of New Jersey's property-tax system until the advent of the county boards of taxation. They were the arm of municipal government that, during their 130 years of existence, performed one of the principal functions of our present-day county boards of taxation.

In 1906, county boards of taxation were established in New Jersey, combining separate duties formerly performed by several municipal and county agencies into a single agency. One of the duties of the county boards of taxation was that of hearing and ruling on tax appeals filed with them by aggrieved taxpayers—or municipalities—from assessments placed by the local assessor. The county boards also equalized property-tax rebatables in the aggregate for appointment of shared budgets within each county. Unlike the hearing of appeals, however, the equalization function was set up to be carried out at the county level rather than at the municipal level of government.

Another important function of the county boards of taxation was the supervision of assessors, which was originally set up to be carried out on the state level of government. The State Board of Taxation, established in 1891, had the authority to direct an assessor to reassess a property deemed to have been improperly assessed, and if an assessor failed or refused to comply with an order given by the State Board of Taxation, the board was empowered to appoint some other person to make the new assessment. The State Board of Taxation also had the duty to investigate methods adopted by local assessors in arriving at their values. In 1905, the State Board of Taxation was abolished and its duties were assigned to the State Board of Equalization of Taxes.

The county boards of taxation and the commissioners of appeals more or less supervised the activities of the individual assessors in New Jersey until recent years. In 1967, the Division of Taxation and the Association of Municipal Assessors in New Jersey convinced the legislature that individuals

109

be required to take a test to hold the office of assessor, providing a method for existing assessors with certain experience to qualify for a certificate. As a result, examinations for certified tax assessor are now given twice a year. The examination tests the applicant for his administrative ability to be an assessor and his ability to appraise and value real property.

Currently, all real property in the state of New Jersey is to be assessed on a uniform basis. A Farmland Assessment Act, passed in 1964, permits lower assessment on farmland used for farmland purposes. Railroad property is assessed by the state at a uniform rate on that portion of railroad property used for railroad purposes only. There is no assessment of personal property, except for that of telephone and telegraph companies, which is assessed at the local general tax rate. Public utilities are assessed by the state insofar as the equipment used to produce services is concerned. Buildings and land are assessed locally in this case. New Jersey has a number of tax-relief measures. A *homestead rebate system* is used to relieve some of the effects of property taxes on residential homes and grants an extra $50 for senior citizens. There is a $50 veteran's deduction granted, as well as a total tax deduction for 100-percent disabled veterans who qualify. In addition, there is a property-tax deduction for qualified senior citizens, disabled persons, and surviving spouses amounting to $200 in 1981.

Administration

In New Jersey, the basic responsibility for assessing lies with the local assessor, who in turn, reports to and through the county boards of taxation. The county boards of taxation are instruments of the state by statute. Through a cooperating committee arrangement, the director of the Division of Taxation supervises and assists county boards regarding regulations, interpretations of the laws, and other related matters.

The next level of administration of property-tax laws in New Jersey is the tax court, which consists of eleven full-time judges who handle taxation matters, including local property-tax appeals from the county boards of taxation and decisions of the director of the Division of Taxation. The members of the county boards of taxation are appointed by the governor with the consent of the senate and are paid by the state. The local assessor is appointed by the municipal officials. The county boards of taxation have from three to five members depending upon the population of the county. In no case should all the members be of one political party.

Public utilities such as telephone companies and electric companies are assessed by the state, except the personal property of telephone and telegraph companies. Nonoperating buildings and land also are locally assessed. Any structure used in the connection with the production of electricity, water, gas, and such are assessed under the public-utility laws administered by the state. *Class II* railroad property in New Jersey is assessed by the Division of Taxation and taxed at a flat rate of $4.75 per $100 of evaluation. Other railroad property used for railroad purposes is exempt from taxation. In all cases, the assessments are made on a calendar-year basis.

The quality of local assessments is reviewed by the county boards of taxation, and also by the Division of Taxation when a revaluation is ordered by the county boards. There are three considerations used in New Jersey to determine assessment quality. The first is the use of the local average ratio, which indicates the relationship between the assessed value and true value of a particular taxing district. The second is the application of the coefficient of deviation, which tends to evaluate the assessors performance. In New Jersey, this coefficient is developed on a nonstratified basis as well as by property class. The third is the knowledge and experience of the local assessor in relation to the two above. Although in New Jersey the standard of assessment is determined by the county boards of taxation, each county board has the standard of assessment of 100 percent of true value, determined by the *willing buyer/willing seller concept*. A review of the local assessor's practices and his problems is conducted basically by each county board of taxation.

A key element in the New Jersey system of property taxation is the Local Property and Public Utility Branch of the New Jersey Division of Taxation. This branch is staffed by approximately 140 employees, both field and office, consisting of appraisers, certified tax assessors, engineers, and office personnel. The branch is made up of seven sections:

Appraisal Section

The appraisal section assists the local assessor in preparing appraisals of difficult and complex properties that normally the local assessor does not encounter on a day-to-day basis.

The appraisal section is responsible for administering the New Jersey Farmland Assessment Act, which literally means that a review of all the approximately 26,000 Farmland Assessment Act applications has to be made.

The appraisal section also has the responsibility of keeping the *New Jersey Real Property Appraisal Manual* up-to-date. This operation, in itself, means revision of at least sixty to seventy pages per year.

The appraisal section is also called upon to value state-owned properties and properties the State Treasury Department is buying and leasing for state use.

Lastly, the appraisal section has the duty of reviewing all revaluation contracts submitted for approval by the director of the Division of Taxation.

Along those lines, the appraisal section requests, reviews, and finalizes financial and qualification statements of appraisal firms doing business in the state of New Jersey.

Sale-Ratio and Electronic Data-Processing

The prime mission of the sales-ratio section is the annual task of compiling the statutorily required *Table of Equalized Valuations*. The information required to formulate this table is the use of the SR-1A Form, which is used by the local assessor, the county boards of taxation, and the state division of taxation, and contains information on each real-property sale in the state of New Jersey.

The primary use of the *Table of Equalized Valuations* is to provide a method by which $800 million worth of state aid is distributed to the local municipalities for school monies. In addition, the table is employed when a municipality wants to borrow money for various public projects. It is also used in connection with distribution and apportionment of the cost of county governments.

This section also computes, through a statutory formula, the distribution of $100 million worth of state revenue sharing and administers the distribution of $12 million worth of state aid, based on state-owned property within the taxing district. This method reflects the state's recognition of the services provided to the state agencies within the taxing districts. In this context, it might well be noted that there are 135,000 parcels of exempt property in the state of New Jersey valued at over $21 billion of state-owned property alone.

Finally, the sales-ratio and electronic data-processing (EDP) section supervises, maintains, and revises the New Jersey computer tax system, which is a tax listing and billing method used throughout the 567 taxing districts in the state.

Public-Utility Tax Section

This section computes, for state use, the public-utility taxes that are apportioned to the individual taxing districts on the basis of the public-utility property located in each taxing district. Currently, the amount of money that is raised from this operation is about $475 million. It should be pointed out that this section operates with a maximum of six employees.

This section also inspects utility installations to assure the allocation is assigned to the correct taxing district.

Engineering Section

The engineering section annually computes the railroad tax assessment for all operating railroads in New Jersey. In conjunction with this particular assignment, it computes the New Jersey railroad franchise tax and also computes and allocates the state aid to municipalities. The engineering section also approves tax maps.

Assessors' Assistance and Certification Section

This section provides the field staff that contacts the 567 taxing districts and the 21 county boards of taxation to provide direct assistance in solving day-to-day administrative and property-assessment problems.

This section also makes sure that a new assessor has the two primary tools the state provides, namely, the *Assessor's Handbook*, and the *Real Property Appraisal Manual for New Jersey Assessors*.

This section also provides for training sessions for assessors and supplies instructors for assessors' courses at the state university. One of the most important functions of this section is the biannual preparation of the examination for assessors (certified tax assessor) and the administering of same.

The personnel from this section in the last recorded year contacted the local assessors about 9,600 times and investigated 28,000 sales for the sales-ratio section.

Statistical Section

This particular section is further divided into three sections: The first, for the want of a better name is the *statistical section*, which handles complaints against the *Table of Equalized Valuation* each year. County equalization tables are reviewed and corrected where necessary.

The second subsection is the *realty transfer-fee section*. This section collects about $2 million a month under the provision of the Realty Transfer Fee Act and also contacts the county clerks in New Jersey on a monthly basis when errors have occurred. Another of its functions is the preparation and issuance of the *Local Property and Public Utility Branch Newsletter*, a publication sent to all local assessors and county boards of taxation that updates them on current changes in laws and regulations as well as other related data.

The third subsection is the *homestead-rebate section*, which processes 1.45 million homestead-rebate applications. The total homestead rebate, statewide, amounts to $280 million. This subsection also answers approximately 15,000 taxpayer inquiries and responds to about 18,000 telephone inquiries, all concerning the homestead rebate.

Administrative Section

The administrative section handles the processing of new employees, all special mailings of instructions, copies of the law, guidelines, and regulations that are sent out to all assessors and collectors throughout New Jersey.

In addition, the county boards of taxation are informed of all of the above changes in the law or regulations on a regularly scheduled basis. The fiscal and personnel problems in this branch are also handled by the administrative section.

In addition, state assessments of utilities and railroads are made and supervised by the Local Property and Public Utility Branch of the Division of Taxation. As stated before, assessors also receive assistance and direction from members of this branch.

Fiscal Importance

The total property-tax levy for the year 1980 for the state of New Jersey was $3.797 billion. In 1970, the total tax levy was $1.967 billion, and in 1960, it was $834 million.

From our records at this time, we are unable to determine what is the cost of providing the local assessment function because salaries, office-space rental, personnel, and such are paid out of local municipal budgets. The state of New Jersey pays the salaries of the twenty-one county boards of taxation at a cost of $650,000. According to our most recent records in all the taxing districts, there are 2,315,629 line items that reflect an assessed value of $101.728 billion. In addition, there are 138,072 line items of exempt property that reflect a value of $21.042 billion.

Policy Framework

The Division of Taxation, through its Local Property and Public Utility Branch, along with the Association of Municipal Assessors and the twenty-one county boards of taxation, are continually investigating, reviewing, and checking just how well the local property-tax system is working in New Jersey. A continual program of education for the public is available through the above agencies. The legislature determines the needs of its citizens and passes laws and budgets accordingly each year. The county governments also need a certain amount of revenue, and that revenue is raised through local property taxation and allocated by formula. The cost of schools and the running of local municipal governments is also a part of the tax levy and is reflected in the local tax rate.

By and large, it is felt that the administration of the local property-tax function is carried on well within the statutory restrictions of budgets and personnel. From the figures above, it is easy to realize that the local property tax is a viable source of revenue for local and county governments. The state receives no property-tax revenue. Many recommendations are made yearly by the legislature and taxpayers' associations for improvement of the taxing system. Some of the recommendations and laws that have been passed tend to erode the tax base and shift the burden from one taxpayer group to another.

Fortunately, in New Jersey, there are two organizations that provide a watchdog service to the legislature and also to the Division of Taxation. These are the New Jersey Taxpayers' Association and the New Jersey State Chamber of Commerce. There are many areas in the field of local property taxation which can be improved and are being continually studied at the present time. Among them is the computerized annual reassessments program—a more sophisticated sales-analysis program for use at the local and county levels that would, by proper application, assist the local assessors in arriving at an assessed value that would reflect equity and uniformity of treatment for all taxpayers having an interest in real property in New Jersey.

12 The Role of the State in Property Taxation in New York

David Gaskell

Legal Framework

The property tax in the state of New York is levied entirely by localities. It is levied on real property only, and all revenues from the tax are used for local-government purposes. Although New York has had a property tax for over two hundred years, its history has been one of poor administration and unsuccessful attempts to improve assessment practices. Despite the statutory requirement—going back to at least 1788—that property be assessed at full value, fractional assessments became the rule, and the use of fractional assessments in property valuation became so haphazard that eventually there was widespread inequity in the treatment of taxpayers.

Again and again, assessment reform was demanded by the courts and urged by state committees and commissions. During the eighteenth and nineteenth centuries, it was clear to many that property assessments in New York were often arbitrary and unjust and that the state government lacked the power to restore equity to property-tax administration because it had no supervisory authority over the actions of local assessors. Although the courts emphasized the need for compliance with the full-value standard of assessment, their concern was limited to ensuring that property owners would not be assessed at more than full value. If a taxpayer was assessed at less than full value, the courts saw no cause for complaint, even if the taxpayer could show that he was assessed at a percentage of full value greater than the average for his community.

In 1923, the U.S. Supreme Court, in the *Sioux City Bridge* case (260 U.S. 441) decided that, even though a taxpayer is assessed at less than full value, he has a constitutional right to a reduction in assessment if his assessment is at a percentage of full value greater than the average for his assessing jurisdiction as a whole. The effect of this ruling was to divert whatever interest the state courts may have had in full value as the underlying principle of all property assessment. From that point on, both the courts and property owners directed their attention to reducing assessments that were already below full value.

Interest in full value as the most workable and fairest standard of assessment was eroded further in 1964, when the state's highest court determined that the law did not mandate assessment at 100 percent of full or

117

market value. Rather, the court found that the law required only that every type of property in an assessing unit be assessed at a uniform percentage of full or market value (16 N.Y.2d 779). This interpretation continued to be the accepted meaning of the full-value standard in New York until 1974.

Concurrent with these decisions, the state made efforts to improve the quality of property-tax administration. In 1959, it created the permanent and independent State Board of Equalization and Assessment. One of the board's most important responsibilities was the establishment of equalization rates, which reflect the average ratio of assessed value to full value of taxable property in a municipality.

In 1969, another step was taken to improve the administration of the property tax. State law was amended to allow parties in inequality proceedings to introduce the state equalization rate established for the roll containing the assessment under review as part of their proof of the ratio of assessed-to-market value. The intent of the amendment was to improve the system of assessment review and, particularly, to lessen the cost to the taxpayer of obtaining a meaningful reduction in an inequitable assessment.[1]

In 1970, with the enactment of the Assessment Improvement Act, the state undertook a comprehensive program designed to help localities upgrade assessment administration. The act: (1) provided for the appointment of county tax directors to coordinate local assessment functions; (2) provided for appointed assessors in cities and larger towns but allowed smaller towns to retain elected assessors; (3) established an assessor-training program; (4) created boards of assessment review in each municipality; (5) required all counties outside New York City to provide assessors with up-to-date, accurate tax maps; (6) established minimum qualifications and certification for appointed assessors; (7) provided for advisory appraisals by the state of complex industrial and utility property and large forest tracts; and (8) funded the establishment of a state computer-assisted mass-appraisal system.

These state actions in 1959, 1969, and 1970 did not address the fundamental causes of poor property-tax administration directly—general noncompliance with the full-value standard of assessment and haphazard application of other assessment standards. They did, however, do much to improve the day-to-day operation of the assessment function, and they provided the taxpayer with some protection against the inequities inherent in the property-tax system.

The long-standing central issue in property-tax administration in New York—the full-value standard of assessment—finally was confronted in 1975. In the now famous *Hellerstein* case (37 N.Y.2d 1), the state's highest court declared that the law requires all real property to be assessed at full value. As one would expect, this decision caused a tremendous upheaval in assessment administration. While the immediate public reaction in the legislature was a positive response to carry out the court requirement, the legislature needed time for further study of possible new legislation. Ultimately, its follow-up reaction has been the introduction of several bills seeking to overrule the *Hellerstein* decision, or at least continue the postponement of its implementation. In the interim, full-value assessment has proceeded, quickly at first but more slowly of late.

The schedule for achieving compliance with the full-value standard of assessment was eased by the legislature in 1977, and limited extensions in the time frame for implementing full-value assessment have been granted several times since then. Progress toward full-value assessment was encouraged through state financial assistance: in 1977 a law was enacted providing aid payments of ten dollars per parcel to each assessing unit that proceeds with a full-value revaluation in conformance with state standards.

It bears notation that while the *Hellerstein* decision accelerated the progress toward full-value assessment, it obviously has not been the only stimulus to revaluation. Full-value rolls had already been filed by 13 cities and 141 towns by the time the *Hellerstein* case was decided (New York has 60 cities and 931 towns).

When we look at the overall history of the progress toward full value, we find that, outside New York City, 22 cities and 329 towns completed revaluations between 1970 and 1980—about a third of the municipalities in the state. Only 16 of these revaluations were court ordered; the other 335 were all done voluntarily. If all goes as scheduled, more than half of the municipalities in the state will have completed revaluation by the end of 1982. However, the momentum following the *Hellerstein* decision is now dissipating in the absence of a clear legislative statement of property-tax policy. Few, if any, revaluation projects are now being undertaken, and many assessment rolls that were revalued are not being updated or maintained.

The staff of the State Board of Equalization and Assessment has studied the impact of each revaluation completed with state assistance between 1978 and 1980. (To date, the impact in five cities and eighty towns has been analyzed.) Their most important finding has to do with the tax-liability shifts experienced by the major property classes (residential, farm, commercial, and vacant land): revaluation in New York usually has resulted in a greater redistribution of the tax burden *within* classes, rather than between classes. For 69 percent of the residential parcels studied in 1980, 83 percent of the farm parcels, 82 percent of the commercial parcels, and 90 percent of the vacant-land parcels, revaluation resulted in an intraclass shift in tax liablity of 10 percent or more. Intraclass shifts during revaluation basically reflect the prior existence of inequitable assessment practices. For the three years studied, the shift to the residential class from other classes has averaged 3.7 percent. The most underassessed class in the vast majority of cases has been vacant land.

Tax-Relief Programs

In New York, probably more so than in most other states, there are available a large number of property-tax exemptions that are intended to act as incentives or subsidies for the furtherance of desirable social purposes. During the 1970s, New York used the property tax as a major vehicle to achieve state social- and economic-policy objectives—a result of which has been a proliferation of exemptions. Proper administration of the tax has become well-nigh impossible under the load of administrative complexities involved in the various exemptions. An assessor must understand and work with over two-hundred different exemptions, including those for property for the development of the ideals of good sportsmanship, fallout shelters, steel manufacturing, solar energy, telephone equipment, condominiums, plus innumerable housing exemptions as well as numerous more conventional exemptions. An assessor, to do his job correctly, must be an expert in a great many fields besides appraising.

One result of these exemptions has been the steady erosion of the tax base. With each year, additional exemptions have been granted and none have been removed. While each individual exemption may be justifiable, cumulatively they have resulted in massive tax shifting. At least 33 percent of all real property in New York is exempt from taxation. About $100 billion in real property is off the tax rolls—in fact *supported* by the slightly over $200 billion in taxable property. The percentage of exempt property as compared to taxable grows with each passing year. In our cities the problem is particularly acute, where the average of exempt property to all property is 41 percent. In the period from 1972 to 1978, forty-six of our sixty-one cities witnessed an increase in the portion of their property exempt from taxes. On balance within all cities, there was a shift of 5.6 percent from taxable to exempt during this six-year period. These numbers on exempt property probably are actually on the low side, as exempt properties tend to be assessed at lower ratios than taxable properties. Clearly, this fact helps to explain why many of our cities are in a financial bind and are faced with high effective tax rates.

New York has two programs of tax relief that are geared to alleviating the tax burden of homeowners of limited income: the aged exemption and the circuit breaker. The aged exemption allows an exemption of 50 percent of assessed value on residential property owned by persons aged sixty-five or over whose incomes do not exceed $9,200 a year. Localities are allowed to choose whether to grant the exemption, and they also are allowed to lower the income ceiling for eligibility.

The circuit breaker is a credit against the state income tax—or a refund in income tax—available to aged and other homeowners whose incomes do not exceed $13,500 a year. The credit or refund allowed is equal to a percentage of the amount by which qualifying property taxes exceeds a threshold percentage of gross household income; the threshold varies with gross household income. The maximum credit allowed for the aged is $250; the maximum allowed for other homeowners is $45.

Although it is not a relief program based on personal income, another exemption should be mentioned since it has recently been adapted for the specific purpose of neutralizing the effect of full-value assessment. This program is the veterans exemption, which for most veterans traditionally has been limited to a maximum $5,000 reduction in assessed value. The exemption has been changed so as to allow, after revaluation, the same ratio between exempt and assessed value that existed prior to revaluation. Currently, preserving the ratio is mandatory in those municipalities that are court ordered to convert to full value; in municipalities that voluntarily convert to full value, preserving the exemption ratio for veterans is optional.

Tax and Debt Limitations

Tax and debt limitations—which apply to counties, cities, villages, and city school districts—in New York have existed since the late 1800s. While they vary somewhat, the highest limit is 2 percent of "the average full valuation of taxable real estate" for any of the municipalities. Towns, school districts, and special districts are not subject to the tax limitations. Thus, property in overlapping taxing jurisdictions, may be taxed at several times the limit for any one jurisdiction.

Excluded from the tax limits are taxes levied to pay interest and principal on indebtedness. Another exclusion is for expenditures from borrowing for noncapital budget items with periods of probable usefulness. Under this exclusion, the legislature exempted from the constitutional limits certain municipal tax levies for pension and retirement payments. The court, after several years of amendatory legislation and litigation, reasoned that if such expenditures had useful lives then nearly all municipal expenditures could be considered similarly.

Tax-exempt property is excluded from full value in calculating constitutional limitations. Thus, as new exemptions are created or existing exemptions expanded, the tax limit becomes constricted. Given New York's standard of assessing of full value, calculation of the tax limits has presented no serious difficulty. Rather, the problem has been that many cities and city school districts have been levying taxes at or near the limit. With the court decision restricting legislative exclusions, the legislature has made direct appropriations in recent years to city school districts to offset the amount of their budget requirements in excess of the tax-levy limit. With expenditures rising far faster than taxable value is increasing, the problems of meeting city and city-school-district financial needs will become ever more acute.

Classification of assessments is now under active discussion in New York. No question arises as to the legality of classification—which, clearly, is a form of exemption—as long as properties within a class are treated similarly. The issue is whether the amount of property value that is exempt from assessment through the operation of a classification system is to be included in taxable property in the jurisdiction for the calculation of the limits. Such modification of the assessment standard runs the risk of resulting in reductions in local tax revenues leading to personnel layoffs and service cutbacks, through reduced-borrowing-power restrictions on funds for repair and replacement of capital improvements and impairment of the security of bonds. Should classified assessments be enacted, the courts would be required to resolve this difficult issue.

Administration

Local Responsibility in Property-Tax Administration

Local assessors are responsible for identifying and valuing property, preparing the assessment roll against which property taxes are levied, and reviewing assessed valuations for the correction of inequalities. New York has some 1,539 assessing units. In two of the fifty-seven counties outside New York City, the assessment function is centralized at the county level. Other assessing districts include 61 cities, 919 towns, and 557 villages, about half of which do not actually do their own assessing but, instead, accept the town rolls. City and town rolls are used by other taxing jurisdictions as required.

While state statutes do not specifically require a frequency of assessment, the implied frequency is one of annual updating of assessment. Nevertheless, only a small number of cities and towns annually update. Many of the assessors that have gone through reassessment update on a two- or three-year cycle.

Assessors are either elected or appointed to their positions, and there are many variations in organization for property-tax assessment throughout the state. All but two cities have a single appointed assessor or appointed boards of assessors. Village assessors are appointed, and villages have either one or three assessors. As mentioned earlier, in 1970 the smaller cities and smaller towns were given the option of converting from elected to appointed assessors. About 56 percent of the towns have retained assessment by elected assessors.

The compensation, especially of part-time assessors, is generally low. No current statistics are available, but little progress has been made in improving salaries in line with the new requirements and responsibilities of assessors.

In each municipality there is a board of assessment review, whose function is to hear complaints from taxpayers about their property assessments. Each board is made up of three to five members; no one who has a direct or indirect interest in any property under review may be a member of the board. The only requirement for being a board member is a general knowledge of real estate.

State Responsibility in Administration

Although the property tax in New York is primarily a local responsibility, the State Board of Equalization and Assessment plays an essential and multifaceted role in its administration. The board provides a wide range of services to local governments through its staff, the State Division of Equalization and Assessment. In addition to its establishment of equalization rates, the board also directly assists localities (through four regional offices) in improving the administration of their property-tax systems.

The staff of the board trains assessors and other local officials and employees working in the property-tax field. Training includes a certification program for those local-government staff required by law to complete a course of training. The training program for assessors consists of two four-day courses: assessment administration and introduction to property valuation. In 1980, the administration course was held in twenty-one different locations throughout the state; 435 people, mostly assessors, attended the course, and 86 percent of these passed the course examination. The valuation course was conducted seven times during the year, with a total attendance of 740; 59 percent passed the course examination. Training programs for other local-government staff (such as members of local boards of assessment review) were also held during 1980; a total of 1,523 attended these courses.

The board is responsible for certifying locally prepared tax maps (as required by the Assessment Improvement Act of 1970) and for certifying state-aid payments (of one dollar per parcel) to localities that prepare and maintain tax maps. As of 1 June 1980, tax maps for 50 percent of the parcels outside New York City were complete.

The board also certifies state-aid payments to local governments that implement improved systems for property-tax administration. Payment is made in four steps: (1) two dollars per parcel for the first assessment roll completed after 1 April 1977 that conforms to state standards for the preparation of tax rolls and tax bills; (2) three dollars per parcel for submission of a plan conforming to standards for the collection and maintenance of property-valuation data and the maintenance of records of property transfers; (3) two dollars per parcel for satisfactory completion of the plan; (4) three dollars per parcel for the first assessment roll completed after 1

April 1981 that conforms to state standards for full disclosure to property owners of the estimated effect of changes in assessed valuation.

Furthermore, the staff of the board assists local governments in the installation of computer-assisted tax-accounting systems and full-value programs. By mid-1981, computerization of tax-accounting systems utilizing the state system for 61.5 percent of the upstate parcels had been completed or was in process. The assistance given to localities in implementation of full-value assessment includes: evaluation of the tasks to be accomplished during the two to three year period of conversion to full value; help in the preparation of specifications for consultant work required in revaluation; on-the-job training for local officials, participation at public meetings; the editing of computer files; and, analysis of the impact of conversion to full-value assessment.

The board also supervises and reviews local assessment and administrative decisions. Its staff issues legal opinions, promulgates rules and regulations for administration of the property tax, issues forms and instructions to assessors, and conducts hearings as required for public review of state and local actions in tax administration.

Additionally, the staff of the board provides localities with advisory appraisals of highly complex properties (public-utility, railroad, industrial, and commercial property) and privately owned forest land in excess of 500 acres, upon request. Lastly, the state is responsible for establishing assessments on taxable state-owned lands and special-franchise property owned by public utilities, and for establishing ceiling values for qualified railroad and agricultural properties.

The assessment of taxable state-owned land involves determining the full value of the lands—through periodic sample appraisals—and establishing their assessments at the same fraction of full value used by a locality for the assessment of privately owned property. There are now over three million acres of land on which the state permits itself to be taxed.

Assessment of public-utility special-franchise property is done annually by the state and includes all privately owned lines, cables, and pipelines located on public property. In 1980, the state established about 7,500 special-franchise assessments for property owned by over 300 public-utility companies.

Railroad ceilings, the maximum amount on which taxes may be levied, are determined annually by the state. The assessment of properties that qualify for railroad ceilings is the responsibility of local assessors. However, because of the difficulties involved in the valuation of railroad property, most assessors adopt the state ceilings, or variations thereof, for assessments on such property.

The establishment of agricultural-value ceilings, which is done annually, involves the valuation of farmland on the basis of its use for agriculture (rather than for some other purpose). Ceilings currently are determined on the basis of income capitalization and a land-classification system reflecting agricultural productivity.

Fiscal Importance

The Property Tax as a Local Revenue Source

Between 1969 and 1979, the changes that occurred in the amount and make-up of local-government revenues in New York were in several respects notably different from the changes experienced nationwide. First, in New York the overall growth of local revenue was slower than the national average. Second, revenue generated by local governments themselves in New York grew more than revenue received from outside sources (state and federal aid), and in 1979, locally generated revenue continued to produce as large a proportion of total revenue as it had in 1969. Third, the importance of the property tax as a producer of local revenue remained more stable in New York during the decade than it did nationwide.[2]

In 1979, local-government revenue in the United States was almost three times what it had been in 1969; in New York between 1969 and 1979, the rate of growth in local-government revenue was lower than the national average, and, unlike the United States as a whole, New York experienced a slowdown of local-revenue growth during the decade. Local revenue in New York in 1979 was $27.8 billion, a little less than 2 1/2 times the 1969 level, whereas in the previous ten years local revenue had nearly tripled, from $4.16 billion to $12.3 billion.

Nationally, between 1969 and 1979, locally based sources of revenue (the property tax, other local taxes, and locally collected nontax revenue) grew by 156 percent, while intergovernmental (state and federal) aid to localities grew by 236 percent. Also, the importance of locally generated revenue relative to intergovernmental aid declined considerably during the period; by 1979 the revenue obtained through local collections had dropped from 64 percent to 55 percent of total revenue. In New York, the trend was different. Locally generated revenue increased by 134 percent, slightly outgrowing intergovernmental aid, which increased by only 128 percent. In addition, the contribution of local collections relative to intergovernmental aid remained constant, continuing to account for about 56 percent of total revenue.

Some interesting differences appear when New York is compared with the nation as a whole in terms of the role played by individual revenue sources in the growth of local revenue between 1969 and 1979. Nationally, the largest contributor to overall-revenue growth was state aid (accounting for 36 percent of the growth), followed by the property tax (23 percent), locally collected nontax revenue (18 percent), federal aid (13 percent), and local nonproperty taxes (9 percent). In New York, the largest contributor was the property tax (accounting for 29 percent of overall-revenue growth), followed by federal aid (25 percent), state aid (19 percent), local nonproperty taxes (17 percent), and locally collected nontax revenue (11 percent).

In New York, as is the case elsewhere, the property tax is the final revenue source available to local governments in the municipal budgeting process. The amount of revenue that must be collected through the tax is determined only after revenue from all other sources is estimated. Therefore, the importance of the property tax relative to other revenue sources changes from year to year as these other sources become more or less productive. Given current federal and state fiscal policies and constraints, the pressures to make greater use of the property tax in the immediate years ahead will be inordinate.

The property-tax yield in New York in 1979 was $8.66 billion; in 1969 the yield had been $4.16 billion, and in 1959 it had been $2.06 billion. Between 1969 and 1979, property-tax revenue grew at about the same rate in New York as it did nationwide, and its growth during that period was slightly higher than it had been the previous decade.

Between 1969 and 1979, property-tax revenue in New York increased by 108 percent. During that period its rate of growth was higher than the increase in state aid, which grew by only 74 percent, but lower than the increase in federal aid (287 percent), nonproperty-tax revenue (185 percent), and locally collected nontax revenue (164 percent).

The importance of the property tax relative to other sources of local-government revenue has been declining in New York, although this decline, at least in the past ten years or so, has not been as sharp as it has been nationwide. Between 1969 and 1979, property-tax collections as a percentage of total local-government revenue in the United States dropped by 11 percent, from 41 percent to 30 percent. In New York during the same period there was a decrease of only 4 percent, from 35 percent to 31 percent; with an 8-percent decrease for municipalities (counties, cities, towns, and villages), from 30 percent to 22 percent, offset by a 7-percent increase for school districts, from 43 percent to 50 percent. The percentage decrease was the same for New York City and its school district as it was for municipalities and school districts in the rest of the state.

While the property tax continued to be a major revenue source for all government units in New York from 1959 to 1979, the degree to which individual units of government relied on property-tax revenues shifted considerably. In 1959, the property tax produced at least half of the local revenues of five out of seven government units: the New York City school district (66 percent), towns (65 percent), villages (57 percent), cities outside New York City (55 percent), and counties outside New York City (51 percent). By 1969, only three out of seven government units had continued to receive at least half of their revenues from the tax: towns (65 percent), villages (50 percent), and the New York City school district (50 percent). By 1979, the number had fallen to two out of seven: the New York City school district (55 percent) and towns (53 percent).

Between 1959 and 1979, the greatest decrease in reliance on the property tax as a revenue source occurred for cities outside New York City, where property-tax collections as a percentage of total revenues dropped by 30 percent (from 55 percent to 25 percent), for counties outside New York City (which experienced a decrease of 28 percent, from 51 percent to 23 percent), and for the New York City government (where a decrease of 24 percent, from 39 percent to 15 percent, occurred). New York City differed from the rest of the state in the mix of nonproperty-tax revenues that grew enough to allow for the decreased contribution made by the property tax. In the city the offset was produced by state and federal aid, which together increased as a portion of total revenue by 26 percent. Outside New York City, it was a combination of state aid, federal aid, and nonproperty taxes that produced the offset, with an increase of 31 percent for cities and 27 percent for counties.

More and more of the property-tax dollar in New York has gone to school districts. In 1959, school districts received about 42 percent of total property-tax revenue; by 1969 their share had risen to 45 percent; and by 1979, they were receiving more than half of the property-tax yield (53 percent). Between 1959 and 1979, the share commanded by the New York City school district grew very little, from 18 percent to 19 percent of total property-tax revenue. For school districts outside the city, however, the share increased from 23 percent in 1959 to 34 percent in 1979.

Of the other local-government units, only counties and towns increased their share of total property-tax revenue—and for both the increase was small. The county share of the property-tax dollar rose from 13 percent in 1959 to 14 percent in 1979, while the share received by towns during that period grew from 7 percent to 9 percent. The portion of total property-tax revenue received by New York City decreased from 28 percent to 17 percent, and the portion received by cities outside New York City fell from 8 percent to 4 percent. For villages, the share remained roughly the same from 1959 to 1979, about 3 percent.

Cost of Collecting the Property Tax

The collection cost of the property tax in New York has recently been estimated from 1979 and 1980 financial reports filed by local governments. In terms of tax revenue, the local cost was found to be less than 1 percent of revenue collected, with expenditures of about $7.70 per $1,000 of revenue. State expenditures in support of local administration of the property tax added another $1.20 to the cost of collection.

The total local and state cost per parcel was $16.20, with local governments spending about $14.00 of this amount. Of the $14.00, localities statewide spend about $7.70 per parcel on property assessment; the rest was spent on tax collection, costs incurred on property acquired for taxes, and general administration of the tax. The average assessment cost per parcel was $7.30 upstate (with a good deal of variation between counties) and $9.30 in New York City.

Policy Framework

The property tax in New York is under attack. Questions of inequity and of fractional assessing have been brought into public focus primarily because of the ever-increasing reliance on the property tax as a revenue source. Yet, relatively little attention has been given to the level of taxation or to the incessant erosion of the tax base. To date, the focus has been almost exclusively on the assessment process.

The problems with New York's property tax are long standing and well documented. Studies by a variety of governmental and nongovernmental organizations are done year after year, pointing out the serious flaws in our property-tax system. A study sponsored by the Ford Foundation in the early 1970s found that assessment "in most municipalities does not differ significantly in accuracy from what might be obtained by lottery." Studies of subsequent years have supported such a conclusion.

Despite the clear identification of inequity and erosion, little progress has been made in redressing the problems. The time for recognition and acceptance of the fact that reform was necessary has long since passed. Yet, New York is no closer to resolution of these problems than it was several years ago.

The issues that prevent resolution are fourfold. First, a wide difference exists in the current perception of assessments. No one disputes the inequities, but questions exist as to whether they are intentional or unintentional. On one side, a belief exists that what is on the assessment roll is by conscious intent and design—and thus merits preservation and protection from change. On the other side are those who believe that the results are unintentional and come from a lack of attention to the assessing process.

Second, wide differences exist over the role of the state in determining property-tax policy. Since the property tax is solely a local revenue source, one approach would be reduce the state's policymaking role to the absolute minimum. A converse view is that the state and its local governments are so intertwined (over 60 percent of all state revenues flow back to local governments) that the state has a major stake in the preservation of a viable and equitable property tax. Under the first approach, local government would have great flexibility in assessing practices; under the second, a high degree of uniformity would exist across the state.

Third, New York is a most diverse state. The property-tax system that has evolved in New York City is very different than in the rural areas of the state. In fact, New York—perhaps unconsciously—has developed two property-tax systems: one in New York City and one for the rest of the state.

Fourth, until recently, the state's cities and towns had not played an active role in the property-tax debate. Only during the past year have the various local-government organizations developed thorough and well-thought-out positions on the kind of property-tax system they would like to have.

The legislative response, at best, has been confused. With an affirmative court decision upholding the full-value standard, the legislature responded by providing a state assistance program for municipalities undertaking reassessment. At the same time, the effective date for implementation of reassessment was delayed and further studies of the property tax undertaken.

Moreover the legislature became increasingly uncomfortable with the property-tax issue, an issue that for every winner there was a loser—with the losers likely to make more noise than the winners. During the past years, five major bills have been put forth by the legislature. While very different in approach, four of these bills have very similar themes. The objectives of each of the bills were to the maximum degree possible leave policymaking on assessments to each local government; and, to the maximum degree possible retain the status quo. All of the bills repeal the full-value standard and take an antireassessment position.

The fifth legislative bill accepted the full-value standard and the necessity for reassessment. To mitigate the effects of reassessment for homeowners, a local-option homestead exemption was included, along with state assistance for local governments maintaining their assessment rolls.

During 1981, Governor Carey presented to the legislature a comprehensive package of thirty-two bills on property-tax reform. Of that number, the only major bills to pass were the exemption legislation on nonprofit organizations and cemeteries.

Despite the recent legislative impasse, New York has the potential for having one of the best property-tax systems in the nation. The computer-assisted mass-appraisal system that has been developed is one of the best in the United States. The administrative framework, while needing some modification, is largely in place. What is needed is an accepted legal framework.

The issue of property-tax reform is not likely to be resolved soon. The courts will continue to have a significant role. Indeed, it is possible through either legislative action or inaction that the courts will have the major role.[3]

Notes

1. There is still some confusion about whether or not the equalization rate may be used in inequality proceedings.

2. Based on New York state data from N.Y.S. Department of Audit and Control and U.S. data from Tax Foundation, Inc., *Monthly Tax Features*, June-July 1981.

3. Since preparation of this chapter, the state legislature in November 1981 passed major legislation amending property-tax administration and assessing standards. Governor Carey vetoed this legislation, but was overridden by the legislature in December 1981.

This legislation will have a sweeping and long-range impact on the property tax in New York. The historic assessment standard of full value was repealed. The new law states that "the existing methods in effect in each assessing unit . . . may continue." All property in each assessing unit shall be assessed at a uniform percentage of value.

For assessing purposes, the state is divided into two categories. New York City and Nassau County (the state's largest county) are in one category and all other assessing units in the other. Within New York City and Nassau County, the new law is quite specific with most provisions mandated. Among the new requirements for New York City and Nassau County are the following:

1. Four classes of property shall be established: residential, apartment, utility, and all other.
2. No residential assessment may be increased by more than 6 percent in any year or by more than 20 percent in any five-year period.
3. Within New York City all residential assessments increased by more than 20 percent in 1981 returned to 1980 assessment.
4. Any assessment increase on other than residential property shall have a five-year transition.
5. Class tax shares shall be calculated for the four classes based on the 1981 assessment roll, which shall then be used to determine the amount of taxes to be paid by each class (differential tax rates based on 1981 relationships).
6. Within Nassau County, class tax shares shall be determined for each school district, village, and so forth (128 portions × 4 classes = 512 class tax shares).
7. The class tax shares can only be modified or changed as follows:
   a. Modifications may be made to reflect new construction, demolition, and exemptions.

b. At local-governing-body discretion a tax share may be increased or decreased by 5 percent a year.

c. The state board beginning in 1985 and every two years thereafter shall modify the class shares to reflect market trends (roughly a four-year lag).

8. Nassau County villages (sixty-four) are treated like the rest of the state, except they may opt to come under New York City and Nassau County provisions.

In the rest of the state all the provisions of law are permissive rather than mandatory. There are no required provisions. An upstate assessing unit may seek to be an *approved assessing unit*, which requires that a reassessment has occurred pursuant to state regulations. Once approval has been obtained, the certification is permanent and does not require review or renewal. The certification is based on the latest final assessment roll or, for a current revaluation, the new roll being completed.

For approved assessing units two local options are provided. First, new assessments may be phased in over five years. Second, a two-class system may be established of homeowners and all others. The class shares are established based on the assessment roll as it existed in the year prior to the reassessment.

As with Nassau County, the class shares are based on the portions of taxing units in each assessing unit (a typical town has five to six school-district pieces). The number of portions in New York will be approximately 4,800 with a resulting 9,828 class shares.

The class shares can only be modified at the local level by an annual adjustment for new construction, demolition, and exemption changes and by a very complicated and small discretionary increase in the homeowner class share. The state board on a three-year cycle shall modify the class shares for market trends, so that appreciation will be captured on roughly a six-year lag basis.

This explanation unfortunately oversimplifies the changes made in New York's real-property-tax law. Other significant changes were made restricting taxpayer grievances, limiting the valuation of cooperatives and condominiums, creating class ratios, and modifying the market-value surveys done to establish equalization rates.

The impact of the new legislation is still unclear. Litigation is only just beginning and may well take several years before the many issues posed are resolved. Prior to 1981 about one hundred cities and towns initiated reassessment projects each year. In 1981, there were no new starts. In 1982, only two cities are expected to start reassessment projects. Clearly, one impact is a wait-and-see attitude by local governments.

13 The Role of the State in Property Taxation in Ohio

Frederick D. Stocker and
John H. Bowman

Ohio illustrates several distinctive features of property-tax law and practice. For many years, constitutional property-tax limits in Ohio have been among the most stringent anywhere in the country. Statutory enactments operate so as to virtually eliminate any revenue growth due to inflationary adjustments to assessed values of real estate. State legislation designed to prevent inflation-caused increases in property-tax bills has complicated calculation of the tax beyond the comprehension of the ordinary property owner—and even of most tax administrators. Moreover, Ohio relies heavily on state administration for the tax on tangible personal property (business machinery, equipment, inventory, furniture, and fixtures) and derives an unusually large amount of revenue from this component of the tax base. Lastly, the assessment function—including periodic reappraisals and, in many counties, maintenance of the rolls as well—is performed by private-contract appraisal firms rather than by the assessor's own staff.

Legal Framework and Fiscal Significance

The property tax in Ohio, as in other states, is a collection of levies that apply in somewhat different fashion to various kinds of taxable property.

Besides real estate, the property tax applies in Ohio to tangible personal property: machinery, equipment, inventories, and business furniture and fixtures. Only business-owned tangible personal property is taxable. Household belongings are exempt, as are automobiles, pleasure boats, and airplanes. Commercial motor vehicles are also exempt from Ohio property tax.

In 1980, the taxable value of tangible personal property in Ohio was listed at $22.6 billion (including that of public utilities), or 28 percent of the

This chapter is adapted in part from previously published studies by the authors, notably Stocker's *The Ohio Real Estate Tax: Its Role and Possible Alternatives,* Center for Real Estate Education and Research, The Ohio State University, March 1980, and *Financing Ohio's Schools and Other Public Services,* National Education Association, September 1980. Part is adapted from *Fiscal Options for the State of Ohio,* vol. 2: *Property Tax Issues,* by John H. Bowman, Frederick D. Stocker, William A. Testa, and Daniel E. Chall, Academy for Contemporary Problems, June 1980.

total property-tax base. Considering that Ohio taxes neither automobiles nor trucks, this share of property-tax base is unusually large compared with other states.

In addition, there is a property tax on intangible personal property: investments, deposits, credits, mortgages, cash and shares in financial institutions, and dealers in intangibles. In calendar year 1980, the various classes of intangibles generated about $250 million in state and local revenue.

The property tax is the largest single source of state-local tax revenue in Ohio, generating an estimated $2.793 million in fiscal year 1978-1979. Local governments derived $2.660 million from the property tax, accounting for 51 percent of local own-source revenue in 1978-1979. Ohio school districts especially rely on the property tax, as it provides almost every penny of school district own-source tax revenue ($1.834 million in 1978-1979). Municipalities in Ohio are less dependent upon property taxes than those in most other states, since many municipalities levy taxes on earned income. Municipalities in Ohio derive only 27 percent of own-source tax revenue from the property tax, compared to a national average of 56 percent.

The real and tangible personal-property-tax base in Ohio, calendar year 1980, can be summarized as shown in table 13-1.

There is no indication that the property tax is overworked in Ohio. In 1978-1979, per-capita property-tax revenue was 12 percent lower than the national average. Ohio's property taxes were only $33 per $1,000 of personal income compared with the $38 national average.

The relatively low level of property taxes in Ohio reflects the application of nominal rates that, statewide, average very low, to a tax base that is

Table 13-1
Property-Tax Base in Ohio, 1980

Classification	Amount	Percentage
Real property (total)	$57,212.7	71.7
Agricultural	6,025.1	7.5
Mineral	82.2	0.1
Industrial	3,952.7	5.0
Commercial	9,752.9	12.2
Residential	36,695.5	46.0
Public utility	704.3	0.9
Tangible personal property (total)	22,600.6	28.3
Manufacturing machinery and equipment	5,373.1	6.7
Manufacturers' inventories	4,681.8	5.9
Merchants' inventories	3,140.6	3.9
Furniture, fixtures, and all other	1,824.0	2.3
Public utility	7,581.1	9.5
Real and tangible Personal property (total)	79,813.3	100.0

broader than that found in most states. Moreover, Ohio's property-tax base is augmented by inclusion of an unusually large amount of tangible personal property in the form of business machinery and equipment, inventories, and furniture and fixtures. The result is that the average Ohio homeowner's property taxes are even lower relative to other states than is indicated by overall comparisons.

Perhaps even more surprising than Ohio's low tax rate is the decline in Ohio's effective tax rate during the past decade. A number of causes of this decline may be noted. Property assessments have failed to keep up with inflation in real-estate values, and voters have increasingly defeated tax-levy proposals. Under 1976 legislation, percentage reductions in tax liabilities are applied to real property that is reappraised or revalued. Finally, since 1972, real-estate owners have received a 10-percent rollback in their annual property-tax bill (now 12 ½ percent for owners of residential property).

The Property Tax and the Schools

To a significant degree, more than in most states, the property tax in Ohio is a school tax. In 1978, 72 percent of the taxes levied on real estate and tangible personal property were levied by school districts. Municipalities received under 10 percent in 1978. Counties and special districts received about 15 percent and townships, 4 percent.

These percentages would change slightly, with the school-district share being a little smaller, if the tangibles tax were included. This tax has two parts. The *local-situs* portion, consisting largely of taxes on the income yield of stocks, bonds, and mortgages ($105 million in 1980), goes almost entirely to support public libraries. The *state-situs* portion, including chiefly the revenue from taxes on the deposits and shares of banks and other financial institutions, goes mostly into the Undivided Local Government Fund, from which it is parceled out to local governments. The revenue from this portion of the property tax amounted to $145 million in 1980.

The dominant role of school districts in the Ohio property-tax structure is a result of Ohio property-tax law (in particular the ten-mill limit) and state tradition. Just as the state government a half century ago withdrew from taxation of property (except intangibles) for state purposes, Ohio municipalities in the years since World War II have largely given up on the property tax, except for their *inside millage* (that is, their share of the ten mills that can be levied without referendum). Because of the difficulty of securing voter approval for levies outside the ten-mill levy, and because they have power to levy taxes on earnings, municipalities have tended to leave the property tax to the schools. Counties and townships, though less significant fiscally, also have tended not to rely to any great extent on voted levies.

As a result, most of the voted millage in Ohio, along with the major portion of the inside millage, goes for schools.

This linking of school finances so closely to the local property tax in Ohio has been a subject of some criticism. In the recent case of *Cincinnati* v. *Walter* (58 Ohio St., 2nd, 1979), it was argued that heavy dependence on locally voted levies, along with uncomfortably large interlocal disparities in taxable wealth, deprived school children of equal access to education. The implication of this line of argument is that schools ought to be supported in greater proportion from state revenues, presumably—but not necessarily—drawn from sources other than the property tax.

Another criticism derives from the view that property taxes should be used only for support of *property-related services,* and schools and other human services should be financed from other kinds of taxes. While this viewpoint is certainly an oversimplification, it has considerable plausibility, especially as it relates to business property. It provides at least part of the rationale for the recommendation urged by many that the state governments should themselves assume the major responsibility for financing schools, from state-tax sources, thereby freeing up the property tax for support of municipal (largely property-related) services.

The fact that the supreme court of Ohio has found that the present system poses no constitutional violation does not put to rest the fundamental criticism. The decision does suggest, however, that Ohio school districts will continue to depend heavily on voted property levies until such time as the general assembly works up the courage to undertake a fundamental restructuring of the school finance system.

Tax Limitations

Ohio stands out among the states for the unusually restrictive limitation that the constitution and statutes place on property-tax rates. This limit—the so-called ten-mill limit—restricts to ten mills (1 percent) the aggregate tax rate that can be imposed on property without voter approval. The available ten mills (referred to as the inside millage) is divided up among overlapping county, municipal, township, and school-district governments according to a formula dating back to the late 1920s. Levies in excess of this limit must be placed on the ballot and approved by a majority of the voters.

The ten-mill limitation, established by constitutional amendment in 1931, is made especially restrictive by the custom of interpreting the limit as though it applied to *taxable value.* The constitution itself defines the limitation as "1 percent of true cash value." There may have been a time when taxable value closely approximated true cash (market) value, on the average but that no longer is true. Today taxable value is defined by statute as a *fraction* of true cash value, at present averaging around 23 percent. Still, the tax-rate limitation applies to taxable value as though it were the same as cash or market value. The ten-mill limit, highly restrictive in original intent, has thus come to be applied in a way that makes it something less than a two-and-one-half-mill limit.

The result is particularly severe in its effects on schools. School systems are made dependent on voter-approved levies for the revenues without which they literally cannot continue to function. In effect, the local electorate has been given the power to veto the local school system. Whatever appeal this arrangement may have to proponents of decentralized fiscal power, there can be no question that it contributes increasingly to Ohio's school-finance plight.

Another feature of the Ohio property-tax system is the *ten-percent rollback* in real-estate taxes. Under legislation first effective in 1972, as an offset to the then-new personal and corporate income taxes, real-estate owners pay only 90 percent of the taxes levied on their property; the other 10 percent is paid by the state in the form of a direct reimbursement to the local governments levying the tax. In 1979, the rollback was increased to 12 ½ percent for residential properties. The cost of this state-financed reduction in real-estate tax levies has grown steadily, and in 1980 amounted to $253 million.

Perhaps the most significant feature of the Ohio property tax, in terms of explaining Ohio's recurring problems in financing schools, is the unique tradition in Ohio with respect to voted property levies (that is, those outside the ten-mill limit). One would normally think that a voter-approved levy of, let us say, five mills, would authorize collection of a five-tenths of 1-percent tax on the taxable value of property and that as this taxable value rises, so would the revenue from the voted levy. This view is not accepted in Ohio. Instead, a voted levy is considered to authorize collection of only a certain number of tax dollars from existing properties. Long-standing custom, implemented over the years in a variety of ways, holds that an increase in assessed values on existing property should not be allowed to cause an increase in taxes from voter-approved levies.

Prior to 1976, this philosophy was implemented by a rollback in the tax rate at the time of a reassessment of property. The reduced rate, however, applied to tangible personal property as well as real estate, even though only real estate is involved in the reappraisal.

To confine the tax reduction to real estate, at the same time observing the legal requirement of uniform tax rates, legislation (HB 920) was enacted, which established a system of tax credits designed to return to real-estate owners an amount equal in the aggregate to the tax revenue that would otherwise have been generated from voted levies by a revaluation of property. Rising market values of real property thus lead to higher assessed values. Automatic property-tax revenue increases, on the other hand, result only from: the first ten mills of the total millage rate; that is, the inside millage; new construction, including improvements to existing real property; and, increases in value of tangible personal property, as tax-reduction factors do not apply to tangible property-tax payments.

Calculation of these tax credits *(tax-reduction factors)* is unbelievably complex. The original difficulty caused by the necessity to calculate—and adjust for—the inflationary increase brought about by each reassessment (or update) since 1975 has been multiplied by 1981 legislation requiring that the calculation be done separately for each of two classes of property (*Class I*—agricultural and residential; *Class II*—all other). These state actions have undermined the uniform ad valorem operation of the tax. They also have made it practically impossible for the taxpayer to understand, or the tax collector to explain, exactly how a property owner's tax is determined.

This system is very favorable to real-estate owners, who, to a large extent, are shielded from tax increases caused by inflation and reassessment. The system, however, has put the schools (and other units of local government to the extent they depend on voted levies) in a fiscal straitjacket. They are forced to meet inflationary increases in operating costs from a revenue base that is prevented from growing with inflation.

For schools, the fiscal problem caused by the HB 920 credits is made even more severe by the design of the formula for basic aid. Under the equal-yield formula adopted in 1975, each school district's entitlement depends in part on its property-tax capacity (taxable value) and its tax effort (effective tax rate, after allowance for the HB 920 credits). A reassessment of real estate (which by law occurs every six years) or an update of assessments (which occurs in the third year of the sexennial cycle) thus causes taxable values to rise and tax effort to fall. Both effects reduce the amount of state aid under the formula. But the revaluation produces no increase in property-tax revenue, except from the small part of the total rate that represents the district's inside millage.

Real-Estate Classification

Ever since the early 1970s, when the general assembly, under court mandate, took steps to enforce the constitutionally required uniformity principle in real-estate assessments, a segment of public opinion has favored amending the constitution to eliminate the uniformity requirement. Various such proposals have been put forward in the general assembly, always in the face of strong opposition from the business community.

In November of 1980, however, the voters approved a constitutional amendment that expressly authorized lower effective rates of tax on farm and residential real estate than on other kinds of property. The differential would come about through a complex arrangement giving different percentage credits to owners of different kinds of property when property values are increased by a reappraisal. The possibilities that this amendment opens for classification of real estate could basically alter the Ohio tax structure and the reform options. Until further legislation and court decisions clarify the situation, at present one can only speculate about the long-term consequences.

Administration

Administrative Structure

In Ohio, the property tax—as it applies to intangible and tangible personal property—is largely administered by the state. Intercounty corporations (those having tangible personal property located in more than one county) must file returns annually with the State Tax Department, setting forth the book value of their tangible personal property within the state. These valuations must be made according to the strict rules promulgated by the tax commissioner and are subject to audit by tax-department staff. The valuation of property, as determined by the tax department, is allocated to the counties in which the property is located and certified to the county auditor. This valuation is then incorporated into the tangible-personal-property tax duplicate of the counties. The appropriate tax rate, as developed by the taxing jurisdiction, is levied and certified to the county treasurer for collection.

Corporations operating in a single county and unincorporated businesses with tangible or intangible personal property valued at more than $5,000, or producing an income in excess of $500, are required to file returns with the county auditor (acting in this capacity as deputy of the tax commissioner). A duplicate copy is also forwarded to the appropriate district office of the Department of Taxation, where it is subject to audit.

Local-size unincorporated businesses (those below the statutory limit in value of taxable property and income) file returns with the county auditor (serving as deputy of the tax commissioner) who, himself, assesses the tax.

In the taxation of intangibles, the tax commissioner has exclusive responsibility for administration of the tax on utilities and intercounty corporations. The tax commissioner and the local county auditors share responsibility for administration on individuals, unincorporated businesses, and single-county corporations, with the commissioner being involved with those of larger (state) size.

Real-property tax administration differs from that of tangible and intangible personal property in that: (1) primary administrative responsibility rests with county auditors, although the Department of Tax Equalization provides state-level supervision and, (2) the primary administrative task (valuation) is on a multiyear, rather than an annual, cycle.

Ohio property-tax law requires that each parcel of real property be assessed at 35 percent of its market value. This fractional value is known as the *taxable value*, or *assessed value*. An exception is agricultural land, which, at the option of the owner, may be valued according to its agricultural-use value. Administrative responsibility for valuing real property lies with the county auditors, under the supervision of the State Department of Tax Equalization.

Each parcel must be physically inspected in a mass reappraisal, or reassessment, every sixth year to establish a new assessed value. A different group of counties is reassessed each year. Counties undergoing reassessment after 1971 were required, between 1973 and 1976, to update assessed values annually. The updating process did not require physical inspection and, therefore, was unlikely to detect differences among parcels. In 1976, this annual updating requirement was abandoned in favor of a triennial update in the middle of the sexennial reassessment cycle.

The Department of Tax Equalization inspects the tax duplicate of each county to determine adherence to the legal requirements. The department calculates assessment-sales ratios to assist in its oversight of local calculation and state appraisals also are made of some properties for this purpose. Information from these and other sources is used by the department to suggest target increases in assessed values for a reassessment or update. Since 1976, however, the department has not been permitted to require a change in values other than in the reassessment and update years.

This administrative system has not met the prescribed assessment level and uniformity standards. The Department of Tax Equalization prepares and publishes semiannual assessment-sales ratios for each of several types of real property by county. Residential ratios are more reliable than nonresidential ratios, both because of the more numerous sales of such properties and because of the greater similarity of residential properties in comparison with agricultural, industrial, or commercial properties. The statewide average residential ratio for the last half of 1977 was 27.3 percent, with the county averages ranging from 23.1 percent to 33.2 percent. Ratios for the other classes reveal a similar situation. By and large, the 35-percent assessment standard is not achieved.

The Census of Governments, taken every five years, develops coefficients of dispersion in addition to assessment-sales ratios. The 1977 census, reporting data for 1976, contains information for forty-two of Ohio's eighty-eight counties. If they are grouped according to the year of the most recent reappraisal as of the 1976 survey period, counties reassessed more recently come closer to the assessment standard, and the interim updating appears to be relatively successful in this regard. In those counties last reassessed in 1971, real-property values had not been updated between 1971 and 1976. Counties reassessed in 1976 had current (as of the 1 January 1976 tax-lien date) assessed values during the census bureau's survey period. The other four groups of counties all had values on the books intended to be appropriate as of 1 January 1975, either because an interim update to 1975 had been made or they were reassessed in 1972, 1973, or 1974.

In addition to the assessment ratios, the census bureau also calculates coefficients of dispersion for residential properties within the county areas. The coefficient of dispersion is a measure of assessment uniformity. It expresses, as a percentage of the median ratio, the average absolute deviation of the separate assessment-sales ratios for each of the parcels from the median ratio. Thus, a higher coefficient implies a greater degree of nonuniformity of assessments.

The most recent assessments generally are the most uniform (that is, the most accurate.) Unlike the assessment-ratio experience, the interim updates of values do not seem very successful in improving assessment uniformity. This result is not surprising because the interim updates generally are accomplished by application of uniform multipliers (percentage-adjustment factors) to individual property values to raise the average assessment level. Updating so performed is not capable of altering relationships among individual parcels. In all but a few counties, however, the coefficients of dispersion are quite high, often above the 20-percent level regarded by many as a minimally acceptable degree of uniformity.

The picture that emerges, then, is one of marked differences between assessment law and accomplishment, although census-bureau data for the several states show that Ohio's performance does not differ greatly from the average.

The Appeals Process

To assure the fair and uniform application of the property tax, it is generally acknowledged that taxpayers: (1) should be given all the information needed to evaluate the fairness of their assessed values and, (2) should have available an inexpensive and easily accessible means to appeal assessments thought to be inequitable. If the property-tax system is opened to taxpayers in these ways, it is reasoned, assessors will be kept on their toes by taxpayer scrutiny, and flagrant errors should not occur. But when errors do occur, redress would be readily available. The expected result is a more equitable set of assessed values.

In Ohio, the first step in the appeals procedure is the county auditor, with whom complaints must be filed. The auditor places the complaint before the county board of revision, which is comprised of the county auditor, the county treasurer, and the president of the county commissioners. The board must render its decision within ninety days after the complaint is filed. From the county board of revision, complaints may be taken either to the court of common pleas or to the State Board of Tax Appeals, with appeals from either of these bodies going to the Ohio Supreme Court.

Little is known at the state level about the functioning of the appeals process, because the county boards of revision are not required to report to any state agency on the number, types, or disposition of complaints filed. Only those cases not resolved at the county level, which then are appealed to the State Board of Tax Appeals, are reported to state tax agencies. Reportedly, most of the appeals coming to the state level are by business-property owners.

Without knowing the details of the complaints filed at the county level, together with their disposition, it is difficult to know how effectively the appeals process really works. Two diametrically opposed hypotheses are suggested by available information. One is that the appeals process is, in practice, available only to business-property owners, a possibility suggested by the predominance of such appeals reaching the state level.

The alternative hypothesis suggested by this same observation is that the county-level appeals process adequately redresses the grievances of the residential- and agricultural-property owners, so that appeal to the state level is not necessary. Reportedly, some 14,000 appeals were filed in Cuyahoga County following the 1976 reappraisal, with most resolved at the county level. Whether this volume of appeals from over 440,000 parcels (nearly 400,000 residential) is as large as would be desirable is unclear. Also, the basis for deciding when to make adjustments, and by how much, is not known.

The need for better information on the local appeals process is underscored by the relative weakness of the taxpayer notification process in Ohio. At the time of a reassessment, or update, when all real-property values in a county are likely to change, the only notice that is legally required is advertisement of the fact of the completion of the general reassessment, or update, in a newspaper of general circulation in the county. Such advertisements are to be made in each of the three weeks preceding the issuance of the tax bills. Only when individual parcels are revalued (as opposed to mass, or universal, revaluation) do individual property owners receive mailed notices of the value changes.

Technical Proficiency in Assessment

Ohio is unusual, if not unique, in the degree to which it relies on private-contract appraisal firms for the performance of the assessment function.

Nearly all counties contract with private appraisal firms not only for mass reappraisals but also for maintenance assessment work (for example, keeping the roles current by deleting demolished structures and adding newly constructed ones). Because hired professionals typically do the actual assessment work, the fact that the assessor (that is, county auditor) is elected rather than appointed and does not have to meet any assessing proficiency standards, seems not to be a cause for great concern.

Positive changes that might be made in Ohio include the issuance and required use of a standard appraisal manual and the insistence upon tax maps. Ohio has had no standard appraisal manual for several decades. The Department of Tax Equalization issues rules and suggested procedures, but they lack the specificity of many state appraisal manuals. In the absence of standard manuals and their required use, each county apparently is free within relatively broad limits to decide exactly how to implement the assessment function. For example, no standard cost schedules are issued by the Department of Tax Equalization. Also, the assessment-sales ratio studies that are prepared are used only as general indicators of the prevailing level of assessment and, therefore, of the degree of change needed.

The problem is compounded by the fact that the department's staff is too small to conduct extensive checks on the accuracy of tax abstracts. Although the number of full-time assessors employed by the department has risen from one to twelve in recent years, there still are too few to permit much spot checking of assessments. The state assessors have to be used almost exclusively in valuing commercial and industrial properties in counties undergoing reassessment or update.

Similarly, staff limitations prevent the department from offering much technical assistance for valuing difficult properties. The staff attempts to deal with individual questions that are raised, but there is no strong, extensive state technical-assistance program. Finally, tax maps, often considered essential to effective and efficient assessment, are not required in Ohio. Although most counties nevertheless have tax maps, their quality varies substantially from one area to another.

The department currently uses assessment-sales ratios to help determine the degree of change in values that is needed at time of reassessment or update. Consideration might be given to using them to identify types of property or areas within a county needing reassessment. While current law apparently keeps the Department of Tax Equalization from ordering a county auditor to change values in other than reassessment or update years, the county auditor apparently has the discretion to make such changes at any time, and assessment-sales ratios could be invaluable in determining the need for such changes.

It seems, therefore, that one possible cause of Ohio's less-than-satisfactory assessment performance is the absence of a strong state-oversight role. The Department of Tax Equalization is constrained by its inability to order determination of new assessed values in all but two of the six years of the sexennial assessment cycle. Budgetary limitations also preclude truly meaningful supplementation of assessment-sales ratios by state appraisals. Moreover, the preparation and publication of assessment-sales ratios involve a considerable time lag that limits the usefulness of the data that are available.

Another promising area for change is improved taxpayer notification. Armed with more assessment information, taxpayers could become more effective in policing assessment quality. If they were more aware of the degree of assessment nonuniformity, they might file more appeals and cause more adjustments, which should improve overall assessment quality. Ohio taxpayers apparently are given too little information to take full advantage of the relatively simple appeals system.

Equalization

Ohio law does not require annual equalization. Between 1972 and 1976, annual updates were required in counties having undergone mass appraisal in 1972 and later years to keep assessed values near the legal standard of 35 percent of true value in money (that is, full value). House Bill 920 in 1976 replaced this requirement with a provision requiring the updating of assessed values only in the third year after a mass appraisal. Thus, both equalization of existing assessed values and establishment of new assessed values are required every sixth year, with the two separated by three years. The Department of Tax Equalization is not empowered to require equalization in any county more frequently than every third year.

The Department of Tax Equalization conducts assessment-sales ratio studies every six months. Such ratio studies are required to be performed and used in arriving at estimated values in the reassessment and update years. But there is no requirement that these ratios be used to equalize—for any use—the end results of the mass appraisal and the interim update, either in the years of reappraisal or in the intervening years. However, the Department of Tax Equalization must determine whether real property is assessed at the legal level in reappraisal and triennial update years. If it is not, appropriate adjustments must be ordered. Assessment-sales ratios are one of the important pieces of evidence used in making such determinations and any adjustments indicated. The department also used these ratios to help set the targeted percentage increases sent to a county auditor going into the appraisal or update period. Thus, Ohio attempts to equalize the original assessments, rather than use specified multipliers in aid-distribution programs.

The data suggest that Ohio's equalization efforts are not very effective. Substantial deviation from the 35-percent assessment standard still remains.

Just as there is variation among the types of properties, so too is there variation among the counties for a given type of property. For example, in 1977, industrial ratios ranged from 16 percent in Stark County to over 57 percent in Muskingum County, and residential ratios from 23 percent in Pike County to 33 percent in Marion County.

In summary, more frequent—perhaps annual—reappraisal or assessment equalization seems necessary if the uniformity required by law, and equity considerations, is to be achieved. Most states permit property-tax revenue to grow after reassessment (although perhaps by a smaller percentage than the average assessed value increase). This arrangement recognizes the fact that government costs rise over time, so that the amount of money authorized in an earlier period to provide a particular service probably will not be adequate now. Ohio law strips out the revenue growth that otherwise might occur from voted millage on pre-existing real property. In principle, this makes the assessor's task more acceptable. Attaining more uniform property assessment—the real reason for periodic reappraisal or equalization—does not lead inexorably to a higher level of taxation. If assessments were adjusted annually, any resulting property-tax increases might be more acceptable than those that would result from triennial updating, because annual adjustments would be smaller.

One of the most promising avenues to improved equalization on a more timely, yet efficient, basis is computer-assisted assessment using multiple-regression analysis. Just over a decade old, this technique generally has produced relatively uniform assessments at reasonable costs, although it is not a cure-all for assessment problems. An accurate data base in machine-readable form must be developed and maintained for regression-based estimation of sales prices. Although several Ohio counties have begun to introduce computer technology into the assessment process, only a few of these have carried it to the level of development required for computer-assisted estimation of values. Careful consideration should be given to the development of this capability throughout the state, with technical assistance available through the Department of Tax Equalization.

14 The Role of the State in Property Taxation in Texas

Kenneth E. Graeber

The system of property-tax administration in Texas is currently undergoing major revisions. In 1979 and 1981 laws were enacted to implement constitutional amendments providing for expansion of preferential tax treatment for agricultural and timber lands, creating new homestead exemptions and exempting livestock, intangible property, and household goods. A State Property-Tax Code was also enacted, which codified existing statutes, created a State Property-Tax Board, and provided for the implementation of single-appraisal districts in each county by 1982.

Legal Framework

The Texas Constitution establishes three principles for property-tax administration: property is taxable unless exempted by federal law or the Texas Constitution; taxation shall be equal and uniform; and property shall be valued according to market value, unless constitutional authority exists for preferential assessment. As in many states, however, past assessment practices have included forms of de facto classification and exclusion of certain properties from taxation without constitutional authority. Such practices should decrease significantly with full implementation of the single appraisal districts.

Certain exemptions of property are specified by the constitution; others are specified by statute based upon constitutional authority. Additionally, the legislature has enacted statutes that attempt to exempt property without constitutional authority. While these statutes consistently have been invalidated when challenged, some local taxing units continue to grant the exemptions they provide.

Total Exemptions

The following total exemptions, having constitutional authority, exist in Texas:

> Intangible property, with the exception of stock of common carriers, contract motor carriers, banks, mutual life-insurance companies, pension

or profit-sharing funds, savings and loan associations, and insurance companies. Special provisions exist for taxation of these intangibles.

Household goods and personal effects not used to produce income.

Private automobiles not used to produce income are exempt unless the governing body of the taxing unit votes to tax them.

Public property used for public purposes.

Farm products in the hands of the producer, and family supplies for home and farm use.

Property designated as a cultural, historical, or natural-history resource.

Actual places of religious worship and any property used exclusively as a dwelling place for the ministry of such worship, whether for a church or an organized religious society.

Burial places not held for private or corporate profit.

Solar and wind-powered energy devices.

Institutions of purely public charity.

All property, both real and personal, owned by a person or an association of persons and used exclusively for school purposes.

All property used by an association exclusively and reasonably to conduct the trifold purpose of religious, educational, and physical development of boys, girls, young men, or young women.

The constitution provides that by general law, the legislature may exempt all or part of the personal property homestead of a family or single adult.

Recent revisions of the Property Tax Code contain exemptions of farm and ranch personal property, including livestock and machinery. Uncertainty exists whether the general authority in the constitution allows these exemptions.

Total exemptions provided for by statute, without constitutional authority, include property owned by the following organizations if not held for gain: veterans' organizations; Federation of Women's clubs; Nature Conservancy of Texas; Texas Congress of Parents and Teachers; private-enterprise demonstration associations; theater schools; biomedical research corporations; and community-service clubs. Lastly a statute provides for an exemption for buffalo and cattalo used for experimentation and breeding purposes or to preserve the species.

Partial Exemptions

Currently, Texas homeowners are eligible for six different homestead exemptions, depending upon age, disability, and the option of the governing units. These exemptions include: $5,000 for school-tax purposes and $10,000 if sixty-five and over or disabled, also if sixty-five and over, the school taxes are frozen based upon the taxes paid the first year the property qualifies; $3,000 if sixty-five or over or disabled by local option; not to exceed $3,000 based on the degree of disability for disabled veterans; and $3,000 for state ad valorem tax purposes, and for taxes levied by counties for farm-to-market roads or flood-control purposes.

The legislature has passed a proposed constitutional amendment, subject to voter approval that would establish authority for a local-option general-homestead exemption. The amendment would provide that a local governing body could exempt up to 40 percent of the market value of the homestead in 1982-1984, up to 30 percent in 1985-1987, and up to 20 percent thereafter. If locally opted, the unit must grant a $5,000 minimum exemption. The exemption would be in addition to other exemptions granted.

Preferential Valuation

Two constitutional provisions exist related to special valuation of land. The first provision—enacted in 1967—applies only to agricultural land and contains the following restrictions, which have limited its application: the land must be owned by a natural person (land held in partnership or corporate title cannot qualify); the land must have been in agricultural use for three years prior to claiming this kind of valuation; the owner must file a sworn statement about use of the land; and, the agricultural business must be the primary occupation and source of income of the owner. While no constitutional or statutory guidelines exist for a method to determine these agricultural values, the income-capitalization approach has been upheld by the courts as an accepted technique.

The second provision, enacted in 1979, applies to land used for agriculture or timber purposes and has few restrictions that would limit its application. Under this provision: agricultural land must be currently devoted principally to agricultural use to the degree of intensity generally accepted in the area; and, timberland must be used with the intent to produce income and be currently and actively devoted principally to the production of timber or forest products to the degree of intensity generally accepted in the area. This provision also specifies that the land must have been in agricultural or timber use for at least five of the last seven years. There is no requirement that the land be owned by a natural person, and the agricultural or timber use need not be the primary occupation or source of income of the owner. The statute specifically requires the use of the income-capitalization approach and sets the capitalization rate at the Federal Land Bank interest rate on December 31 plus 2 1/2 percent, or a minimum of 10 percent. The capitalization rate for 1981 was 12.75 percent.

Both provisions provide for rollback or recapture should the land be converted from a qualifying use. The rollback is based on taxes that would have been paid, based on market value plus interest. The first provision provides for a three-year rollback and is also triggered by a sale. The second provision provides for a five-year rollback and is only triggered by a change in use.

Tax-Limitation Provisions

Tax-rate limitations exist in law and vary by the type of governmental unit. Schools are limited to a tax rate of $1.50 per $100 of value for operational purposes, with no limit on the debt-service tax rate. Schools, however, are subject to a limitation of 10 percent of their assessed valuation on the amount of bonded indebtedness. Home-rule cities often have charter provisions that limit tax rates. General-law cities are limited to total tax rates not to exceed $2.50 for cities of over 10,000 population, and $1.50 for those under 10,000. Counties are subject to a total limit of $1.25, with specific limits placed on individual rates set for different purposes.

As a practical matter, increases in property valuations associated with the establishment of appraisal districts and the removal of fractional assessment will minimize the effect of tax-rate limitations in Texas.

Truth-in-Taxation

The Property Tax Code and its revisions, however, enacted several major provisions directed toward limiting increases in property taxes. These provisions are generally referred to as the *Truth-in-taxation* sections of the code and have not been received warmly by local government officials or administrators.

Truth-in-taxation requirements include:

The taxing unit must send a reappraisal notice to taxpayers whose property is increased in value by more than $1,000.

The tax assessor must calculate a rate that will generate the same level of revenue as levied in the prior year and publish the rate in the local newspaper.

If the governing body intends to adopt a tax rate that exceeds the calculated rate by more than 3 percent, it must first run two quarter-page newspaper advertisements stating its intention and announcing a public hearing (and then a public meeting) for the specific purpose of adopting the rate. The members of the governing body are required to show how they voted on the intent to increase taxes as a apart of the advertisement.

Effective in 1982, if a governing body increases its rate by over 8 percent above the calculated rate, the public has the right to petition for a tax-rate rollback election. The petition must contain signatures of 10 percent of the qualified voters and be filed within ninety days after the tax is adopted. The tax limitation, if adopted, is effective for the current tax year for all jurisdictions other than for schools, where it is effective the following year.

Administration

This review of responsibilities for property-tax administration will be based upon provisions of the Property Tax Code to be fully implemented in 1982. At the present time, local units of government maintain their individual offices for appraisal of property. Effective as of January 1982, local units will utilize appraisals made by a single appraisal district established in each county. Recent revisions to the code provide for a local-option postponement of one year (or for a three-year phase in) for implementing the single-appraisal concept. Very few counties are considering postponement, due to additional costs that would occur if the system were delayed.

Local Administration

Effective 1 January 1980, an appraisal district was established in each county with the responsibility for listing and appraising taxable property in the district and providing local remedies for dissatisfied property owners. Effective as of 1 January 1982, property taxes for all local taxing entities will be based on the district's appraisal. If a school district, an incorporated city or town, water district, or junior-college district overlaps two or more counties, it may choose to have all its taxable property appraised by only one appraisal district. Costs of appraising territory outside the county are allocated to the taxing unit that chooses to add that territory to the appraisal district. Should two or more taxing units add the same territory, the additional appraisal costs would be divided between these units in proportion to the total dollar amount of taxes each such unit imposes in that territory.

Each appraisal distrtict is governed by a board of five directors, serving two-year terms beginning January 1 of even-numbered years. Members are not compensated for service on the board but may be reimbursed for expenses. The governing boards of the school districts, incorporated cities, towns, and counties participating in the appraisal district elect the directors. Although they participate in the appraisal districts in all other respects, the remaining property taxing units (for example, water districts, hospital districts, junior colleges) are not entitled to vote in selecting the directors.

Within an appraisal district, the number of votes a voting taxing unit may cast is determined by dividing the amount of property taxes imposed by that unit (that is, tax levy, not tax collections) for the preceding year, by the total amount of property taxes imposed that year by all voting taxing entities. A taxing unit participating in two or more districts is entitled to vote in each district, but only the taxes imposed in a district are used to calculate voting entitlement in that district. A majority of taxing units having the right to vote can veto the appraisal-district budget, or any action of the district's board of directors.

Each appraisal district has an appraisal office, which is administered by a chief appraiser (who is employed by the board of directors). The chief appraiser may be compensated under the budget adopted by the board and may hire necessary personnel as authorized by the district's budget. Instead of establishing its own office, however, a district may choose to have a taxing unit within the district, or the appraisal office for another district, perform appraisal functions for it. If a taxing unit performs the appraisal office's duties, the assessor for the unit is the chief appraiser. A district may also contract for a private appraisal firm to perform appraisal services.

The chief appraiser must prepare a budget for district operations for the following tax year and submit copies to each participating taxing unit and to the district's board of directors. An estimate of the budgetary costs to be allocated to each taxing unit must be included. Each unit's portion of the total cost is determined by the proportion its total property-tax levy bears to the total amount of property taxes imposed in the district by all participating units.

Equalization Boards

Each appraisal-district board of directors appoints an appraisal review board. This group normally consists of three members, although counties can locally opt to increase its membership. A person must both be a district resident and also have resided in the district for at least two years to serve on the appraisal review board. Members serve two-year terms, beginning January 1 and staggered so that as close to one-half the positions as possible expire each year. Members may receive per diem set by the appraisal-district budget as well as reimbursement for expenses.

A property owner may protest the appraised value of his property as not complying with the law. Any taxing unit required to use appraisal-district values may challenge the value placed on a specific property until 1984. Beginning that year, they can only challenge the level of appraisal. The appraisal review board must decide all challenges by written order before approving the appraisal records.

State Administration

The State Property Tax Board, created 1 January 1980, consists of six gubernatorial appointees serving six-year, staggered terms. A board member must have been a Texas resident for at least ten years to be eligible to serve. After 1 March 1983, at least two members must be certified by the Board of Tax Assessor Examiners.

Unlike similarly named entities in other states, the power of the Texas State Property Tax Board is heavily circumscribed. The Texas Constitution contains a specific prohibition against statewide appraisal of property. No central assessment of utilities, mineral, or industrial properties exists in Texas. While the board does provide technical assistance related to property valuation, the agency does not value classes of property or individual properties for local districts.

The board's assistance to local tax administrators includes a monthly reference bulletin, numerous publications on compliance with laws and rules adopted by the board, development of both general and specialized appraisal manuals, development of educational programs, and technical assistance on specific problems. It should be noted that appraisal manuals developed by the agency are not mandated for use but serve as optional guides to assist the appraiser.

The board maintains advisory committees of local administrators to assist in the development of rules affecting record requirements and educational programs. The most popular service offered involves inward WATS lines, which allow local tax administrators and officials to call and obtain technical assistance on daily problems encountered. More specifically, the board prescribes the record system for district appraisal offices and all property tax forms, and effective in 1984, the board will be required to conduct ratio studies to determine the average level of appraisal in each appraisal district and publish its findings.

Collection of Taxes

Local governments retain the authority to collect their own taxes under code provisions. These units will set their rates, prepare tax statements, and make collections using appraised values provided by the appraisal district.

In the majority of counties, attempts currently are being made to voluntarily consolidate these functions either with the appraisal district or in a central collection office. It is anticipated that collection functions will be consolidated in the majority of counties by 1984. Under the code, governmental units could voluntarily implement the appraisal district prior to 1982 using interlocal governmental contracts. Voluntary early implementation occurred in approximately 80 of the state's 254 counties.

Prior to passage of the Property Tax Code, there were approximately two thousand individual offices appraising property for tax purposes. To a certain extent, this system resulted in two thousand different interpretations of the term *equal and uniform*. While some excellent tax offices existed, they were clearly in the minority.

Generally speaking, governmental units did not provide adequate funds to support the operation of a good office. Tax records maintained by individual offices lacked any significant degree of uniformity. School districts, which are most dependent upon tax revenues, typically maintained more current values on property than other units of government.

Moreover, the majority of local governments were extremely reluctant to reappraise local properties. Many units maintained values on local properties that were thirty years or more out of date, and certain local properties were often omitted from the tax rolls. Industrial, utility, and mineral properties were normally appraised on an annual basis. Thus, over time, significant disparity developed between classes and within classes of property.

To a certain extent, this lack of uniform records and property valuations has benefited the implementation of the single appraisal districts. Since it was not possible to use existing records and values to set up a good system, the majority of counties are building new systems in compliance with State Property Tax Board rules. Additionally, the vast majority of counties are conducting complete reappraisal programs for the establishment of the initial values for the single appraisal district. One revision to the code designed to protect the system from reverting to practices of the past is a provision that requires a reappraisal of property at least once every four years.

The cost of implementation of the appraisal districts has been the subject of considerable discussion. In many counties, these costs have exceeded the combined prior expenditures of existing units for property appraisal. Much of the increased cost, however, relates to the fact that little was being spent previously on property-tax administration, and to develop a reasonably sound system, expenditures must rise initially.

Associated with the implementation of the appraisal districts has been a general increase in compensation to local property-tax administrators. Texas has a reasonably sound base of trained and experienced professionals to administer the local appraisal offices adequately. As in all professions, the geographic distribution of these individuals is not balanced with where they are needed. However, increased compensation levels and the potential consolidation of collection offices have significantly increased the mobility of many administrators.

Much of the credit for the large number of trained and experienced tax administrators should be given to the Texas Associaton of Assessing Officers. This association has provided an excellent program in past years. The state property tax board works closely with the association in the design, development, and conduct of educational programs. In addition, the board conducts regional training programs related to revisions of the laws, record-system requirements, and local administration. Continuing-education and formal degree programs have been developed by the board in conjunction with colleges and universities.

Another significant revision to the Texas property-tax system was the creation of the Board of Tax Assessor Examiners (BTAE) in 1977. The BTAE is charged by law with the registration and professional certification of individuals appraising property for tax purposes. Individuals may challenge a person's registration should they believe the person has violated provisions of the certification act. The existence of the BTAE significantly has increased participation in training programs available for tax administration.

Fiscal Importance

Texas is a property-tax haven compared to other states. The per-capita property tax levied ranks Texas last or almost last in the nation. However, Texas is relatively dependent upon the property tax, with approximately forty cents of each state and local tax dollar coming from the property tax.

Table 14-1 lists property-tax levies during the past decade by type of taxing unit.

Significant increases have occurred in property-tax levies during 1980 and 1981. While all data has not been compiled, property-tax levies will have increased between 15 and 20 percent. Schools, which levy approximately half of all property taxes, increased levies by 18.8 percent in the past year.

The property tax has a diversified base in Texas. Table 14-2 lists, by major category of property, the approximate percentage of taxes levied and the level of appraisal based upon the 1979 study of school-tax rolls.

Appraisal and Collection Cost

No comprehensive study has been conducted in Texas to analyze costs effectively at this time. The State Property Tax Board currently is collecting data that would provide for such analysis.

Table 14-1
Property Taxes Levied by State and Local Governments in Texas, 1970-1980
(millions of dollars)

Year	Total	State	Total Local	Counties	Cities	School Districts	Special Districts
1969-1970	1,521.6	$69.0	1,452.6	213.5	369.2	737.0	133.0
1970-1971	1,680.2	67.4	1,612.8	234.4	408.5	821.4	148.4
1971-1972	1,823.2	62.7	1,760.4	255.3	450.9	892.8	161.4
1972-1973	1,980.4	60.1	1,920.3	279.0	487.6	975.0	178.8
1973-1974	2,181.4	53.8	2,127.6	308.4	530.2	1,085.9	203.0
1974-1975	2,486.5	47.6	2,438.9	343.4	599.6	1,260.7	235.2
1975-1976	2,808.4	38.9	2,769.5	387.7	665.4	1,434.2	282.2
1976-1977	3,154.5	44.5	3,110.0	439.3	734.3	1,619.4	317.0
1977-1978	3,501.7	46.6	3,455.1	522.0	794.2	1,767.1	371.7
1978-1979	3,856.6	52.5	3,804.1	586.4	857.1	1,939.4	421.1
1979-1980	4,214.3	59.8	4,154.5	651.8	946.0	2,086.4	470.2

The state provided a limited amount of funding for the implementation of appraisal districts. These amounts were $2.8 million in 1980, and $7.8 million during 1981. The allocation for 1981 amounts to approximately $.94 per real parcel of property statewide. No further increase in state funding is anticipated.

Appraisal district budgets totaled approximately $7.5 million in 1981, for a statewide average cost of $9 per parcel of real property, or $7.70 per parcel of real and personal property combined. Appraisal-district costs represented 1.5 percent of total tax levies in 1981.

Table 14-2
Tax Base by Category of Property, Texas
(in percentage)

Category of Property	Percentage of Taxes Levied	Estimated Actual Level of Appraisal
Single family residential	25.92	60
Multifamily residential	4.14	67
Vacant lots	3.34	55
Acreage	8.74	33
Farm improvements	1.34	47
Commercial/industrial real	19.08	77
Minerals	13.16	96
Banks	2.31	81
Utilities	7.38	78
Business personal	11.72	77
Other personal	.50	53

Policy Framework

Texas is undergoing what one member of the legislature termed "a noble experiment which the public will reject." From a tax administrator's view, however, the revisions to the system should improve equity in the valuation of property significantly and promote better management in the system as a whole.

The major public concern expressed at this time relates to shifts in tax burdens associated with reappraisal. The legislature has responded to this concern by expanding exemptions to homeowners, expanding preferential assessment of land, and including exemption of certain other properties. While doing this to mitigate tax shifts, the legislature has maintained the concept of assessing property equitably in relation to market value and avoided a property-classfification system.

Numerous groups representing taxpayers' associations and governmental units have been involved in the development of revisions to the Texas property-tax laws. The majority of concerns have been expressed and considered in legislative revisions to be law.

It would appear that 1983 will be the critical test of the new system in Texas. Tax notices for 1982 are mailed in October, immediately prior to the November general elections. The legislature convenes in January 1983. At this time, the new system will be tested to determine whether it was a just noble experiment or is indeed a sound system for property-tax administration in Texas.

15 The Role of the State in Property Taxation in Utah

Gary C. Cornia

Legal Framework

When Utah was admitted to statehood in 1896, its constitution was designed to limit the power of the state legislature in many areas, including taxation. Specifically it established the property assessment level and the requirement that all property be equally assessed. Over the years, however, these and other provisions in the early constitution either have been disregarded by administrative agencies or removed by a series of legislative or constitutional changes, while several tax-relief programs have been adopted.

Utah's tax-relief and limitation programs presently include circuit breakers for both homeowners and renters, tax abatement, tax deferral, tax exemptions for disabled veterans and blind individuals, farmland exemptions, budget limitations, and levy limitations. Still, the most significant tax-relief program is the constitutional exemption of land owned by governmental bodies and by religious and charitable institutions. It is estimated that 80 percent of real property in the state is not subject to any form of property taxation. The majority of property exempted under this provision is owned and managed by various departments of the federal government, which in some counties owns over 90 percent of the land. Another substantial share of exempt property is owned by various units of the dominant religion in the state.

Levy and Revenue Limitations

The tax-limitation policies employed by the state generally have been in the form of controlling the maximum number of mills adopted by a specific type of local government. Counties depending upon gross assessment may impose up to sixteen or eighteen mills, cities up to thirty-five mills for general purposes, plus additional levies for specific purposes.

A more general limitation is the state's requirement that revenue generated from the property tax for a unit of government cannot increase more than 6 percent from the previous year's collection. Revenue from any type of taxable new development is omitted from this restriction, as are capital outlays for schools and levies for bonded indebtedness. Annual revaluations of 10 percent or less are automatically exempt from the 6-percent limit. The severity of this limitation, however, is reduced since it is only imposed during the first year following a revaluation.

Circuit Breaker

The circuit-breaker system, only recently adopted, is designed to provide property-tax relief to older and low-income residents. It covers homeowners, mobile homeowners, and renters. Qualifying homeowners receive a credit against their property tax ranging from $50 to $300, based on annual income. The average payment to a homeowner in 1980 was $151. Renters can also receive a credit up to $300 based on a sliding scale of income. In 1980, the average renter received $66 under the circuit-breaker program. The program is administered and funded by the state and had a per-capita cost of $1.61 in 1980. Just over 18,000 of the estimated 30,000 eligible senior citizens were using this program in 1980.

Abatement and Deferral

Utah citizens can also take advantage of tax-abatement and tax-deferral programs. As with the circuit breaker, these programs were designed to aid older citizens in the state. To qualify, an individual must be sixty-five years or older and a homeowner. In the case of tax abatement, physical disability (or extreme financial hardship) also may qualify an individual. Income cannot exceed $7,500 ($8,000 for couples) for each program. Under the abatement program, homes cannot exceed $70,000 in value, and under the deferral program, the taxpayer cannot own any assets that could be liquidated to pay taxes.

Deferred taxes accumulate as a lien against the property. An interest charge of 6 percent is assessed on the deferred taxes. The abatement program allows the homeowners to avoid up to 50 percent of owned taxes, but this amount cannot exceed $300.

Blind and Veteran Exemptions

Two other exemption programs—one for the legally blind and another for disabled veterans—are mandated by the Utah Constitution but are funded and administered by counties. These programs also are available to the widows and minor orphans of the blind and to the surviving spouses and minor orphans of veterans. There is no income limit under the program for the blind, but veterans cannot have income sources, other than disability payments, that exceed $12,000 per year.

Real property up to $2,000 of assessed value is exempt from the property tax of blind individuals. The veteran program exempts up to $3,000 of assessed value. These exemptions are substantial, given the low assessment levels found in most Utah counties. It is estimated that over ten thousand individuals and families participated in these programs in 1980.

Farmland Assessment

Since 1968, the state has allowed farmland to be assessed at use rather than fair market value. Exemption is limited to parcels of land of at least five acres in size that gross a minimum of $1,000 a year from the sale of agricultural products. If the land is converted to other use there must be paid up to five years of back taxes equal to the difference between the taxes under the new use and those under the agricultural use.

Administration

Prior to the 1970s, local property assessment primarily had been a function of the county government. In 1969, the state legislature enacted legislation to improve the quality and frequency of property assessment in the twenty-nine counties. Included in the act were provisions for the training and state certification of county assessors and their staffs, plus a program for the revaluation of property on a county basis every five years. The program was designed to have professional staff from the State Tax Commission assist the county assessor in the reassessment of property. Under the act, the state was to pay 70 percent of the cost of all reappraisals.

There were a variety of reasons why the state wanted to take a more active role in reappraisal. The issues of uniformity and equity were becoming serious. In addition, there was indication that many county assessors had insufficient resources—and in some cases, training—to administer effectively the duties of their office. But the major reason for the adoption of this bill centered around the financing of public education, which now accounts for close to 30 percent of all state and local expenditures.

Under Utah law, all school districts are required to impose 23.5 mills for the support of the Basic School Program. The Basic School Program, however, does not consider the effect of low assessment levels on the amount of revenue collected, and any school district that cannot meet the costs of the program through property-tax collections can have the difference made up through transfers from the state-financed Uniform School Fund. As a result, counties have been encouraged to keep assessments low and receive a larger share of state funds—something that has provided a strong incentive for the state to become involved in improving property-tax administration.

The results from the uniform assessment program have been mixed. It has been more expensive to administer than first estimated—over $23 million during the first eleven years. It has required much more time to reassess property in the state than was originally intended—at least double. And, worst of all, it has not mitigated the problem of intercounty assessment nonuniformity.

Two major problems contributed to the increased cost and length of this project. The existing tax information was inadequate in some counties: many parcels had never been included on the tax rolls, improvements to land or building had gone unrecorded, or tax rolls were almost nonexistent. In addition, inflation was increasing so rapidly that anything short of annual reappraisal would prove little more than cosmetic.

In spite of the cost and time overruns, the program made several important improvements in reassessment practices, including the eventual development of a reasonably progressive computer-assisted assessment program. This program, however, was not developed until most of the initial reassessments had taken place. Under this process, information on all taxable parcels of land were entered in a data-storage system maintained by the Local Valuation Division of the State Tax Commission. This system was designed so that during any subsequent reappraisal, existing data from each parcel could be combined with current data to establish a new appraisal value. To date, fifteen of the twenty-nine counties in the state have been placed on the system.

Unfortunately, current legislature essentially dismantled the reappraisal program. First, it amended the law requiring the reassessment of real property every five years, and now there is no mandatory reappraisal of locally assessed real property in the state. Furthermore, counties do not have to contract with the state for reassessment assistance. Counties can, if they wish, still enter into such contracts, but the cost is now shared on a 50-50 basis. The legislature also substantially reduced the budget of the division responsible for state-assisted revaluation.

There were several reasons—mostly political—for the actions of the legislature. First, perhaps as many as one-third of the county assessors (primarily from rural areas) had long opposed the approach. They felt the state was moving too fast and causing too many political problems for them in its efforts to achieve uniformity. Second, a new wave of conservative state legislators was elected which was committed to "less government" and budget cutting. Given this mentality, the program for property reassessment was relatively easy to drop. Finally, because the program had not appreciably improved the uniformity of assessment, it was difficult to defend. In spite of the problems, the decision by the legislature to drop the reassessment program promises to increase the lack of uniformity in the state property-tax system.

To further complicate matters, the legislature also passed a law requiring all property in the state that has been reappraised since 1978 to be rolled back to 1978 levels. Moreover, all subsequent reappraisals were to be set at 1978 levels. The rationale for this policy was that it would place every county on an equal footing, and it would promote eventual intercounty uniformity. The legislature also ruled that all residential property in the state was to be reduced by 20 percent of the 1978 level, citing the argument that market value, by including closing costs and other selling fees, overstated the true cost of a home. The combined result of these two policies was to reduce the assessment level of residential properties to 16 percent of 1978 market value and of all other properties to 20 percent of 1978 cost of replacement.

Just prior to these legislative actions, the State Tax Commission had ordered all counties to factor locally assessed property up to the 20-percent level. The factoring was to be based on the data from the annual-sales-assessment studies conducted in each county. There were two reasons why the commission took this action. First, there was concern about the fiscal integrity of the uniform school fund, and this action was seen as a way to force counties to increase their contributions to education. Second, because some property—such as railroads and public utilities—is assessed annually, it generally bears a higher tax burden than property that is assessed less often. The recently passed Railroad Revitalization Act, however, made this practice unlawful and thus the commission felt it had little choice in the matter. Subsequently, the legislature passed a law requiring counties to refactor on a biennial basis. Some have speculated that this policy was the final blow to the reassessment program. Apparently, the legislature may have felt that if the factoring program would work, there was no need for forced reappraisals.

This policy, given the high coefficients of dispersions found in many counties, has serious implications for both equity in and the administration of, property taxation in Utah. Furthermore, there is considerable ambiguity as to how this factoring must be done. Many counties, for example, have factored residential property at a lower rate than commercial property—thus increasing the tax load of commercial property. This approach is also problematical because the sales-assessment studies conducted by the tax commission allegedly were never intended for anything more than general measures of uniformity, and because in some counties, the data is insufficient to establish accurate ratios.

State Tax Commission

The administration of the property tax is shared by local county assessors and the Utah State Tax Commission. The four members of this commission—two Democrats and two Republicans, as required by state law—are appointed by the governor to four-year terms. The chairman is also designated by the governor, but the legislature sets the salary of the commission, as well as its budget. The current budget is around two million dollars, which is a reduction of about 50 percent from previous funding.

The tax commission has full responsibility for the assessment of certain types of property and may assist local assessors in areas of property-tax administration, such as the development of assessment techniques and standardized forms. The commission has broad administrative powers in the area of the property tax, including the authority to equalize the assessment level in all counties, the authority to increase the Uniform School Levy in a county if the county assessment is below average, and the administrative power to impose guidelines and rules on county assessors. It bears notation, however, that legislative action is usually required for the commission to participate in the assessment of local property or the determination of procedures. In the past, there have been political repercussions when the commission has not first sought legislative blessings for its actions and, as a result, the commission has become reluctant to impose itself on local county assessors.

A major function of all county assessors is the annual reappraisal of personal property, which primarily includes automobiles, commercial and industrial machinery, and commercial and industrial supplies and fixtures. Business inventory and household goods are excluded from taxation.

The primary problems facing local assessors are inadequate staffing and funding. The staffing problem is particularly acute.

The data we obtained reveal that assessors have not been able to increase staff to keep up with the growth in the number of parcels. The problem with funding is similar: there is little evidence that funding has matched growth. When weighted by population, the average county per-capita budget for assessment is $4.48. Per-capita property-tax collections, by comparison, are approaching $300 a year—a ratio of almost seventy to one. Ten county assessors earn less than $15,000 a year, and two of these earn less than $10,000 per year. In at least one county there are now no full-time personnel in the assessment office. Obviously, in many other counties the role of the assessor is very close to a part-time position. One reason that counties are able to get by with part-time assessors is that the property-assessment cycle allows the assessor to share administrative authority with the county treasurer and county auditor.

The Appeals Process

Under current practice, the appeals process is a combination of state and local procedures. Taxpayers can appeal their assessment levels by first appearing before a county board of equalization, which is composed of the county auditor and the county commissioners. As all of these officials are elected, the initial step in the appeals process can easily be influenced by political considerations. In most cases the county assessor also serves in an advisory capacity. If a taxpayer is dissatisfied with the outcome at the local level, he may appeal to the State Tax Commission for a hearing. Prior to the actual hearing, State Tax Commission staff members generally hold an informal meeting with the taxpayer and attempt to negotiate a settlement, and approximately one-half of all appeals are settled in this manner. Following this step, the taxpayer then may appear before the tax commission. If unhappy with the decision rendered after this hearing, the taxpayer may request a second hearing, which will include a transcript of the proceedings. Once these avenues are exhausted, he may then file a claim with either the State Tax Court or the State Supreme Court. There are generally few local appeals in any one given year. The State Tax Commission handles some three-hundred cases a year, and the Supreme Court hears about five cases each term.

State-Assessed Property

According to provisions of the Utah Constitution, the tax commission has the responsibility for the assessment of two major classes of properties: mining and public utilities. Mining assessment is divided into three areas: metalliferous mines, nonmetalliferous mines, and oil and gas properties. Metalliferous mines are assessed according to a state statute that requires that assessors use *net proceeds* in determining value. Net proceeds is defined as the three-year average value of mined metal minus the cost of extraction. (Equipment used for extraction is expensed out the year of purchase.) This figure is then multiplied by a factor of two. Whether or not the ore is actually sold does not enter into the establishment of market value. Current market evidence indicates that this method undervalues mining property. In a recent example, the assessed value of a large copper mine and mill was approximately one-third the purchase price.

Nonmetalliferous mines are valued according to tax-commission regulations, which average the gross income of the mine for the past five years and then subtract the cost of exploration and depreciation which is computed on a straight-line basis. Federal income and state franchise taxes are not deductible. Net income is then capitalized by an interest rate that is established around the rate of long term U.S. government bonds, as modified by such factors as risk, taxes, and liquidity. The capitalized net income is finally multiplied by 20 percent to reflect the current level of assessment. The recent sale of three coal mines in eastern Utah also suggests that this method results in a value that is far below actual market value.

Oil and gas wells are assessed by establishing the annual value of the well-head sales price, minus tax-exempt royalties. This figure is then multiplied by 80 percent to arrive at taxable value. In the case of gas and oil wells—as well as metalliferous and nonmetalliferous mines—the actual tax liability is dependent upon the rate imposed by each taxing district. Capital facilities in all three classes of properties are assessed at cost of replacement, minus depreciation for buildings and the cost of installation for machines. Land owned by mining companies is assessed at a flat rate of $10 per acre (this value is set by the state code). The mining division is responsible for approximately 28,000 parcels owned by 2,200 firms or individuals. In 1980, for every dollar spent on assessment, local governments collected $269 in property-tax revenue.

Public utilities are essentially assessed on a unitary concept. Three factors are considered in developing value: the income of the firm, the original cost of situs property minus depreciation, and the stock and debt value of the firm. The factor that is given the most weight is determined by the practical limit of available information. For large interstate organizations, taxable value is developed in cooperation with the Western States Association of Tax Administrators (WSATA). This process requires substantial cooperation from the firms involved. Once system-wide value has been established, it is allocated back to the individual states on the basis of a WSATA allocation formula. In the case of railroads, the allocation is based on a formula developed by the National Association of Tax Administrators. Smaller intrastate utilities that cross county lines are assessed according to the cost of the replacement of property.

The taxable value allocated to the state is then apportioned to the various counties of situs. The allocation is based on first determining the total value of a firm's property in the state, minus the assessed value of buildings, personal property, and real estate. In the case of a railroad, the remaining value is then divided by total miles or rail operated by the system in the state. Finally, this average value is multiplied by the total number of system miles in the county. The product is then taxed according to the tax rate of the local jurisdiction. Although there is some variation from industry to industry, this basic format is followed for all public utilities. Telephone companies' apportionment, for example, is based on the average value of lines per mile, pipeline companies by the average value of pipelines per mile, and airline companies by average air miles. Truck and bus lines are assessed on a cost basis.

Measures of Uniformity

There are two major administrative classes of assessed property in Utah. The first, state-assessed, represents about 20 percent of all taxable property in the state. It is assessed annually and value is determined on some measure of income. The second is locally assessed property, and while this property is the providence of the local tax assessor, the tax commission has played an important role in its assessment. Except for personal property, no locally assessed property has any current requirement for periodic revaluation. The value of locally assessed property is generally determined on the basis of cost.

In spite of the significant reductions in the required assessment level, a serious problem of underassessed property persists within the state. This condition, however, is not entirely the fault of local assessors. There is little evidence that the tax commission has really pushed for full market assessment—and considerable evidence that the tax commission pursued policies that established assessment at substantially below the level set by state law. In 1978, only one county was within 6 percent of the then legal 25 percent, and the next closest county was almost 5 full points below 20 percent. A total of nineteen counties were assessed below 10 percent. By 1980, only five of twenty-nine counties had moved within 1 percent of the legal level of 20 percent. From 1978 to 1980, the average assessed value in the state fell from 15 to 13 percent of market value.

The movement away from full market value would not be so serious if all property in the state were assessed at the same level. Unfortunately, there is a significant disparity in the level of assessment within the state—on both an intercounty and intracounty basis. In 1978, for example, the ratio of the assessment level of the highest assessed county to the assessment level of the lowest assessed county in the state was 3.4 to 1, but by 1980 this ratio had increased to 4.5. Intracounty coefficients of dispersion indicate that there are instances of substantial disparity in the assessment levels within some counties.

Fiscal Importance

Property-Tax Revenues

A review of property-tax expenditures gives an indication of the relative size of government activity within Utah. Education continues to be the largest single function of state and local government, using over 50 percent of all the property-tax revenue produced in the state. However, education's share of total property tax has been declining, as has the share spent by cities and towns. Much of the reduced importance of the property tax to cities and towns can be explained by the growth of a local-option sales tax. Evidence also indicates that the relative importance of the property tax to Utah counties and special districts has increased since 1960. During this period, their combined share of the local property tax has increased from 18 percent to just over 30 percent.

As one would expect, the gross yield of the property tax has increased substantially over the past two decades. On a per-capita basis, the property tax has also grown rapidly. When compared to increases in the consumer price index or to increases in the per-capita income level, however, the property tax has lost ground. In the past ten years, the proportion of the property tax paid by residential homeowners has increased by a relatively large percentage. At the same time, the percentage paid by agricultural, industrial, and commercial interests has declined. Much of this change can be accounted for by the strong demand for housing during the 1970s and the reappraisal program of the state, which brought the assessed value of homes closer to the assessment level of commercial and industrial properties.

In general, the property tax has slipped in importance to other taxes in the state. In 1960, the property tax represented over 40 percent of all taxes collected; in 1979 property-tax collections represented just over 25 percent of total taxes. During this same period, state and local sales taxes—as well as individual income taxes—increased substantially.

Cost of Administration

No data are routinely available or have been collected on the cost of property-tax administration in Utah. In the development of this chapter the appraiser from Weber County, the fourth most populous county in the state, and the assessor of Salt Lake County, the most populous, produced assessment costs per parcel as follows:

Weber County

Residential	$22.68
Commercial	$81.08
Agricultural and undeveloped	$ 9.73
Average	$37.26

Salt Lake County

Average	$67.00

If rural counties had been involved, the average probably would have been lower; nevertheless, the costs appear high, and no explanation for this fact is available. How much, if any, of these costs may have had their origin in the now-aborted reappraisal program is not clear.

Policy Framework

There are a number of groups and individuals working to improve the administration of the property tax in Utah. The Utah Association of County Assessors and the Utah Association of Counties have each played a role in improving the quality of administration. The Utah Association of Counties has been especially active in this area, and on several occasions they have pressed issues into the court system.

Other groups, such as the League of Women Voters, the Utah Foundation, and the Utah Taxpayers Association, have worked to improve property-tax administration. The league and the foundation try to provide balanced information and have not taken positions on many issues. The Utah Taxpayers Association, however, actively promotes or opposes many tax policies. For the most part, they push policies that could be described as beneficial to the business community. Nevertheless, they have been strong supporters of many policies to improve the overall administration of the property tax, including the reappraisal program.

The factoring program and the rollback of residential property to 80 percent of 1978 assessed value have been criticized by the Utah business community. They argue that such tax breaks should be extended to all property in the state, regardless of ownership and use. Several businesses are now preparing court challenges to this legislation. While the outcome of the litigation is not yet clear, the Utah Attorney General has cautioned county assessors to be ready for a so-called tax shock. Given time, more taxpayers will likely become concerned about the equity of the property tax.

The governor of Utah has also established a committee chaired by the chairman of the tax commission. This committee, the Governor's Tax Study Revision Commission, includes members from the executive and legislative branch, local government officials, and the business community. In the past, they have examined and made recommendations on property-tax-relief programs and funding of schools. They are examining the issue of state-assessed property currently. The Utah legislature also has a standing committee examining the overall issue of taxation in the state. There have been efforts to have this committee and the governor's committee jointly discuss areas of mutual concern.

16 The Role of the State in Property Taxation in Washington

Glenn R. Pascall

To preserve the property tax's role in our tax structure, we need to examine carefully the causes of the two nationwide property-tax revolts experienced during the last fifty years.

Several factors have contributed to these revolts, including the Depression, recessions, and rampant inflation of real-estate values, but the factors I plan to concentrate on in Washington are the following: the administration of the tax in general and assessment policies and procedures in particular; the overall level of property tax burden; limits on year-to-year increases; and, economic distortions resulting from property-tax policies.

If state and local tax administrators and state legislators can provide the proper balance in these four areas in the future, the property tax bill will continue to be a dependable and responsive source of support for those essential state and local programs that it has traditionally supported. On the other hand, if any one of these factors is not properly controlled, I believe we will see the further decline, and the possible demise, of this revenue source.

Legal Framework

In Washington state, property taxes were the dominant revenue source from statehood (1889) to the early 1930s. During that period, there were no tax limitations or any other important state and local tax. Government services expanded and the property-tax burden rapidly increased in this era, peaking at a 3-percent effective rate in the late 1920s. By comparison, California was at 2.7 percent when Proposition 13 passed in June 1978, and in the Boston area effective rates were as high as 8 percent (a nationwide high) when voters approved Proposition 2 1/2.

During the decade of the Depression, total revenue from property taxes in Washington fell by half. This deficit forced enactment of the sales tax, and the voters approved an income tax (but it was stricken down by the state supreme court).

During the Depression, a constitutional limit was set on regular tax levies at 2 percent of value, dropping the rate by about one third and by the early 1950s the effective rate was down to 1 percent.

The pendulum began swinging the other way in the 1950s. In 1955, the legislature passed a revaluation act in an attempt to capture tax-base growth, to improve the quality of assessments, and to distribute the burden equitably. The act increased state supervision, and it required on-site appraisals every four years.

The mid-1950s were also a period during which the ratio between school-age population and taxpaying population dramatically changed—a rapid expansion in school enrollments forced increased use of locally voted *special levies*, which caused the property tax burden to rise dramatically once again.

Legislative budget politics in the 1960s forced further growth in special levies because the state did not fund a stable ratio of the growth in school costs. Then in 1969, the legislature appropriated funds for a program to revalue all property in the state. A "good government" argument for quality administration squared with a pressing need for revenue.

The state revaluation program succeeded in bringing about much-needed uniformity. But the lack of effective limits produced dramatic changes, since there was no limit on annual increases. In 1980, for example, the value of property in Washington increased 24 percent. Even if new construction is excluded, this increase amounts to an average of 20 percent per parcel.

A second major property-tax revolt was in full swing by 1970. In 1972, the voters enacted a 1-percent constitutional limit—nearly six years prior to Proposition 13. Other rate reductions were enacted by the legislature, lowering the rate to about .9 percent by allocating fixed shares to different levels of local government. A very effective annual-increase-limit law was imposed. It operates differently from Proposition 13, which limits assessed values to 1975 levels plus 2 percent a year until the property is sold. The Washington law limits to 6 percent the total amount of additional dollars that any unit of government can collect each year from taxes on existing property.

The impact of property taxation was further softened by a state supreme court decision that declared that the use of locally approved property taxes for basic education was unconstitutional. This was not a *Serrano*-type decision, arguing that differences in local tax wealth should not be the basis for potential differences in the quality of education. Rather, the decision was entirely based on a constitutional provision requiring the state to "support basic education." Special levies were sharply reduced and replacement funding was absorbed by the state without creation of new revenues.

In Washington, the voters adopted a constitutional amendment permitting low-income relief only for senior citizens. Consequently, there are bills before the legislature each year to provide expanded reduction for senior-citizen property taxes up to the average family income level in the state, and no relief for low- to middle-income working families. The focus of our relief program is strictly age-based and not income-based, which leads to a property-tax overburden for those who might qualify on an *equity* basis.

Broadened eligibility requirements, increased income levels, and relief limits were enacted by the 1979 legislature. The number of participants (105,127) and amount of property-tax relief for senior citizens ($18,392,355) attained new highs. The expanded eligibility criteria lowered the claim-filing age to sixty-one years (fifty-seven for a surviving spouse), permitted life estates, and included cotenants as owners. The income limits for complete special-levy relief were increased to $11,000 and to $7,000 for a regular-levy exemption of $15,000 property value.

Total participation in 1980 increased by 17.5 percent from 1979, and the amount of relief increased 36.4 percent. The amount of regular-levy relief increased by 189.4 percent and the number of applicants increased by 13.2 percent. The increased relief from the regular levy resulted from a $1,000 increase in the income level and a tripling of the regular-levy-value exemption. The average value exempted from regular levies was $12,554, with a per-capita tax relief of $119. Regular-levy relief represented 53 percent of the total compared with 24 percent in 1979.

Special-levy relief was $8,638,626, down 14.6 percent. The phase in of full state funding for basic education (lowering special levies) was the significant factor in this reduction, in spite of the higher income levels and greater participation. The average value exempted was $20,818, and the average relief was $82.

Washington also has a senior-citizen tax-deferral program—but with only 112 participants. The reason, according to the leader of a senior-citizens lobby, is that "for people of my age, the happiest day of their lives was the day they burned their mortgage." In other words, older citizens don't like the idea of a lien on their property, so they won't take a deferral. I can certainly understand that feeling, but many younger homeowners may never burn their mortgage.

The 1970 legislature enacted statutes that resulted in reduced assessments on certain lands. The Open Space Taxation Act was enacted by the 1973 legislature, permitting these lands to be valued on the assessment rolls at current use rather than highest and best use.

To receive the reduced assessment, farm or agricultural land must meet acreage and/or gross-income requirements. Local five-person advisory boards assist the assessors in determining current-use value for the different types of farm and agricultural lands. They take into consideration lease contracts or productive capacity for different types of lands in their areas. The assessors annually estimate a true and fair value for the lands *separate* from current-use status. The property owner is liable for a maximum of seven years' compensation taxes based on the yearly difference between current-use and fair-market-value estimates, plus interest and penalties if removed from open-space status within ten years.

Of the current-use value on the rolls for taxes due in 1980, 98.5 percent was farm and agricultural, 0.3 percent was timber, and 1.2 percent was open space.

The program has a serious defect. It always fails on the urban fringe, which is the only area where current-use taxation is really justified as a concept. The penalties are not strict enough to deter sales to developers. As a result, we are protecting not the sincere agriculturist but rather those who hold speculative land for a high price that fully justifies paying the penalties.

Administration

We have observed great swings in the property-tax pendulum. Obviously there are a number of factors that are beyond the control of state legislators and tax administrators. Depressions and recessions limit people's ability to pay, and help create tax revolts. Demographic factors can alter dramatically the ratio between tax payers and tax-supported basic services. Unchecked real-estate inflation is a factor that may be distantly related to government deficits, but it is not a factor we can control directly.

There are other elements over which legislators and tax administrators have much greater control. One is inconsistent and irregular revaluation efforts. Washington law requires that one-fourth of the county be appraised every year. In the affected area, an assessor puts four years of value growth in the current year. Currently this means that the assessment of the average residence is increased 30 percent. One assessor in our state is habitually poised to run for some higher office on a platform of property-tax relief to correct the very situation he is legally required to oversee as assessor.

The five-year history of residential taxes in Seattle is most interesting. The average home had an annual property-tax increase for 1977 to 1981 of 4.5 percent a year, at a time when the inflation rate was at least double that level and the real-estate inflation rate was roughly four times as high. During two of those five years, the tax actually dropped in absolute dollars because of massive state relief on local special levies. Yet when the one-year increase becomes current political reality, people forget the relief they received in prior years.

Irregular and inconsistent revaluation efforts are something we can and should correct. They can have dramatic political consequences if not properly controlled.

Another thing we can do is provide a reasonable limit on year-to-year growth in property taxes. You will recall that in California, before Proposition 13, they had tax *rate* controls. What they did not have was a requirement that tax rates be reduced in equal proportion to value increases. Tax-rate controls are extremely effective in the absence of real-estate inflation.

But with real-estate inflation they failed to protect homeowners, and California adopted the Proposition 13 value freeze with all its mischievous consequences. The Pomona city manager gave me an example of a street of identical homes in his city. The value freeze, you will recall, is lifted when property is sold, but is otherwise capped at 2 percent a year if it is not sold. One homeowner on that street pays $860 a year, and another homeowner of similar property pays $3,600 a year—more than a four-fold gap in property tax.

We can also work to prevent the effective rate from exceeding an acceptable level. When there is an 8-percent effective rate in Boston, for example, and it is reduced to 2.5 percent, you think of an enormous revenue crunch. But in the state of Washington, if the property tax went to 2.5 percent it would be three times the present level—and we would have a revolution on our hands. An acceptable level, therefore, has more to do with people's perceptions and the rate of change than with an absolute level. In California, it was the *rate* of change that was so unsettling.

Another problem is permitting property-tax overburdens to cause social or economic distortions. This statement simply means that even if you are a defender of the property tax, as I am, you've got to recognize the need for low-income relief in certain situations.

The Washington experience has indicated that from 1 percent to 3 percent of properties revalued annually are appealed to local boards of equalization. The political viability of the property tax would be enhanced if, whenever a revaluation notice goes out, it clearly stated the fact that the higher property value will not translate into a tax increase of equal magnitude. The form should explain how tax lids work in as simple terms as possible.

Appeals procedures must be easily understood and have the appearance of fairness. Appeals boards should be composed of residents of the county not involved in the taxing process but possessing a basic knowledge of property valuation. It is not always easy to find people with professional knowledge who are not professionally employed as public officials, but it is possible.

About 5 to 10 percent of appeals to local equalization boards eventually find their way to the State Board of Tax Appeals. The board hears about one thousand property-tax appeals per year, ruling either partially or totally in favor of the taxpayer in about 40 percent of the appeals.

We do not intervene in an individual appeal unless it relates to our assessment-ratio study. We have the responsibility to make sample appraisals to provide ratios between assessed value and market value—partly for apportionment purposes and partly for local adjustment purposes. We also make advisory appraisals on certain commercial and industrial properties in about one-third of the counties. If an appeal to the board involves one of our advisory appraisals, or has a crucial bearing on our ratio study, we would probably participate in the case. Otherwise, it would be between the taxpayer and the assessor.

Each year our staff makes a number of advisory appraisals of large commercial and industrial properties. In 1980, we provided such assistance in fifteen counties and valued properties worth well over $300 million. This figure is exclusive of the $4.2 billion in utility values for which the state is responsible.

We have authority to issue regulations governing the practices of county assessors and their staff. The boundaries of state supervision are not always clear. For example, we have been negotiating complex legislation with the assessors on ratio studies. There are disagreements on how the study concept is applied. A state constitutional provision that the state cannot levy a local tax for use by a local government has been interpreted to mean that we have no power to adjust individual parcel values. We are restricted to adjusting the total county property value through use of the ratio study. In the bill, we were trying to move restrictive language into a limited section.

Marshalling support behind effective tax administration is not easy. Even though the department collects 120 times as much money as it costs it to operate, the legislature may look only at the spending side of the tax-administration budget. Take the example of tax auditors who review the books of companies headquartered out of the state of Washington. These corporations fail more frequently than in-state firms to pay their business and occupations tax, so such auditors are very productive. They cost an average of $40,000 a year in salaries and expenses, but bring in $1 million each as an average. We have only eleven of these people and are unable to fund more.

If the department was a private company, it would hire another dozen auditors to see what would happen. The cost-benefit ratio would appear to support such an approach. But to sell that idea to the legislature is hard. Recently, a supplemental budget request of $425,000 was made for the last portion of the two-year budget period. The outgoing governor's budget office was under orders to come up with a tight budget, and the request was arbitrarily reduced to $275,000. The legislature, after much lobbying, was finally persuaded that the amount of revenue loss created by the cut would have been well over $1 million, and the cut was restored.

17

The Supervisory Role of the State in Property Taxation in Wisconsin

Glenn L. Holmes

The number and mixture of governmental units responsible for assessing and/or taxing the various classes of property in Wisconsin is most likely unique among the states. There are 1,848 municipalities, 72 counties, approximately 250 school districts, and numerous sanitary and lake rehabilitation districts—all with the authority to tax certain real and personal property. This description certainly fits the definition of a multijurisdictional setting.

Public-utility property is assessed by the State Department of Revenue. Residential, commercial, and agricultural classes of property are assessed and taxed at the municipal level of government, with the exception of one county that has established a county-wide assessment system. Under the county-wide assessment system, the state pays 75 percent of the annual operating costs. In 1974, the Department of Revenue assumed the assessment of all manufacturing property in the state, with the local jurisdictions retaining the responsibility for levying and collecting the tax.

There has been a recent reduction in the number of assessors in the state. Since 1976, a type of *quasi-assessment jurisdiction* has emerged. Research done by Professor Richard Stauber of the University of Wisconsin identified 303 multidistrict assessors. Wisconsin's municipalities are each required to have an assessor for the purpose of establishing the assessed value of all taxable residential, commercial, and agricultural property. The term *multidistrict assessor* refers to a person or firm appointed to serve as the assessor for more than one municipality. As can be seen from tables 17-1 and 17-2, this de facto consolidation has, in effect, reduced the number of assessment jurisdictions at the municipal level from over 1,800 to 1,225. Over two hundred municipalities share their assessors with another municipality, and over one hundred share their assessors with two or more municipalities.

Property Valuation

Property valuation in Wisconsin—as might be expected with the large number of assessment jurisdictions—varies from poor to very good.

Printed by permission of the International Association of Assessing Officers (IAAO) and the author. This chapter was originally presented at the 1981 IAAO Washington Forum.

Table 17-1
Multidistrict Assessors in Wisconsin, 1978 Summary

Tax Districts	Share Assessor	Assessor Not Shared	Total	Percentage Sharing
Towns	628	641	1269	49.5
Villages	228	164	392	58.2
Cities	60	127	187	32.1
All districts	916	932	1848	49.6

Note: There were 303 Multidistrict assessors in Wisconsin in 1978.

Wisconsin law requires all property to be assessed at market value. There is no state authority to assure compliance with this requirement, and court cases have held that assessments made at some fraction of market value are permissible so long as all property within a municipality is assessed at the same fraction. As a result, assessment levels in municipalities vary from a low of 5 percent to a high of 135 percent.

As shown in table 17-3 when the assessed value of all taxable real estate is compared to the equalized value determined by the Department of Revenue, property was, on the average, valued at approximately 58 percent

Table 17-2
Assessors in Wisconsin by Number of Districts Valued, 1978

Assessors Who Valued:	Assessors		Municipalities	
	Number	Percentage of Total	Number	Percentage of Total
One municipality only	932	76.1	932	50.4
Two municipalities	201	16.4	402	21.7
Three municipalities	50	4.1	150	8.1
Four municipalities	19	1.6	76	4.1
Five municipalities	13	1.1	65	3.5
Six municipalities	4	—	24	1.3
Eight municipalities	4	—	32	1.7
Nine municipalities	1	—	9	—
Ten municipalities	3	—	30	1.6
Eleven municipalities	2	—	22	1.2
Twelve municipalities	2	—	24	1.3
Fourteen municipalities	2	—	28	1.5
Sixteen municipalities	1	—	16	—
Thirty-eight municipalities	1	—	38	2.1
Totals	1,225	100%	1,848	100%

Table 17-3

Overall Level of Assessment by Class of Property, Wisconsin, 1979

Class	Assessment Value	Equalized Value	Level of Assessment
Residential	$31,399,607,094	$54,002,039,900	58.1%
Commercial	8,662,913,003	12,886,684,500	67.2
Manufacturing	2,566,859,400	4,263,368,400	60.2
Agricultural[a]	8,285,868,567	17,018,162,900	48.6
Total	$50,915,248,064	$88,170,255,700	57.7%

[a]Includes open land, forest, and waste land.

of market value in 1979. A comparison of the level of assessment by major class of property indicates a spread of almost 20 percentage points between commercial property, assessed at 67 percent, and agricultural, forest, and waste, assessed at approximately 49 percent.

A study of assessment performance measured by an assessment-sales ratio analysis indicates an overall coefficient of dispersion of 22 for the state in 1979. A similar study using 1971 data had indicated an overall coefficient of dispersion of 30. This significant reduction in dispersion levels is evidence of an improvement in the quality of assessment statewide.

The uniformity of valuation and taxation required by Wisconsin's Constitution has been preserved generally. Constitutional amendments have allowed different treatment for certain classes of property, such as woodland and open land, but this end generally has been accomplished through direct tax relief in the form of credits, rather than by prescribed assessment levels for different classes of property. This combination— where property under municipal jurisdiction varies in assessment level from one community to the other, coupled with the requirement that all property must be taxed uniformly—creates the need for some additional steps in the valuation and taxation of property under state jurisdiction.

The real and personal property of public-utility companies, including all rights, franchises, and privileges, is valued as a unit at fair market value. The average rate of taxation on other property is determined by the Department of Revenue and is used to compute the tax due on the value of the utility. This approach insures that utilities are taxed uniformly with other property in the state.

Manufacturing property is valued at fair market value, with any objections to that value resolved by the Wisconsin Tax Appeals Commission. Since this type of property is valued by the state, but taxed at the local governmental level, it is necessary to change the value to the same level of market value that the department has determined that the locally valued property is assessed. This process can result in the market value established by the department being adjusted up or down, since some communities in certain years will have property valued higher than the market or equalized value established by the state.

Supervisory Agency

The Department of Revenue is the agency charged by law to supervise assessments in the state to insure equity and uniformity. The Department's effort to carry out this supervisory assignment falls into four general areas: (1) the establishment of equalized values; (2) the development, implementation, and measurement of statewide assessment standards; (3) assessor training; and, (4) direct assistance or service to local units of government.

Equalization

Equalization is the annual establishment of the market value of all taxable general property in each town, village, and city in the state for seven classes of real estate and six classes of personal property. It is necessary to know the value of taxable property in the state and its subdivisions to administer a wide variety of provisions in the Wisconsin Statutes. Some of the major statutory provisions for the use of these values include:

> *Apportionment of Certain Property-Tax Levies.* A number of tax jurisdictions contain more than one municipality. Examples include counties, many school districts, and all vocational, technical, and adult education districts. Property-tax levies of such jurisdictions are apportioned to each municipality on the basis of equalized value. For example, if a municipality on the basis of equalized value contains 10 percent of the taxable value within a county, its residents should pay 10 percent of the county property taxes levied. If the same community contained 30 percent of the taxable value in a school district, its share of the school-tax levy would be 30 percent.

> *Allocation of State Aid to Local Government.* The distribution of money to local governments under several state programs is determined in part by formulas that examine the relative need for state aid in a given jurisdiction, based partly upon the equalized value of taxable property in the jurisdiction. Major programs that rely on the use of equalized value in determining aid distributions include the school-aid formula, VTAE aids, the general property-tax-relief formula, and the aidable-revenues formula within the shared-revenue account.

Calculation of Allowable Municipal and County Levies. Under the levy-limit program, operating levies of county and municipal governments cannot increase at a rate greater than the percentage of growth in the state-equalized value of taxable property.

Calculation of Allowable Debt. The amount of debt certain local governments can incur is limited to fixed percentages of equalized value. Municipalities may not incur debt in excess of 5 percent of their equalized value. Certain school districts have debt limits of 10 percent of the equalized value. Counties, like municipalities, have 5-percent limits.

Determination of Assessed Value of Manufacturing Property for Tax Purposes. Municipalities assess property for tax purposes at different percentages of market value. Each community's assessment percentage is multiplied by the state-established market value of manufacturing property to determine the local assessed value of such property. For example, if a municipality is assessing property at 50 percent of market value, the state's established market-value assessment would be reduced to that level.

Various work methods are employed to achieve the goal of equalization. Generally they can be categorized as sales analysis and property appraisal.

Sales Analysis. Sales are analyzed through two principal methods: market-assessment ratio studies, and unit-value projections. Market-assessment studies compare actual selling prices of bona fide market sales with the locally established assessment of the property sold. The results of these comparisons are then analyzed statistically and used to develop an equalized value, if sufficient sales have occurred within a municipality. Annually, these market-assessment studies include the review of approximately 180,000 real-estate transactions. Unit-value projections involve the development of unit values such as the value per acre sold. These values are then multiplied by the number of units to obtain an indicated market value to be used as a guide in establishing the equalized value.

Sample Appraisals. Sample appraisals are used by the department when the sales-analysis techniques are insufficient to estimate market value. This method involves a randomly selected sample of similar properties to be appraised in detail. The value indicated by the appraisal is compared to the locally assessed value to develop a ratio of assessment to appraised value. The information gained from this analysis is used as a guide in valuing the entire class.

Depending on the type of property and the uniformity of local assessments, any or all approaches to value estimation may be used to establish the equalized value of a particular class within a given municipality.

In addition to this information, local assessors are required to report all changes in property values due to a variety of causes, such as annexation or detachment, new construction, revaluations, or changes in assessment level on property formerly exempt but now assessed. These additions or subtractions are made to the previous year's equalized value, after analysis of the assessor's final report. After the local board of review has met and finalized the local assessment for a particular year, the local clerk is required to report the assessment of property to the department. This report is compared to the assessor's report for any changes made by the board of review. Any required changes are made to the equalized value by the Department of Revenue.

The equalized value of personal property is established each year from various sources of information. Personal property such as furniture, fixtures, machinery, tools, and patterns are difficult to equalize and require periodic sample surveys of the fixed-asset accounts from the income-tax return or from information received directly from the taxpayer.

Using one or more of the techniques described for the development of value, the department estimates the market value of each class of real estate and personal property in each municipality in the state. The municipal totals become the state equalized value.

Statewide Assessment Standards

The number and quality of assessment standards developed by the state has increased steadily in the past fifteen years. In 1965, the Department of Revenue issued the first edition of the *Wisconsin Property Assessment Manual*. As an indication of the growth in the number of standards now available, the manual has grown to three volumes: Volume 1 establishes practices and procedures and explains assessment law; volumes 2 and 3 are basically cost manuals updated every five years. These manuals must be used by Wisconsin assessors.

The state prescribes and/or approves all forms used in the assessment process. Mapping standards have been developed but are not mandatory. Since 1977, all assessment personnel must pass an examination administered by the Department of Revenue to become certified Wisconsin assessors. Individuals must be certified at the appropriate level—as determined by the department—to be elected or appointed to assessor positions. Periodic recertification is required and can be obtained by either re-examination or meeting continuing-education requirements.

Assessor Training

Training is provided assessors by department personnel at an annual training session conducted in each county. In addition, the Department of Revenue, in cooperation with the Wisconsin Association of Assessing Officers and the State Vocational Training System, provides ongoing training in valuation and assessment administration. Courses developed by the Department of Revenue and the International Association of Assessing Officers (IAAO) are presented by certified instructors through the state's vocational and adult training schools. Special courses are developed and presented as needs are recognized.

Service to Local Government

Services provided to local assessors by the state have also increased during the past few years. The state currently provides data-processing programs in valuation, assessment, and tax collection to municipalities. These programs were developed at state expense and are given to local governmental units free of charge. This service could also be considered an assessment standard since the valuation programs are state-of-the-art and as such provide uniform and equitable valuations at market value.

Assessment of manufacturing property by the state reduced the need for direct state assistance to local assessors in appraising complex properties. In the course of its normal work, the Department of Revenue does not make appraisals of individual properties for assessment purposes on other classes of property but does advise local assessors on the appraisal of other complex property upon request.

Revaluation of property is primarily the responsibility of municipalities in Wisconsin. There is no statewide requirement that revaluations be performed at any particular interval, but in practice they occur on an average of once every ten years. Whenever a municipality recognizes a need for revaluation, the usual procedure is to furnish the assessor with assistance by contracting with a mass-appraisal firm to complete the review of all property within one year. The state does become involved if, in the absence of municipal governmental action, taxpayers owning 5 percent or more of the property in the municipality petition for reassessment. Usually when this petitioning occurs, the department orders a revaluation and hires a mass-appraisal firm to do the job under direct state supervision.

The state performs annual sales-ratio studies for all classes of property where sufficient sales data exists. These ratios are an important tool used by the Department of Revenue in establishing the equalized values. To date, the results of these studies have been shared with local assessors but have not been published. Publication will begin in 1981.

Consultation in any area of property-tax assessment is furnished through the Department of Revenue's seven district offices, upon request by a local assessor. Areas most often discussed include determination of exemption; special-valuation problems; forms design; recruitment and training of personnel; and assessment appeals.

One of the most direct impacts of the state's supervisory role is its statutory duty to review and report on local assessment practices once every six years. In one form or another, the department has been making reports available to local units of government for several years. The results and recommendations from these reviews are advisory only. Until a recent change in the format, these reports received little attention or action. A little more than a year ago, the department devised a report format that included a criteria for evaluation of local assessment practices. The criteria includes eight major elements and is very similar to the ten components of an effective assessment system described and recommended by the IAAO. The criteria presently in use is as follows:

1. *Overall Assessment Level (0-6 points)*. The points are assigned as follows. Overall level of assessment of:

115 to 85 = 6 points

130 to 70 = 4 points

145 to 55 = 2 points

All other = 0 points

This is to recognize the relationship of level of assessment to quality of assessment. It has been determined that the higher the level of assessment, the better the uniformity of assessment. The inclusion of the concept of a range (that is, 115-85) is in keeping with the Department of Revenue's position that value for assessment purposes is an estimate.

2. *Uniformity between Classes (0-6 points)*. The spread between classes of property must not be greater than 10 percent. A class of property must represent at least 5 percent of all property in the municipality (based upon the department's equalized values) to be considered in determining if this criterion has been met. The ratio for each class of property must be divided by the overall property ratio before determining whether the spread between classes is 10 percent or less.

The assignment of points is as follows:

0 to 10 percent   = 6 points

11 to 15 percent   = 4 points

16 to 20 percent   = 2 points

21 percent and beyond = 0 points

3. *Uniformity within a Class of Property (0-6 points)*. To measure uniformity within a class of property, the coefficient of dispersion derived from an assessment-sales ratio study is used. Uniformity is considered for the major class of property in the municipality, except where there are two classes of property each having significant value. There must be at least 20 vacant and improved (total) sales, or 20 sample appraisals included in an assessment-sales or assessment-appraisal ratio study. Zero points are assigned for coefficients of dispersion above 20; 3 points for dispersions lying within 12.5 to 20; and 6 points for a dispersion of less than 12.5. In the absence of sufficient sales or sample appraisals for the major class of property, 3 points are assigned. In those cases where there are two classes of property that represent most of the value in the municipality, the following point system for each of the studies performed is used: 0 points for a coefficient of dispersion above 20; 1.5 points for a coefficient of dispersion between 12.5 and 20; and 3 points for a dispersion of less than 12.5.

4. *Property-Record Cards (0-6 points)*. Zero represents no property-record cards; 6 points are assigned for municipalities with a set of up-to-date property-record cards completed in accordance with the assessment manual. Point values may be assigned between 0 and 6, depending on the quality and completion of the records.

5. *Land versus Improvements (0-6 points)*. The variance between the aggregate ratio of all classes of land versus the aggregate ratio of all classes of improvements should not exceed 10 percent. These ratios must be divided by the overall ratio to determine if there is a variance of 10 percent or less between land and improvements.

The assignment of points is as follows:

0 to 10 percent	= 6 points
11 to 15 percent	= 4 points
16 to 20 percent	= 2 points
21 percent and beyond	= 0 points

6. *Maps, Aerial Photos, Soil Surveys (0-3 points)*. Zero points are assigned if the assessor has inadequate maps for use in locating, classifying, and grading the properties to be appraised. Three points are assigned if the assessor has a complete set of current and appropriate maps for the specific municipality. Point values may be assigned between 0 and 3 depending upon how current and complete the maps are.

7. *Board of Review and Subsequent Appeals (0 or 3 points)*. Zero points are assigned in those cases where at least 2 percent of the total parcels in a municipality are appealed to the board of review or if the department receives appeals indicating extensive inequities in assessments. Three points are assigned if less than 2 percent of the total parcels in the municipality are appealed to the board of review or if there are no appeals to the department.

8. *Improvements to the Overall Quality of the Assessments (0-4 points).*
Zero points represent minimal qualifications on the part of the assessor and
minimal effort by the assessor or municipality to improve the quality of the
assessments. Four points would represent the reverse situation. Point values
may be assigned between 0 and 4, depending on the attempts made in recent
years by both the assessor and municipality to improve assessments. Elements for consideration include the following:

Assessor	*Municipality*
Continuing education	Adequate budget for assessor's
Appraisal-assessment	office
designations	Monies for revaluation
Annual market analysis	Resources for modernization of
Maintenance of assessments	appraisal systems
Effective cost-market-income	Public-relations relative to
approach to value	assessment function (that is,
Compliance with reporting	annual notice to taxpayers)
systems to state agencies	

A perfect total score would be 40. The present procedure calls for
multiplying the total score by 2.5 to produce a ranking based on a 100-point
scale. This criteria-and-ranking system is currently being reviewed with the
Wisconsin Association of Assessing Officers. The association and the
department have already agreed that areas particularly in need of improvements include items 7 and 8.

From the foregoing, it can be concluded that in Wisconsin the state's
supervisory role in the property tax is at a moderate level. The state is strong
in its support and assistance to local government but has little authority to
force compliance with good assessment practices. The modest gains in the
quality of the valuation of property made during the past few years are due
to the availability of better tools, including automated assessment systems
and mandatory state certification of assessors. At the present time, the
automation occurring in the more urban areas of the state, where full-time
professional assessors are doing a good job, is providing them with the
ability to adjust the value of property annually, resulting in more equitable
assessments. Mandatory certification of assessors has encouraged in many
cases, and required in some, a consolidation of assessment jurisdictions that
is large enough to support at least one professional appraiser. This consolidation has yielded a corresponding improvement in assessments. The
Wisconsin legislature has in recent sessions considered numerous proposals
on consolidation of jurisdictions. However, no major legislation has been
enacted. Local control is valued in Wisconsin, to which movement of the

assessment of property away from the municipal level is considered a threat. Nevertheless, if the Department of Revenue is able to continue its support by furnishing better tools and standards, additional automation and consolidation will occur in Wisconsin—with corresponding improvements in valuation.

18 Conclusions and Recommendations

H. Clyde Reeves

The consensus of the Tax Policy Roundtable is that the property tax has served extraordinarily well as a primary source of local revenue. It serves well as the workhorse for local-government funding and impressively as the instrument for balancing local budgets. Prospects are good that the property tax can and will maintain these characteristics. Most members believe the tax will remain the most substantial source of local revenue, though its relative importance might decline.

Many faults of the property tax are charged with political energy. The upshot of the Roundtable's deliberating is that its faults should be addressed and changed rather than strain at the improbability of finding a replacement revenue source as well suited to local use. The pressure on the property tax is not viewed with alarm, indeed many of the changes in the property tax have made it a better instrument of public policy.

Some members believe the so-called property-tax revolt is caused largely by the load the tax carries in financing state and local government ($73 of $240 billion in 1981); others attribute it to inflated taxable values without compensating reductions in tax rates. These two views may constitute distinctions without a difference. All agreee that lack of diversity in the local-government tax systems and the current disenchantment with government contributes to public dissatisfaction with the property tax. Most Roundtable members feel that state and local government share a responsibility to protect the integrity and usefulness of the property tax by endeavoring to improve its equity, certainty (predictability), and convenience of payment.

The Roundtable urges that high priority be given to evaluating and implementing suggestions for fostering a better understanding of how the property tax works. Principal among objectives should be efforts to separate in the public's mind the technical function of assessment from the political function of levy determination—that is, the total funds required by a local government that result in the tax rate. The Roundtable is persuaded that too often assessors have been saddled with the responsibility of determining values that, when multiplied by a fixed rate, will obtain an increase in funds for local government. The legislature body that consciously attempts to reap a revenue windfall by encouraging or demanding assessment changes without a change of tax rate risks the credibility of the assessment process.

189

While state law establishes the legal framework for the local property tax, state interest has grown in recent years in three areas of concern: (1) rate, levy, and expenditure limitations; (2) relief and incentive measures; and (3) assessment standards and practices.

Rate, Levy, and Expenditure Limitations

Rate limitations are viewed generally as being ineffective in protecting the taxpayer from unanticipated tax increases during times of sharply rising property values. Expenditure limitations are a means of curtailing the level of government operations but are inappropriate when property assessment or tax-equity objectives are the primary concern. Members of the Roundtable hold diverse views about levy limitation (state statutory or constitutional restriction of the total annual levy of the taxing jurisdiction to a percentage, such as 110 percent, of the levy for the prior year plus the levy from additions to the tax roll). Members concur, however, that (a) tax-levying authorities should be required to publicize and hold public hearings where any substantial levy increase is under consideration—after the manner of the truth-in-taxation Florida requirement, and (b) if levy limitation is deemed necessary statutory, rather than constitutional, provisions are preferable.

Relief and Incentive Measures

Generally, homestead exemptions, exemptions for the elderly and veterans, use-value assessments (as for agricultural property), and the exemption of industrial property are seriously defective in accomplishing their presumed intentions and may misallocate economic resources. Each of these kinds of relief or incentive measures shifts the tax burden from one set of individuals to another and not infrequently calls forth another measure of relief or incentive. The Roundtable consensus is that too many nonrevenue objectives have already been introduced into the property tax and that state policymakers should endeavor to prevent the expansion of property-tax relief and incentive measures. Nevertheless, members recognize the strong political support for such measures and suggest that if such measures are inevitable they first should be optional with the local taxing jurisdiction, or secondarily the state reimburse local jurisdiction for any revenue loss. For genuine individual difficulties in meeting property-tax obligations—such as may be the case with farmers, or when age or means tests are applicable—deferred payment of taxes, with reasonable interest charges, stands out as a humane and equitable solution over outright tax forgiveness.

Assessment Standards and Practice

Fractional assessments are viewed as an obscuration of the market or true-value concept that undergirds the fair and equitable administration of the property tax. Members firmly believe that the objective should be to (a) assess all property at its current value, and that (b) if for tax-burden purposes, classification of property is desired, the classification should be made in the rate rather than in the assessment.

The Roundtable is convinced that current technologies now enable the annual revaluation of all property. Members believe annual revaluation would be very desirable and (c) annual revaluation should be implemented promptly with the availability of computer assistance, unless less-frequent revaluation is working satisfactorily.

Responsibility of the state to assess utilities, railroads, and other unitary interjurisdictional property directly is unquestioned. In addition, the Roundtable is convinced that states should: (d) provide local assessors with assistance in assessing large and complex properties and with manuals and guidelines for use in more routine assessment analysis; (e) establish an organizational framework, including financial help with consolidation or merger of assessment districts, to lead to assessment jurisdictions of sufficient size to allow the use of full-time professional personnel and cost-effective utilization of equipment such as maps, computers, and word-processors; (f) encourage the use of appropriate modern equipment by local assessors, monitor its maintenance, and share its cost; and (g) establish qualifications for assessment personnel and enhance the capabilities of existing assessment personnel by providing continuing educational opportunity.

Centralizing the assessment function—the technical valuing process—at the state or provincial level, while maintaining local review and levy functions, may promise cost-effective and more uniform and equitable values without impinging on prerogatives perceived to be local. Maryland and British Columbia represent two models worthy of continued observation.

About the Contributors

Robert H. Allphin is an attorney with offices in Louisville and Warsaw, Kentucky. He received the J.D. from the University of Kentucky in 1949 and was admitted to the United States Supreme Court in 1954. He has served as Kentucky commissioner of revenue (twice), Illinois director of revenue, consultant to secretary of revenue of Pennsylvania, and corporate tax manager for PPG Industries, Inc. His published articles cover a wide range of state and local tax-action topics.

Lyle H. Ask is director of the Property Equalization Division, State of Minnesota, Department of Revenue. He attended Winona State University and the University of Minnesota. He was appointed Houston County, Minnesota, assessor in 1959 and served in that capacity until 1970 when he accepted a position with the Minnesota Department of Revenue. He serves on the IAAO Assessment Standards Committee, has held various offices and committee appointments for the Minnesota Association of Assessing Officers, as well as the Minnesota Chapter of the IAAO, and is a member of the Minnesota State Board of Assessors.

Virgil O. Barnard is the deputy commissioner of the Department of Property Taxation in the Commonwealth of Kentucky. He has been employed by the Revenue Cabinet in various capacities relating to property tax administration since November of 1976. Mr. Barnard received the M.B.A. from the University of Kentucky and the B.S. in commerce from Washington and Lee University.

John H. Bowman is associate professor of economics at Virginia Commonwealth University. His publications include papers on various aspects of property taxation in the *National Tax Journal, American Journal of Economics and Sociology, Public Administration Review*, and *State and Local Government Review*. He received the Ph.D. from The Ohio State University.

Gene L. Burner is director of the Maryland State Department of Assessments and Taxation, where he is responsible for the assessment process for each of the twenty-four jurisdictions in Maryland. He also has served as fiscal advisor to the Maryland General Assembly Fiscal Committees. He received the M.B.A. from George Washington University.

Lyle W. Clark is a graduate of Washburn University, Topeka. He was a public-school administrator for ten years and has been an administrator in the Division of Property Valuation, Kansas Department of Revenue, for the past eighteen years. He has served on state, national, and international committees in various capacities and has spoken before many groups on varied property-valuation and taxation topics.

Gary C. Cornia is assistant professor of public management at Brigham Young University. He received the M.S. in economics from Utah State University and the Ph.D. from The Ohio State University. His published works include articles on state and local economic development, property taxation, sales taxation, and the budget process of local governments.

J. Henry Ditmars is a licensed professional engineer and land surveyor. He has been engaged in the field of taxation for New Jersey since 1947. He was superintendent of the Local Property and Public Utility Branch of the Division of Taxation, 1972-1982.

Seth L. Franzman is assessment standards manager in the Division of Property and Special Taxes, Arizona Department of Revenue. He earned the B.S.B.A. from the University of Denver in 1960 and the M.B.A. from Arizona State University in 1965. He has completed additional graduate studies at the University of Birmingham, England, as a Rotary Foundation Fellow, and has been employed by the state of Arizona since 1965 in various phases of property-tax administration.

David Gaskell is executive director of the New York State Board of Equalization and Assessment in Albany. He received the B.A. from Amherst College and the M.B.A. from Cornell University. He has held a number of positions in New York State government, including positions with the Department of Audit and Control, the Temporary Commission on State-Local Fiscal Relations, the Division of the Budget, the Ways and Means Committee of the State Legislature, and the Department of Social Services.

Steven D. Gold is director of Intergovernmental Finance Project of the National Conference of State Legislature. Before joining NCSL in 1981, he had been professor of economics at Drake University. He received the B.A. from Bucknell University and the Ph.D. from the University of Michigan. He has written numerous articles and books on state and local government finance. Among the books are *Property Tax Relief* (Lexington Books, 1979) and *State Fiscal Indicators* (1982).

Kenneth E. Graeber is executive director of the Texas State Property Tax Board in Austin. He received the B.S. and M.S. in agricultural economics

from Texas A & M University in 1972. He has served as a real-estate economist, project coordinator for the Market Value Study in the Governor's Office, and associate director for valuations for the School Tax Assessment
Practices Board. His published works include articles on property-tax laws
and property-tax reform.

J.T. Gwartney is assessment commissioner and chief executive officer of
the British Columbia Assessment Authority and president of the Real Estate
Institute of British Columbia. He received the B.S. in real-estate economics
from California University at San Diego. He has served as city assessor in
Hartford, Connecticut; deputy county assessor in Sacramento, California;
and City Assessor in Southfield, Michigan.

R.L. Halperin is state tax assessor, Maine. He graduated from Bentley
School of Accounting and Finance and worked twelve years with the Inter-
nal Revenue Service before beginning employment with the Maine Bureau
of Taxation in 1959. In 1982 he was elected vice-president of the National
Association of Tax Administrators.

Glenn L. Holmes is director of the Bureau of Property Tax, Wisconsin
Department of Revenue. He received the B.S. from the University of
Wisconsin-Madison in 1958. He directs the activities of staff responsible for
the establishment of statewide equalized values; for assessed values for
manufacturing properties in the state; for supervision, training, and certification of local assessors; and for review of assessment practices in each
taxation district in the state. He is or has been a member of the International Association of Assessing Officers, National Association of Tax Administrators, National Tax Association—Tax Institute of America, and the
American Society of Public Administration.

R.W. Meskers is the director of operations, Bureau of Taxation, State of
Maine. He received the B.S. and M.S. in agricultural economics from Rut-
gers—The State University. He has been employed by the bureau since 1972.

Rodney S. Nedeau was an economist for the Division of Ad Valorem Tax
of the Florida Department of Revenue for seven and one half years. He
received the B.A. in economics from the University of South Florida and
the M.S. in economics from the Florida State University. He recently left
the department to form a computer-processing firm.

A.J. Neves is the director of research, Bureau of Taxation, State of Maine.
He received the M.S. in pure mathematics from the University of Connecticut in 1968. His published works include articles on the theory of
dynamical systems and the assessment of public-utility property.

Stanley T. Ooka is head of the Technical Office of the Real Property Assessment Division of the City and County of Honolulu. He is a graduate of the University of Illinois in engineering. He holds a Certified Assessor Evaluator (CAE) designation and his published works include the Valuation of Golf Courses for Property Taxation.

Glenn R. Pascall is an economic and public-affairs consultant in Seattle. He is a former Washington State revenue director and served as president of the Washington State Research Council. Mr. Pascall received the B.A. from Pomona College in 1964 and the M.A. from Sacramento State University in 1968.

Frederick D. Stocker is professor of economics and public administration at The Ohio State University and a member of the Tax Policy Roundtable. He has written extensively on topics in state and local finance, including property taxation, school finance, and intergovernmental fiscal relations.

Richard Thalheimer is executive director of the Office of Revenue Estimating and Economic Analysis, Kentucky Revenue Cabinet. Dr. Thalheimer has published articles relating to property taxation and valuation in the *Assessors Journal, Southern Economic Journal*, and the *American Real Estate and Urban Economics Association Journal*. He has been involved in various facets of the state property-taxation field, with particular emphasis on sales-ratio studies and automated property-valuation methodology.

About the Editors

H. Clyde Reeves is chairman of the Tax Policy Roundtable of the Lincoln Institute of Land Policy and a member of the Kentucky Council of Economic Advisors. He became commissioner of revenue of Kentucky in 1937 and pioneered property-assessment improvement and statewide assessment-ratio-study development. He has taught public-finance-related subjects at the University of Kentucky, the University of Louisville, and the University of Alabama in Huntsville, where he was the executive vice-president. He is a past president of the National Association of State Tax Administrators and the National Tax Association—Tax Institute of America and was director of research of the Council of State Governments (1973-1975). He has been a consultant to the United Nations and various federal government agencies, states, and industries. His publications include articles in the *National Tax Journal, Property Tax Journal*, and *Public Administration Review.*

Scott Ellsworth, a Washington-based writer and historian, has served as an editorial consultant to the National Academy of Public Administration, the Lincoln Institute of Land Policy, and other public-policy organizations. He received the Ph.D. in history from Duke University.